THE LIGHT SHALL

SET YOU FREE

By
Dr. Norma J. Milanovich
and
Dr. Shirley D. McCune

ATHENA
Publishing

THE LIGHT SHALL

SET YOU FREE

The temple of wisdom is within each of us....
We need only journey there to find it.
Once found, freedom is assured.

ATHENA
Publishing

Albuquerque, NM

Third Printing 1997

ISBN 0-9627417-5-2

Library of Congress Catalog Card Number: 94-78618

Cover Design: Rudy Milanovich, Jr.

Cover Illustration: PAZ

**Published by
ATHENA PUBLISHING
Mossman Center, Suite 206
7410 Montgomery Blvd. NE
Albuquerque, NM 87109-1584
Phone: (505) 881-9618   FAX (505) 880-1623**

Printed in the United States of America
12 11 10 9 8 7 6 5 4 3

One day, while writing this book, we decided to ask the Ascended Masters for their opinions of its contents. Not knowing who would come through, we opened the floor up to anyone who wished to speak. With a smile in our hearts, we offer a summary of what the Ascended Masters are saying about *The Light Shall Set You Free.*

Truly an armistice for healing humanity's heart.
Hilarion

This book contains preliminary keys and codes for unlocking the secrets of Merlin's cave. Soon, after its release, the world shall experience Camelot in the Seventh Golden Age.
St. Germain

A document that gives testimony to the growing need and urgency for infusing the feminine goddess energy on Earth. My Son is well pleased.
Mother Mary

To the people of Earth, I offer my power and assistance in helping you implement the wisdom in this book. The knowledge cannot be underestimated.
Quan Yin

Read the content three times to understand it with your heart; read it seven times to infuse it into your soul. Then, come join us in Shamballa at the Feast of the New Beginnings.
Melchizedek

May the God Force be with you as you open your minds to a higher consciousness, destined to transform your essence. The frequency in this book will do just that. Be prepared to change!
Archangel Michael

Integrate the messages in this book into the meaning of the song, "It's a Small World," and hold the vision of how alike all of humanity really is. Then raise your understanding to include the animal and elemental kingdoms as well, for they too need your strength, compassion, and assistance to evolve. This book is a treatise to their worlds, too.
Walt Disney

TABLE OF CONTENTS

Prefatory Material

Part 1 — Understanding the Basic Concepts

Part II — Understanding the Universal Laws

Part III — Journeying into the Fifth Dimension

End Matter

DEDICATION

We dedicate this book to you, the reader, who has struggled through many incarnations to achieve alignment with the Divine. We hope this book reinforces your efforts. We also offer this instruction to all others who are just beginning to awaken spiritually and are looking for ways to enhance their paths.

It is with deep gratitude that we also dedicate this book to the Ascended Masters and all Celestial Beings of Light who have been with us from the beginning of time, working endlessly to assist us on our journeys. Without their support and guidance, received through numerous transmissions and meditations, this document would not be possible.

In one transmission, Ascended Master Kuthumi affirmed the willingness of the Celestial Realms to guide any person who requests their help:

> *We come to assist all souls who wish to find their connection back to the Divine. We come in many forms and many shapes, each with a job description to enhance the fulfillment of God's plan to raise Earth into the glorious millennium awaiting. We assist within the silence of your hearts, and provide protection and guidance to all who see it and connect to our essence.*

> *We are One and are One with you. You are the creative mind of God. We come to assist you to realize this.*

ACKNOWLEDGMENTS

*T*he origin of this book lies in the authors' search for the kind of information, meaning, and guidance in their own lives that assist us all on the spiritual path. Although information continues to flow, frequently it is available only in fragmented bits and pieces, the connections of which are difficult to see. Consequently, the application of such information to our daily lives often is lost.

It is ironic that in an age where information is readily accessible on an apparently unlimited number of topics, it is difficult to locate complete information regarding the spiritual processes of ascension and enlightenment. This book contains knowledge that finally ties these processes together, and its design was made possible only through the love, guidance, and dedication of the Ascended Masters.

It was they, and, in particular, Ascended Masters Kuthumi and El Morya, who first sparked the interests of the authors by suggesting that a document be developed on Universal Laws and empowerment. The book began as a discussion of the Universal Laws, but quickly expanded to provide the content for understanding them as well. Much of the information in this book was channeled from the Ascended Masters. The authors then researched a variety of metaphysical writings and resources to expand the meaning of the channeled transmissions, and the results of their efforts are contained within these covers. The expansion of the information and its implications reflects the authors' understandings to date, and the information is likely to change in meaning as we continue to evolve. That is the beauty of the journey. Consequently, the readers are encouraged continually to explore other resources as well, in order to find alternative versions of these truths for their own lives.

Writing this book with the Masters was a profound experience and one which involved discipline, focus, excitement, and love. We are grateful for the experience of producing this document cooperatively.

But others had a hand in its production, too, and we would like to recognize them at this time.

Rudy Milanovich, Sr. for his support and for his constant attention to life's logistics and details that provided Norma with the freedom to complete the document.

Pat Lawrence and **Dr. Reeve Love** for editing and refining the book in ways that made it more accessible and easier to understand for readers from all walks of life.

Rudy Milanovich, Jr. for typesetting the book, completing the cover layout and design, and never complaining about making the tedious editing changes that enhanced the quality of the final product.

Jerri Dickinson for her endless enthusiasm in assisting with the research and the word processing of the document.

Amber Williams for eagerly assisting with the word processing, as well as the final proofing of the book.

PAZ for producing the art work for the cover design, which became a labor of love that captured the essence of freedom that all souls seek to find.

Carolann Signorella for volunteering to read and edit the book before it went to press. Her offering of the heart was indeed appreciated by all and her skills added perfection to the final document.

A special thank you goes to the people who attended the workshops facilitated by Norma Milanovich. They helped to clarify issues, identify implications of the information presented, and affirm the need for this book.

Finally, sincere appreciation goes to our friends in Sweden and England who continually pushed and encouraged us to finish this document. Without their constant support, this book might still be on the drawing boards. These special people are:

Lennart Dage
Liselotte Berg
Sue Greaves

The beauty of the Ascended Masters' messages stands alone, so their words have not been changed. Their transmissions remain untouched, to assure that the vibrational frequency of their words remains pure. To them, our hearts are forever grateful.

CREDO FOR THE LIGHT
WORKERS OF THE WORLD

By wisdom is a house built;
by understanding is it made firm.
And by knowledge are its rooms filled with
every precious and pleasing possession.
                                    Proverbs, Chapter 24

B eliefs that underlie the teachings of this book
and the journey for the Children of Light
worldwide...

* ❋ There is one Creator.
* ❋ Love is the creative force of the universe.
* ❋ We are all children of one God.
* ❋ There is only Oneness, and we are all mirrors of one another in this vast creation.
* ❋ Humans are radiant beings of Light with unrealized power, waiting to become transformed into higher-dimensional forms.
* ❋ We each have a Higher Self that is waiting to be realized and that will transform us.
* ❋ Humans are co-creators with God, and each person has been sent to Earth to fulfill a mission.

CODE OF BEHAVIOR

1. Your mind can hold only one thought at a time. You must choose either thoughts of hope, love, and Light, or thoughts of fear and negativity.

Become the dreamers of Thoth. Hold the perfect vision in your mind for yourself, your loved ones, and the world. Let no mortal take that vision from you.

Follow your dreams and never stop believing in yourself. You will become more powerful than individuals who have knowledge, but do not have the courage to realize their dreams.

2. Never put energy into responding to those who try to tear you down. Feed only the positive, and keep this energy flowing into your accomplishments. Negative forces divert your energy and prevent you from realizing your dreams.

3. Hold the Light for the world. Never underestimate the effect of a kind action or word. Stand firm with your integrity, even under adversity, and be kinder than necessary.

4. Commit your attitude and behaviors to self-improvement. See pain and disappointment as opportunities to accept greater challenges, and then forge boldly ahead to become the person you are destined to be!

5. Compare your behavior with that of others and become more positive than anyone you know. Strive to embody a positive attitude, and watch your performance soar.

6. Take responsibility for all aspects of your life by watching every thought, word, action, and feeling that you emit. End the practice of blaming others, and see that all pain and disappointment are only opportunities for growth and mastery.

7. Smile, for the gift of a smile is free. Let your smile grow into laughter, and share this with the world.

8. See the Light of the soul within all people, knowing that each is a child of the one Creator. Treat all as you yourself would like to be treated, even though some individuals may challenge your patience.

9. Never give up on those who appear negative, for the truth is that their need to find love is greater than yours.

10. Never forget that a person's greatest emotional need is to feel appreciated.

11. Boldly carry the banner of St. George into battle, and feel victory at your side. Winners go where losers do not care to journey. Something deep inside you remembers what it is like to be fearless.

12. In mastery, one must be willing to assist others out of the brambles. You must be willing to obey your own inner guidance. Find the teacher inside and listen to the wisdom. You not only will become enlightened, but you also will become a Master.

13. Never forget that we have embodied in order to live in harmony with others and with the Earth, and to increase our awareness of the God-self within. Harmlessness is a basic part of our consciousness, and must be accessed if we are to become Masters.

14. For every moment of every day, there is an appropriate prayer to say. Find the prayer that is right for you in this moment, and give thanks that you have the wisdom and insight to recognize it.

FOREWORD

reetings, Dear Children of Earth.

I AM Kuthumi, coming through this frequency bringing words of wisdom and delight. I hail from the stars and the seventh-dimensional frequency and come to Earth as the Ambassador of Love and Light.

To some I am known as World Teacher. To others, I am the spokesperson for enlightenment and education for the Galactic Command. To others, I am the essence of Spirit. One's title is of little significance, for the importance of one's essence lies not in the title, but in the impact one's message has in changing consciousness and "ways."

I begin in this manner, for my message of today is designed to assist many to understand the concept of the "one way." This instruction is necessary for entry into the Fifth Dimension. It is also timely, for humanity is quickly approaching the portal of time/space that will open to allow entry into this new world.

There is much urgency on Earth during these troubled times. It is my hope that my role as World Teacher will be earned through the imparting of this critical message, designed to assist humanity on how to move gracefully through the turmoil in the days and years to come.

I am one of many who represent the Galactic Command of The Most Radiant One. We have journeyed to your system to accompany Earth on her mission and destiny into the Fifth Dimension. In the twinkling of an eye, you will soon see the beautiful solar body on which you reside turn into a bright star in the Heavens. This transformation will be witness to the fulfillment of many prophesies. In that moment, many will tremble in the remembrance that their journeys have come to an end. With this introduction it is my intent to promote hope, and not fear.

For centuries, negativity on Earth has consumed all that glistens, until it runs like molten lava within the veins of the beautiful Terra. Many have taken this condition, have internalized it within the heart centers, and have become consumed by these lower vibrations of fear and despair. This condition is destined to end, but not until the present level of negativity has run its course and the cycle of energy moves "full circle," returning to the source.

During the next few years, many changes will consume the Earth. This must come to pass because of the transformation that is destined to be fulfilled. In the transformation process, there will come Light and love. In addition, in the process, hope and faith in The Most Radiant One will be restored, for we are bringing back to you the Creator of Light and love. We are returning to you the source of power for which each soul has yearned since the beginning of time.

The closer His radiance comes to Earth, the more intense is the process of transformation in your hearts. As the vibratory frequency becomes intensified, many souls are abandoning former positions of negativity and slowly releasing lower vibrations from their paths. To do so takes courage, strength, commitment, and willingness. Overcoming the grip of evil and darkness is difficult for those who have only experienced soul poverty.

In the years to come each soul on Terra will be touched by this energy and must face the choice of his or her destiny. The choices are simple—one selects either peace, harmony, love, and Light, or fear and darkness. There is no middle compro-

PREFACE

his book is not about religion, conversion, or forming a new church. Instead, it is about US and our humanity, how we have lost our direction and power, and how we can find them again. The contents contain information destined to help humanity, worldwide, to relearn who we are and how we are connected to one Creator—the Creator of All. It's about...

Empowerment...

Thinking for yourself...

Discernment...

Hope...

Universal Laws...

Wisdom from the ancient mystery schools...

Knowledge that we are all created equal...

Oneness...

The path to freedom for everyone in the world...

Integrating spirituality into life.

Within each of us is a spark of Light which connects us to our Creator. This point of energy is the reason why we have come into embodiment, although few understand this to be true. It is the life-giving force of the universe with which we are connected, and this point of Light stimulates each breath that we take and every electrical impulse that charges our body.

On Earth we perceive the dense world of matter primarily through our five senses—sight, smell, hearing, touch, and taste. Since this Light is within, buried deep within our etheric and physical bodies, most individuals do not even know that it is there, or that this Light is our life force. The density of the physical world around us prevents us from piercing the veil and seeing this power within.

This tremendous source of power can be accessed only by going within with the mind's eye and by listening to the silence. There is a "still voice" that speaks to each of us that is connected to this Light. It is the Higher Self, the true self that is waiting to be discovered by every soul in embodiment.

For many, it is difficult to grasp the concept that we are more than our human form and that we are also beings of Light. Consequently, training the mind to accept expanded concepts of who and what we truly are can be an arduous task, requiring time, patience, and a desire to explore areas not commonly taught in the classrooms of today.

When one acquires the ability to connect with the Light within, everything observed and experienced through the five senses in the outer world takes on a new meaning, which releases the child within to want to relearn that which we already know. This path requires a whole new curriculum and set of guidelines to describe our existence.

Most of us spend our childhood and youth dealing with the problems of establishing our identity, gaining knowledge and skills for adult life, and establishing a family and career. As some of these issues are addressed, we may turn our attention to a deeper consideration of the meaning of life. Many are motivated by the question, "Is this all there is to life?" We search for understandings that will help us see the world and our experience in new ways. The still, small voice within us keeps asking the questions:

* Who am I?
* Why am I here?
* Where am I going?
* What is my purpose in life?

When we ask ourselves these questions, we are forced to "see" the limits of our experience in the physical world. We begin to explore another reality—one based on an inner sense of knowing and believing that there are other worlds for us to explore. We may simply "know" that there is more.

This is a book designed to assist all on a spiritual path to understand the world within that is connected to the Light and source of all power. It is a book on Universal Laws that teaches of the interconnectedness between humanity and the universe—the concept of Oneness. Ultimately, it is a book about you, life, and the freedom to manage your life. It is a book about truth.

To find freedom in the Light is what every soul has come to Earth to learn and experience. The answer to our struggle is that simple. It is the Light that sets us free. It is discovered in the NOW, for the Light is within us always, silently waiting to be discovered, to show us the way back to our divinity.

When one discovers this truth and begins to make the journey home, exciting things begin to happen. Things once thought to be "coincidence" suddenly take on a new meaning of order. Miracles begin to be expected. Peace and harmony become the routine of the day, replacing chaos, harm, and negativity with order.

Artwork by Richard Pulito

Chapter 1

INTRODUCTION TO THE BASIC CONCEPTS OF TRANSFORMATION

Nothing we ever imagined is beyond our powers, only beyond our present self-knowledge.
                              Theodore Roszak

In several messages received over the last few years, the Ascended Masters have spoken of the transformation Earth is presently going through. Often they included descriptions of changes that would occur, to both land and people. They called it the birthing process for the planet and stated emphatically that it is part of Earth's evolutionary path.

This transformation into the New Age was described once, by the Arcturians, as the birthing of a planet (Earth) into a star in the Heavens. They said that it has been written since Babylon that the Earth would journey into the Age of Aquarius and become a Garden of Eden in the universe. They also explained that this event was happening because of the precession of the equinoxes, and that Earth's position in this universal parade of stars was guided by forces higher than we can imagine.

Transformation intrigued us because the messages implied a total change, for both humans and the Earth. Kuthumi, El Morya, and Sananda made this clear on many occasions. They spoke of the mysteries, keys, and codes that unlocked the answers to these changes, and often sent us on journeys that assisted us to discover the answers for ourselves.

In several transmissions they suggested that we "follow the thread!" They implied that if we journeyed backward in time and researched major teachings recorded centuries ago, we would discover the secrets to life itself. Never would they give us the answers. Instead, they only provided guidance and advice, allowing us to work in whatever time frame and mode we chose. In short, they were excellent teachers.

The search for answers was sparked by their clues and discussions of past knowledge that none of us had. They moved us through time/space with such rapidity that at times we felt our heads spinning with information and truths that we did not know even existed. They found us to be serious students and, at times, rewarded our efforts by giving us gifts from the etheric. Sometimes books (that none of us had ordered) would appear mysteriously in the mail, providing precisely the reading material that was needed to help us gather the information. At other times strangers would introduce themselves to us by phone or personal visit. "Coincidentally," we always had the information we needed to proceed to the next step. Other times, information was accelerated through our dream states or consciousness, leaving us to decode it.

Transformation, says Kuthumi, is a journey that the human race has taken since the beginning of time. Therefore, in order to understand transformation we have to research the ancient truths from the beginning of recorded history. Records and old libraries, such as the library of Alexandria, contained much of the world's wisdom, but through the actions of unenlightened souls these treasures and gifts were destroyed. That which was not destroyed will be rediscovered in this period, for the time is right for bringing these truths to the world once again. Much of this ancient knowledge will come forth in the same manner in which this book is being developed.

Hearing this bewildered us. Learning that there was even a possibility that there was a master plan for the unveiling of these events was staggering. Receiving this information made us inherently suspicious that this Ascended Master Brotherhood of the All, called in many books the Great White Brotherhood (white in this context meaning white Light), has been in charge all along.

These Masters appear to be members of a group that oversees the entire plan of operations—at least for this section of the universe. Emphatically, they state that they work for God. They are here to assure that all details of this plan run on schedule. Throughout history, when the time was right, they have communicated with souls such as ourselves. They cite Noah's being notified of the upcoming flood or John the Baptist's foretelling the coming of Jesus as examples. These historical figures received their messages in the same way that many are receiving this kind of information today.

Only the Masters appear to have access to the entire master plan; we receive pieces that fit our missions. They oversee the tactics and maneuvers and monitor the proceedings. We are rewarded for our progress and accomplishments with more assignments and hard work. We also are rewarded by knowing that God's plan is actually developing as planned and that each of us, in our own small way, is contributing to its success.

Kuthumi explained that transformation takes quantum leaps around the turn of each millennium, but the effects are even more noticeable when each New Age begins. The vibrational frequencies automatically change with the precession of the planets and stars, and in this scientific motion, consciousness also adjusts.

They define consciousness as the foundation for all there is, for they say that God is thought and out of thought came Light, from which all things are manifested.

They say that the world is a microcosm of the universe

which is our macrocosm. They say that all is energy and that energy is Light. Out of Light energy came sound energy in the original creation. Out of Light and sound comes the formation of all that is. Each object, whether solid, liquid, or gas, has its own code, which is a vibratory frequency. This vibration is created out of Light. Since humans contain a consciousness that can be controlled, and since consciousness is thought, then each individual is actually a co-creator with the Divine.

This is the lesson we have journeyed to Earth to discover. This is the reason for life and for our incarnation in this lifetime. Few will find the answers to these mysteries, for an individual has to experience enlightenment to be able to grasp this truth. Most will scorn this principle, for to accept it demands accountability for our actions. Not many are ready to accept this kind of responsibility. Most, in fact, will try to provide explanations contrary to these facts. Therefore, few are ready for the transformation that is destined to consume the Earth over the next several years.

The date for entry into the Fifth Dimension is scheduled for the year 2012, says Kuthumi. He emphatically states that all vibrational conditions will be in place for this transformation to occur by the year 2011. This, he calls the "end of the world." This, he also says, must be the turning point for all the cleansing to be complete, for it will be at this moment when the critical mass should be ready to take that leap of consciousness into the Fifth Dimension of time/space.

This phenomenon will consume all that has existed before. Some will not recognize their abilities as they are today, but will actually take on a higher form of what is closer to what our Arcturian friends described in the book, *We, The Arcturians*. Some are destined to become the Adam Kadmon species, a highly evolved group of beings with abilities not presently understood on Earth.

The world will be in the at-one-ment with the Creator. The planet will understand the harmony and peace for which it has yearned for many centuries. The decade of the nineties and the beginning of the millennium will test many who are in doubt today, and provide each with the exact tests they will need to overcome their fears and doubts regarding this transition.

Since the human form is destined to change (precisely how, we are not clear), then new rules (books, if you will) must be written that will contain the information to help each soul evolve to this new state of consciousness. The information provided in this document, we were told, would contribute to this evolutionary leap for humanity. Much will be transmitted over the next two decades, but only the souls who are ready to receive the new curriculum will elect to raise their vibrations to match those required to enter the New Age.

The word *vibration* is the key. All humans who will journey on to this new world in the Fifth Dimension of time/space must have a vibrational frequency, earned through raised consciousness, that will match the vibrational frequency of the New Age. This phenomenon is absolute and will be measured by individuals' abilities to be open-minded, loving, centered, tranquil, peaceful, and devoted. Since these characteristics are more closely aligned with the higher states of consciousness, these individuals are defined by the Masters as being more godlike. These individuals will command the vibrational frequency closer to the speed of Light which will be in alignment with the Age of Aquarius.

Kuthumi described this whole phenomenon as a scientific one. He stated that our physicists were already beginning to make connections among these principles and concepts and soon would be able to document the concept of Oneness which is a part of the millennium which we are entering.

Since we are entering the home (or perhaps *dimension* is a better word) of higher level beings, they are our teachers. Soon, they have said, we will have an entirely new curriculum that we must master. They proposed the outline for this book as a part of that curriculum and said that those souls who journey into the higher realms will have to understand and master it. This curriculum includes the Universal Laws.

In the etheric, one behaves at one with the All. In order to do so, the soul must follow certain rules. These rules are the Universal Laws. The laws, Kuthumi said, were provided to Earth by many known as ancient masters, one of whom was Hermes Trismegistus, the "ancient of the ancients."

It was the Egyptians, he said, who later understood these laws and used the power that this existence of at-one-ment provided to them. That is why they built such a great civilization. When one is in harmony with the Universal Laws, then all things can be created and manifested, for the beings who incarnate are truly co-creators with the All. In this state of balance and perfection come the application of ancient mystery school teachings and the keys to eternal salvation.

The key to understanding a higher consciousness is actually to strive to be one with it. When the rules and the laws are followed with mastery and discipline, then all else follows in harmony. In order to become one with one's own divinity, however, one must have the mental discipline and intellect to understand it.

Central to understanding and employing knowledge about the Universal Laws is the understanding of how the human mind works, for the mind holds the keys to transformation. Since scientists are only now beginning to map the paths of intelligence, memory, and consciousness, we asked Kuthumi to explain his viewpoint on the nature of intellect to us so that we would be better equipped to understand the information that was about to be transmitted for this book.

He responded in a way that at first appeared to evade the question, then proved in the end to be very powerful. As usual, he did not provide us with the textbook explanation that we wanted. His explanation provoked us to think, and employed abstract concepts, analogies, and truths that were greater than what we were accustomed to hearing.

After reading the entire transmission, we felt humbled for having doubted his ability to provide the answer. His answer challenges one to see through different eyes—eyes that see us as beings greater than what we believe ourselves to be, and as energy that is only color and sound. It is apparent that the title of "World Teacher" was given to Kuthumi with good reason. The following is his transmission.

Greetings, Daughter,

I am pleased to address your question of concern today regarding the nature of intellect, for in the answer comes more than the understanding of it. In the answer comes also the secret to the heart. Planet Earth cannot survive in the days ahead if the total picture of intellect and its connection to the heart is not clearly understood.

While this unsubstantiated statement may sound abrupt in its present form, allow me to explain why we, on the Ascended Realms, make such a dramatic statement. Remember, please, that my discourse represents the Tribunal Council's collective intellect and the vibrational frequency of the evolutionary process through the seventh dimensional frequency. This is of importance to know, for this states that the wisdom to be imparted represents the collective voice from the ancients. This explanation is shared in hopes that your ears will ring in tune with the sounds of the Temple of Wisdom, and that you will carry this message to the masses so that they may hear the same. We ask not that you necessarily believe all that will be transmitted, but that you consider the possibility of its truth. So, let us begin.

The nature of intellect is nothing more than one's perception of reality. In the universes, of which there are twelve, humans appear to limit themselves and their realities with the concept of closed-

Hitler
ISIS

mindedness. This is not to be taken as criticism. We begin this way because in our observations we note the masses on Earth operate more in the mode of closing their systems rather than in that of opening to new ones. We challenge you to contemplate this observation.

This state of mind is equivalent to the times wherein individuals groped and found comfort in the dark for their security. We believe you have termed such eras the "Dark Ages."

Only during times which your civilizations call "Ages of Enlightenment" have groups of individuals incarnated and brought great progress and intellectual stimulation to help humanity complete evolutionary leaps. While you read about these periods of accomplishments with great admiration and awe, know that these were painful times for the masses. The average human throughout all recorded history has not enjoyed change. This quality has been consistent throughout humanity's development.

What created success during the "Ages of Enlightenment" was that during those eras, many enlightened souls chose to incarnate for the purpose of initiating change. Conversely, during each Dark Age, fewer enlightened souls chose embodiment, making it more difficult for change to occur.

In this last example, we bring you a mathematical problem. What, then, is the variable or factor that makes the difference for the initiation or hindrance of change? The variable is the quantity of humans who come together to rule or provide direction for a particular civilization. In addition to the quantity of individuals, one also needs to include the na-

ture of reality which each holds within his or her consciousness. When one understands that consciousness is volume measured by mathematics and that each person's reality is part of the universal consciousness, then one is well on the way to understanding the nature of intellect.

The universe in which you reside is magical and powerful. It is the totality of universal consciousness and is mind energy. It is also perfect. It contains the sum of all that was and ever will be for your existence while you reside within it. It is the macrocosm of which you are the microcosm. Therefore, your intellect, which is a part of this universal consciousness, has no boundaries. You are one part of the total sum of all there is.

Your intellect has barely been tapped, Oh Children of the Divine. The key to tapping the wonders of your power and happiness lies only in your ability to open your minds to the possibilities around you. When you choose to do this, you open the doors to endless opportunities and become the true co-creators with the Divine. This is truth.

Intellect, therefore, is one's ability to pursue the opportunities around. It demands the discipline and the focus of energy within, to be used for the fulfillment of pursuit. Intellect is that which enables one to reason without anxiety, and to address the questions that challenge one's concept of reality. Intellect is freedom and the courage to explore areas where others dare not go.

The blockages that bar one from using intellect are those which exist within the mind. All blockages are present because of three kinds of memory: genetic, past-life, and cellular memory accumulated

TIME

from the present incarnation. An understanding of these terms incorporates the passing of time. We use these terms for your convenience and understanding only. For, in reality, there is no such thing as time. All time exists in the present moment of time and space. Since you exist, however, in a three-dimensional reality that has created time as a component to organize your reality, we use these as examples or analogies to accommodate your perceptions.

Reality

Energy blockages are perceptions of reality that cause one to become out of harmony with the universe around. When one is not in harmony, difficulties and frustrations occur that are stored in the mind. The mind encompasses all you are, as your essence exists in a thought-form that represents the reality of who and what you are. This thought-form is pure energy that can be shaped in any form of your choosing. Reality, which encompasses intellect, is the manifestation on the outside of what you believe on the inside. All vibrations, good and bad, are stored within this mind and your essence.

Let us stop here for one minute to test you. Considering the information we have just delivered, how would you measure your level of receptivity? Are you accepting these statements as reality or are you closing your minds to the possibility that these might be truths? Thus, do you enhance our original observation provided earlier, or do you discredit it? Note your station at this point, for the additional explanations we will provide are more complex. If you are having difficulty following these statements thus far, perhaps you might like to rest or reread the information that we have transmitted. For those who choose to continue, we deliver this additional information for your consideration.

The intellect of the mind is that rational process that governs the thought-forms which shape reality. All mind and processes are energy. Energy can neither be created nor be destroyed; therefore, all energy is transformed. Energy is also neutral. Intellect is the governing and transforming power of the thoughts used to dictate the shape.

ENERGY

Let us digress here for a moment and discuss the nature of energy. Energy is that which comprises the universe in which you reside. The basis for all creation is the thought-form, which controls and creates out of Light. Light is that which governs and dictates the molding and processing of all that exists; thus, gases, liquids, and solids are only processed forms of energy.

The universe is a perfect, pulsating, rhythmic mechanism that sings the music of the spheres. As the embodied Pythagoras, I brought to the world this understanding of mathematical reasoning. And in my instruction I delivered the secrets of the coded mysteries for both the macrocosm and the microcosm, for they are both One. One of the secrets brought forth was that everything can be measured mathematically because of the vibrational frequency each form emits. Since all is created from Light, which is the manifested energy of thought, then each creation is a unique frequency measured to be less than Light.

Your Earth scientists will soon discover frequencies above the speed of Light. When they do, they will understand our definition of Light. Your present understanding measures Light as the frequency that contains all color and is separated into frequencies called the rainbow. Our definition is that Light is the Great Central Sun, a phenomenon you

Light

*will discover when you fully enter the Age of
Aquarius and the fifth-dimensional frequency. For
our purposes in this discourse, however, we state
with much assurance that either definition suffices
for your understanding of the concepts of which we
instruct.*

*What is important to grasp here is that everything
is energy and that each form sings its own, unique
song which comprises its existence. Since this is so,
and since all parts are interrelated in the macrocosm, then it is of equal importance to note that
sound vibration is also created out of Light.*

*But how do the human factor and the nature of in-
tellect fit into this explanation, you might ask? We
tell you that intellect was created out of Divine
thought and given to each of you because you are
the co-creators of Heaven and Earth. In this plan,
all of humanity was made in the image and like-
ness of God. Therefore, all of humanity have the
tools within their consciousness to become or not
become the totality of what they were created to experience. But, we wonder, how many of the souls in
embodiment will understand this? Do you, Oh
Daughter, know precisely what it is that we say?*

*We have already stated that energy follows thought,
in that what is within an individual's consciousness is that which is manifested on the outside.
Therefore, the energy of thought is that which must
be ruled and governed by each individual. This is
essential, for the changes that will soon ravage
Earth will challenge many enlightened souls to
seek solutions to many problems. Energy is neutral
and travels the path of least resistance. Understanding this brings to light the importance of the
individual's power to shape destiny and the future,*

for not only the one but also the many.

Remember our earlier question regarding the solution to the riddle? What variable, at any given moment, dictates whether a civilization is enlightened or in the dark? If you recall, the answer was the number of souls who choose to move the energy and create that which is in their vision. What they choose is what they will create. What is your vision for the future?

All of your creation will be manifested through Light and sound. For where the human species stands in the evolutionary scale, there are no other phenomena that apply. Therefore, this is the curriculum that must be mastered before journeying further. Since sound and Light are measured mathematically, then we conclude that each form and creation has a mathematical formula that comprises its essence. Does this not make sense?

The coding and encoding of the formulas for creation are written within the Universal Laws. These laws, which are the rules of this universe, are constant, unchanging, and unbending. They are embedded in your concepts of physics, yet comprise the essence of spirituality. They employ the rules of the ancients and speak to the songs of the highest civilizations that have graced your planet. They are truths that many have understood, but few have practiced.

As the new kingdom of Adam Kadmon approaches, many yearn for the new agenda for survival. This fifth-dimensional reality will not be the same as that which has nurtured existence for the past several thousand years. The higher frequencies of the Age of Aquarius, which approach the speed of

*Light, demand a form of mental and emotional dis-
cipline that few have mastered today. The higher
frequencies require adherence to Universal Laws.
The outcome of such obedience would align you
more closely with the behaviors associated with
love and Light.*

*It is because this is so that we transmit this forth-
coming, basic curriculum. Revealed within the instructions are the keys and codes for understanding
the paths both to enlightenment and to the Divine.
The content, which you call the letter of the law, is
not as important as the spirit of the information received, for it is in the application of the information
that the connection to Spirit will be made.*

*Have we answered your question on the nature of
intellect? We say no, but request that you decide. In
making the decision, we ask that you study what
we have transmitted and interpret its significance
from your heart. The heart is the center of all wisdom, for the heart is the connection to the Divine
through the subconscious mind. Follow its guidance and therein will your answer lie. Through the
heart shall your question be answered.*

*Know that when the mind is not connected to the
heart, ego rules. The ego sees separateness and
loneliness in the world and not Oneness or connection. If ego is left unattended and rules intellect,
then that which manifests is reflective of this state
of consciousness.*

*To nurture intellect requires the continual develop-
ment of open-mindedness. Look for new ideas, Dear
Ones, and find the courage to see through eyes that
understand energy and Light. Know that in the
seeing will come great rewards, for new sight brings*

new knowledge. The heightened knowledge will increase intellect, feeding the path to higher consciousness.

We conclude this transmission with one last thought of caution. Look beyond today for your future, for the future is closer than you think. Feel the vibrations of this message and know that in the Fifth Kingdom come the love and happiness for which you have yearned. The key to accessing this dimension is through the heart. Cast off your judgments and cloak yourself with the Light. Judgments will carry you back to the Dark Ages of the remembrances of your souls. You have travelled long and far to complete this journey, and we await to welcome you at the threshold of your destiny.

We who serve on the Tribunal Council of the Galactic Command thank you for this opportunity to deliver these words to you. Adonai, our Sisters and Brothers of the Universe.

I AM Kuthumi.

Summary

Transformation, or the fulfillment of Earth's evolutionary path, is a process which human beings have chosen since the beginning of time. The process speeds up near the end of each millennium and becomes even more noticeable as we approach each New Age in our development. Characteristics of this New Age may be viewed as follows:

* Planet Earth is going through the birthing process of becoming a fifth-dimensional star by the year 2012.
* Moving into the Fifth Dimension requires us to earn a higher vibrational frequency that matches the frequency of the Fifth Dimension.
* The universe is governed by Universal Laws which are the guidelines for our movement into a higher consciousness and vibration.
* Change results when a quantity or critical mass of humans comes together with some perception of reality.
* Intellect is our ability to reason without anxiety and to address questions which challenge our views of reality.
* The Age of Aquarius requires us to observe the Universal Laws and to master higher forms of mental and emotional disciplines.
* Nurturing intellect requires an open mind and an ability to process our actions with our hearts, our connection to the Divine through our subconscious minds.

God is thought and out of thought came light - "Let there be light."

Chapter 2

THE ASCENDED MASTERS

Healing comes only from that which leads the patient beyond himself and beyond his entanglements with ego.

Carl Jung

e are the caretakers of Earth and have come here for experiences that assist us to evolve. We originate from the Creator as a spark of Light, and to this Source we must return. Our incarnations in many areas of the vast universe assist us to grow. These incarnations provide us with a variety of adventures so we may taste what is offered in all realities, including the material world. Our ultimate goals, however, are to become masters of self and masters of matter, eventually returning to God.

We advance when we act responsibly and when we learn service to others. Every deed and action we perform is monitored and recorded in our own Akashic Records, the data banks that store all the forms of Karma accrued on our journeys. Our progress is noted, and teachers are sent to us when we need guidance or answers to help us evolve. As we accomplish greater works, we inevitably are led to assuming more responsibilities, even throughout the galaxy, when we don the robes of other forms of existence.

In the past, however, many generations of people were reluctant to evolve, acquire higher consciousness, and learn the lessons that come with higher truths. History reveals that Earth has gone through cycles called Dark Ages, when consciousness slipped into the abyss and evolution was stalled.

When these periods were experienced, great Masters were sent to Earth to show the way. These Great Ones were often called Illumined Ones. Today, the common term is Ascended Masters. They are also referred to as The Elect, a term used more than 2,500 times in the Bible. (Stone, 1992)

The Ascended Masters

Ascended Masters are highly evolved souls, working for God, who come to Earth to serve humanity. They are illumined beings of Light who have incarnated on Earth not only for their own spiritual growth, but also in service to humanity. In the past, when they have come, each has left a legacy of accomplishments and contributions, documented in the annals of history. They brought knowledge and wisdom far ahead of the times. Some were prophets who could see into the future. Others incarnated into specific craft and skill areas and left artistic masterpieces and architectural structures that baffle even the most profound thinkers today. Still others were philosophers and poets who left their legacies on paper.

In all cases, they came to serve, to evolve, and to shed their Light on the world. Yet, in spite of their contributions, most were scorned and ridiculed by the masses, for no reason except that they saw the world through different pairs of glasses.

Humanity holds an unfortunate track record in terms of what unawakened souls did to these Great Ones. And for what reason? In most cases it was because these beings were different, possibly even eccentric!

The title Dark Ages was earned. People resisted change and were generally very closed-minded to new ideas. Anything outside of what would be termed a normal existence in the physical world was to be feared, scoffed at, and denied, causing problems for those trying to implement or teach the higher truths. Because this was so, many of these Masters were forced into seclusion just to learn and teach.

Not all chose to go into hiding, though. For those courageous enough to remain in public, the price was high, for many underwent tragic deaths. The most classic example of all is the death of Jesus, the Christ, which occurred as a result of the masses' misunderstanding of the higher truths he was presenting to humanity for only one purpose: that we might learn, practice, and become, so that our souls would be set free.

Consequently, becoming a high Initiate took great courage and faith. Many who made their way into history did so carrying heavy loads because of the commitments they made. Upon examining the lives of these Great Ones, one wonders how they endured, since their endings were so unfitting the dignity that they deserved. Witness only a few who serve as examples to illustrate this point.

Pythagoras, the first philosopher who brought to the world the higher concepts of mathematics, sacred geometry, and the music of the spheres. He was murdered. His school was burned, along with many of his disciples.

The Disciples of Twelve who surrounded Jesus. They departed this world in turmoil, for nearly all were attacked by the masses who could not see the gifts of the Spirit, nor hold these gifts in their consciousness.

Joan of Arc, the victorious Light who challenged the politicians. She suffered the flames for the voices she heard and the higher truths she fought to instill in the world.

Galileo, the famed astronomer and mathematician who proved the Copernican theory. He was condemned by the masses during the Inquisition and forced to denounce his own discoveries to avoid being burned at the stake.

John the Baptist, the messenger to the world. He met his fate for the truths he dared to speak. He was imprisoned and beheaded for his courage and fortitude.

This was the fate of many of the elect in the past. Yet, today, each is a hero, a heroine, or a legend. In some cases they are worshipped.

A further description of who the Ascended Masters are is provided in the book entitled *The Keys of Enoch* by J. J. Hurtak (1977). He describes them as the:

> Masters who have served several incarnations in the lower Heavens teaching the Cosmic Law of the Universe and who have ascended back into the presence of the Father from whence they receive new assignments to teach a wide variety of worlds because of their greater love. (p. 567)

Mission of the Ascended Masters

These highly evolved beings have been monitoring the world and our progress from the beginning of time. They have assisted whenever humanity and Earth needed it. They are Masters of love and are sensitive to the changes that we are going through and how these changes affect our emotional bodies. Since our mental, emotional, and physical bodies must be integrated with our spiritual bodies, the Masters move very carefully when guiding us, for they do not want to lose any soul in the process.

They have incarnated numerous times on Earth, each time leaving wisdom and knowledge to help us grow. Although we cannot see them with the physical eye when they are not in embodiment, we are always in their presence. We do not always know that they are with us, but they are. It has often been said by the Ascended Masters:

IF YOU ONLY KNEW
WHO WALKED BESIDE YOU,
YOU WOULD NEVER FEEL ALONE

When the Masters speak these words, they are referring to the presence of the Illumined Ones who know our every thought, word, action, and deed. They include the essence of Jesus, as well, when they make this statement.

Ascended Masters do not always have to incarnate physically to work with humanity, for there are many other ways in which they can assist us, such as through dreams and visions. Another way involves telepathic communication with individuals on Earth whose vibrational levels are high enough to receive the Masters' transmissions. An individual may raise his or her vibrational frequency through dedication and service to the spiritual path. Often this takes several lifetimes and extreme discipline before one earns a higher vibrational status. Only a few have been known to do so in a short amount of time.

To raise one's vibrations to a frequency of love and Light requires purification of body, mind, and Spirit, and demands that the emotional and mental bodies be kept in check. A higher vibrational frequency for the individual is secured by unconditional love and acceptance for all and the feelings that come with this state of mind. When an individual has the ability to hold this state of mind (called enLIGHTenment), the Ascended Masters can connect more easily to the person and begin to communicate with the soul. After this connection is made, they send through messages of wisdom, guidance, love, and support to assist that person to evolve.

Before a person reaches this state of enlightenment, which takes discipline, the individual is essentially left alone to wander on the path of learning lessons. This is not done to punish the soul, but out of the respect and wisdom the Masters have for our free will. In each new lifetime, individuals are tested for seven years before the Masters begin to make their presence known. This assures that the soul is indeed ready to assume the responsibility for the individual's own actions and thoughts and that the person is sincere about the direction in which he or she is headed. What is so fascinating about this process is that it is applied to everyone who comes into embodiment. Even Jesus had to undergo this experience, for Earth is a karmic planet, which means that the veil must go down for each person once the soul arrives on the planet.

Since the Earth plane is such a difficult place to learn the lessons because of the thickness of the energy surrounding the planet, all souls must undergo the same and equal treatment each time they come into embodiment. There are no exceptions. It is the intensity of the Light within each person, the character of our souls, and the choices we make that determine advancement through the tests. Our progress determines how quickly the Masters will make their presence known to us in a more direct manner.

Every soul on Earth is assigned to what is called the *ashram* of one or more Ascended Masters. An ashram is a secluded place where religious and spiritual teachings are learned and practiced. Each of us is assigned to a Master in the Cosmic Hierarchy, whether we know it or not on a conscious level. When the seven years of testing are complete, the Master makes contact with the student. The saying is:

 WHEN THE STUDENT IS READY, THE MASTER (TEACHER) WILL APPEAR

Every person on Earth is included within the Christ consciousness ashram, whether one follows the Christian religious belief or not. For, you see, contrary to popular belief, the Ascended Masters do not follow one religion. They follow the beliefs of Oneness and enLIGHTenment. That means they honor the teachings of all the Great Masters who have come before and left their teachings to assist us to evolve. This truth is evident when you look at history.

Whenever one of these illumined beings came to Earth, there were no religions. Yet all of these Masters were Divine in their own right, even though they were not born into a specific religion. It was only after beings like Jesus, Buddha, Zoroaster, and Mohammad left the Earth plane that religions sprang up. Humans designed the rules and regulations that the Masters' followers were required to obey in order to achieve salvation. This process should not be attributed to the Masters who came to Earth to serve. All of these Masters were recipients of Divine words and did their best, in each of the civilizations into which they were born, to bring higher truths and wisdom to assist people to evolve. The messages that were sent from above matched the needs of the particular civilization.

The Celestial Hierarchy's plan today decrees that no more Ascended Masters will come to Earth one at a time. This time, the journey is OUR journey. It is up to us now. We must learn the truths and live by them. We are being held accountable now for the knowledge that has been delivered to us, and we must integrate these truths into every aspect of our lives. We are the Ascended Masters of tomorrow. We are the Initiates in embodiment who now are being considered for positions in the Ascended Realms.

The Ascended Masters, collectively, see humanity as One. They see the beauty and spark of Light in each person's soul and know that each is a child of one God. They do not see our differences. They see only our similarities as children of the one Creator. They know that we all are struggling to evolve.

Jesus said:

THERE ARE MANY PATHS, BUT ONLY ONE WAY

Translated, this means there are many paths (religions), but there is only one way to salvation—enLIGHTenment. He conveyed this thought in another way in John 8:12 when he told us that he was the way, or the example, if you will:

I AM THE LIGHT OF THE WORLD

Earth's vibrations are being raised and so are ours. This brings us closer and closer to the frequency of the Ascended Masters, and we are slowly closing the gap between their frequency and ours. With this closure, more and more individuals on Earth can now receive telepathic communications directly from the Celestial Hierarchy—a gift that was granted only to the spiritual elite in lifetimes past.

Thousands of people today, worldwide, have begun receiving beautiful messages of encouragement and guidance. For evidence of this one need only look at the hundreds of publications published annually. As vibrational frequencies are raised, clearer messages are being received. This means that the connections are getting stronger, an indication that the vibrational frequencies of some individuals are truly getting higher. The same or similar information is being received by individuals all over the world—a phenomenon that was not possible years ago because the connections were not so clear.

For the average person not aware of the spiritual awakening presently encompassing Earth, the thought of communicating directly with Jesus, Buddha, or some of the other Masters may be alarming, even frightening. After all, was not such communication left only to the saintly in years past? And then, there is the deep remembrance of what we did to the saints for claiming they heard voices or received messages from God. Nearly every one of these souls who achieved sainthood was martyred. Therefore, many deep fears come to the surface and close down our minds to the acceptance that this communication might be a reality for us today. We have been programmed that we are sinners—pathetic souls who have little or no hope for evolvement. So how could we possibly have a direct line to the Ascended Masters?

The Ascended Masters have stated repeatedly that they want for us to know them as our elder brothers and sisters, and as those who have walked the path before us to show us the way. We need to begin to think of them as a team of highly evolved beings who were sent to Earth, one by one, to bring enlightenment over the ages. They were not prophets or beings who contradicted one another for the purpose of starting new religions whose adherents eventually would hate one another and cause wars, hatred, death, and destruction. No! All who chose to come down to Earth to serve were souls who did the best they could with what they had to work with in the civilization in which they chose embodiment. All of them should be honored as a collective team who brought messages of peace, love, and enlightenment to the world. We should be thanking all of them for their commitment to helping us evolve.

A question that needs to be asked today is: If Jesus incarnated today, which religion would he choose to join? Would he choose Catholicism, Methodism, Mormonism, Buddhism, or Judaism? Then, after he chose one, would he berate all other beliefs and publicly tell all others that they were wretched sinners who would perish at the hand of his Father because they were not following the one religion he chose? Would Jesus subscribe to Buddhism, honoring his colleague Gautama Buddha who did what no other human had been able to accomplish until then, or would he choose another religion and then vilify his colleagues and glorify his followers?

The answers to these questions seem apparent. So why do we continue to dwell on our differences and feed on these differences that result from separatism? Why do we not see our similarities and likenesses? When will we evolve to the point where we see only Oneness instead of duality, like

Identify – Don't Compare –

the Ascended Masters?

When a soul chooses to embrace the spiritual path, Oneness becomes the lesson that must be learned. The Ascended Realms work with individuals, lifetime after lifetime, to assist them to achieve unconditional love and acquire a perspective of Oneness. At some time in a soul's evolutionary path it can, while in embodiment, become the recipient of the Masters' direct communications. This is the exact procedure that supported the prophets and Illumined Ones in the past when they received their great teachings and prophesies. Knowledge and wisdom were sent to the Initiate from the Ascended Masters out of embodiment in fulfillment of agreements that were made between lifetimes, because the Initiate's soul was ready for this level of responsibility and growth. Presently, the Ascended Masters are with us again in this way and are delivering messages of hope, peace, love, and wisdom to many people on Earth.

What Is the Cosmic Hierarchy?

There are numerous levels of offices and responsibilities in the Cosmic Hierarchy that governs Earth. There are also many Councils of Light and job titles that are held, each contributing in some way to the fulfillment of God's plan on Earth. The reader might be familiar with some of the common titles of these Ascended Beings because they stem from the different religions of the world. They are: Saints, Buddha(s), Bodhisattvas, Elohim, Angels, Archangels, Gods, Goddesses, and Lords. In addition to these names which appear more frequently than others, there are titles such as: Cosmic Beings, Chohans, Devas, Seraphim, Cherubim, Logos, Planetary and Cosmic Silent Watchers, Kachinas, and Beings of the Elements.

One or more of these Divine presences is behind every intelligent activity completed for the advancement of humanity. Beings of Light have come forth whenever humanity needed a lift. But because of free will, however, whenever humanity withdrew and did not want assistance, they were forced to retreat until a cry for help and an invitation were sent inviting their assistance.

They are with us once again, because a cry for help was sent by humanity's consciousness through the prayers and hearts of millions after World War II. They are among us once again in this closer proximity, working at what they do best—teaching the way to enlightenment and gently guiding our souls to freedom.

There are two primary groups of Ascended Masters that have assisted humanity in Earth's evolution. These two groups are the Great White Brotherhood (or the Brotherhood of the All, as the Arcturians have described it), and the Order of Melchizedek.

The Great White Brotherhood (white meaning white Light) is composed of many of the beings in the Cosmic Hierarchy. This organization includes seventy Orders/Brotherhoods of the universe. Its primary purpose is to assist planets and civilizations to evolve. Since God's plan includes all of creation, the Great White Brotherhood is assigned to observe the evolutionary process of all beings and render assistance when appropriate. The second significant group is called the Order of Melchizedek. This is the group that physically and spiritually completes the work that needs to be done to assist civilizations to evolve. This is achieved in two ways: by orchestrating shifts in consciousness, and through actual accomplishments in the physical world.

Beings of Light can hold membership simultaneously in the Order of Melchizedek and in the Great White Brotherhood. In fact, most, if not all, do belong to both.

One of the beings in charge of organizing the levels of the Heavenly worlds is Melchizedek, an equal with the beings known as Metatron and Archangel Michael. Hurtak's description of Melchizedek's role is that he is:

> ...in charge of organizing the levels of the Heavenly worlds of YHWH for transit into new creation...[for] the "rescue, regenesis and reeducation of worlds" going through the purification of

the Living Light. (Gen. 14:18; Heb. 5:7-10) He is
in charge of the Heavenly Order/Brotherhood of
Melchizedek and the spiritual and planetary
priesthood of Melchizedek. (Ps. 110:4-7; Judges
5:19-21; Heb. 5.9-12) Melchizedek is a manifestation of a 'Son of God.' (Heb. 7:3) (p. 588)

Continuing on, Hurtak reveals the following about the
membership of the Order of Melchizedek:

...The 'elect' of the Order of Melchizedek are Sons
of Light who have chosen to come into the world
of form and manifest the sovereignty of YHWH in
transmuting the earth. They work in implement-
ing the truths of God and, occasionally, even show
themselves as a 'visible Order' administering to
man through the Merkabah, so that the architec-
tonic models in the Heavens can be built on earth
as signposts to the many levels of universal creation. The Melchizedek Order is after the Order
of the Son of God. It governs the quadrants of the
planetary worlds where the Adamic seed has been
transplanted, administering spiritual things to
these worlds. It holds the keys to the opening of
the Heavens with respect to the contact areas on
the earth, and has the ability to commune with the
celestial communities of the Brotherhoods of Light
throughout the Father universes, coordinating the
work of the Christ in the Heavens and on the
earth. The Order is Eternal (Heb. 7:3) and has
foreordained its 'Priests and Programs' before the
world was. In the history of the planet, the Order
of Melchizedek has existed in small family communities of patriarch-priests, priest-scientists, and
poet-scholars who have faithfully attended to the
Word of God. (pp. 588-589)

There is evidence to support the fact that Melchizedek

was the being in the hierarchy who communicated to Jesus during his ministry on Earth. Whenever one is enrolled in this Order, he or she is given the title of Melchizedek. Jesus was referred to as Melchizedek King in the Bible.

Members in the Order of Melchizedek

For readers who are serious students of metaphysics, the names of the Ascended Masters will not be a surprise, for these people consciously communicate with the Masters and know them to be real. The names of the Ascended Masters are included in everyday conversations among this group of Initiates. These individuals know we have the capability of communicating with these beings. Hundreds of documents emerging worldwide testify to this.

To list all of the names of the Ascended Masters would not be possible, for there are so many of them. Many of the names would even be meaningless, for they would be so far removed from each civilization's consciousness. Here is a sprinkling, however, of names of Masters who incarnated in physical embodiment, and some of the names of Ascended Masters out of embodiment:

Abraham	Joseph
St. Anthony	Krishna
Apollo	Kuthumi
Artemis	Lanto
Ashtar	Maitreya
Athena	Mother Mary
Brahma	Michelangelo
Buddha	Monka
Confucius	Moses
David	Nada
Leonardo Da Vinci	Quan Yin
El Morya	Sanat Kumara
St. Francis of Assisi	Serapis Bey
St. George	Shiva
St. Germain	Solomon

Hilarion	Soltec
Isis	St. Therese
Jesus	Vishnu

An examination of the list shows that there are more male names than female names. Even though Ascended Masters are androgynous (possessing equal male and female characteristics within), when the soul ascends, it keeps the personification of the gender of the last embodiment. The gender we command at our ascension will be the opposite of the gender we commanded in our first incarnation when we came to Earth. Since Earth's civilizations have been primarily male dominated, most Ascended Masters selected paths where they could leave legacies as males. Consequently, most kept the personification of male.

Since there appears to be an imbalance of males and females on the Ascended Realms, showing more males, many from the Order of Melchizedek who chose the ascension path in this lifetime have incarnated as female. The goal is to balance the etheric planes by placing more feminine Masters in documented rulership roles after the work on Earth is completed at this time. In truth, however, there is no imbalance.

Ascended Masters Who Contributed to this Book

Four Ascended Masters participated in writing this book. For the reader's information, brief biographies of these Masters are given below. Notice how their present titles and job descriptions relate to the content and instruction they present in this document.

El Morya—Within the Spiritual Hierarchy, El Morya is the Lord of the First Ray and the authority for its actions on Earth. He comes from Mercury and works with one of three major offices of the Spiritual Hierarchy known as the Manu, which is now headed by Allah Gobi. The other two offices are the Office of the Christ, headed by Lord Maitreya (which is shared by Jesus and Kuthumi), and the Office of the

Maha Chohan, recently headed by St. Germain.

The First Ray is a cleanser and changer. Dysfunctional conditions are transformed into more productive means of expression. Those working on the First Ray are chosen for their ability to work with power. El Morya is the representative of God's will, and he supports all who journey to Earth to fulfill the will of God on their journeys.

El Morya is the staunch defender of justice and living up to standards. He is the Master of Universal Laws, truth, and pure communications. In many significant previous lives, he played roles that brought justice and equality to the world. El Morya was Abraham, the father of the Jewish religion; Melchior, one of the wise men who visited the Christ Child; King Solomon; and King Arthur of the Camelot legend. In other lifetimes, Hercules was his teacher, as was the Maha Chohan. El Morya's Twin Ray is said to be in embodiment today, working to assist him in fulfilling Divine justice on Earth.

Kuthumi—Master Kuthumi plays a major role as a teacher with a large ashram of many students. Kuthumi's title is World Teacher, and he holds a position in the Office of the Christ with Sananda, Jesus the Christ. His major teacher was Lord Maitreya, who now heads the Office of the Christ. It is believed that Kuthumi will assume the role that Jesus presently has when, in the future, Jesus journeys into higher realms. The essence of the Second Ray is love/wisdom, inclusiveness, and the power to serve. Kuthumi's role is to bring illumination through education.

In previous incarnations Kuthumi was one of the Three Wise Men who left embodiment after Jesus was born and who quickly came back as John the Beloved, the favorite apostle to Jesus; Thutmoses III of Egypt; Shah Jahan who built the Taj Mahal; St. Francis of Assisi; and Pythagoras. He was also responsible (along with El Morya and Djwhal Khul), for bringing Theosophy, the understanding of Oneness, to the world. His Twin Ray is reported to be on Earth today assisting the Celestial Hierarchy in guiding humanity through the spiritual awakening presently encompassing the world.

Pallas Athena—Known as the ambassador for Cosmic Truth, Pallas Athena was the High Priestess in Atlantis in the Temple of Truth. She was also chief counselor in Lemuria before the maya (or veil) covered the Earth. She fulfilled that role until the vibrations grew so dense that the presence and forms of the Hierarchy became nearly extinct.

Her presence assures that integrity and truth will prevail, and her Spirit directs the will to achieve. All who are on a mission to bring truth to Earth are under her influence. She holds membership on the Karmic Board of the Planetary Hierarchy of the universe along with the Divine Director, Goddess of Liberty, Lady Nada, Vista, Quan Yin, and Portia. Pallas Athena is the Twin Ray of the Maha Chohan.

In Greece the legends say that she was born out of the head of Zeus, she was sister to Apollo, and she is the patroness of Athens and of learning and the secret arts. She guides instruction on the goddess (yin) energy presently being reinstated on the planet today.

Sananda, or Jesus the Christ—He is the image of God, the archetype of God's identity. As Jesus, he was a high priest in the Order of Melchizedek. He came into embodiment from Venus, pure and with no Karma. Jesus is the son of God and man and the personification of godliness living in human form. He represents that portion of the trinity which is found in each of us. We may think of Sananda as the ultimate role model for the behaviors we are expected to learn on our spiritual journey.

His ascension and reunion with the God Force establishes the pattern for our ascension. It is the reunion of our souls with God, the I AM THAT I AM.

Edgar Cayce said that Jesus appeared on Earth as Adam, Enoch, Jeshua, Joshua, and Joseph of Egypt. Others state that he was Elisha. During the last three years of his life he shared his consciousness with his teacher, Lord Maitreya, who is the head of the Spiritual Hierarchy and the Great White Brotherhood, thus facilitating the miracles that he performed. His fourth initiation took place at the time of his crucifixion. Nine years later he reincarnated as

Apollonius of Tyana, one of the greatest Masters who ever walked the Earth plane.

For the reader who is interested in the biographies of the Ascended Masters who wrote the testimonials located in the front of this book, the following information is for you.

St. Germain—He was Lord of the Seventh Ray, which is one of four rays located in the Office of the Maha Chohan. He recently assumed the role of head of the Office of the Maha Chohan and become the Lord of Civilization. This office is concerned with the principle of intelligence on Earth. The Office of the Maha Chohan controls the forces of nature and is the Source of electrical energy. This office is connected with four other rays or departments, three of which are headed by Master Paul the Venetian, Hilarion, and Jesus. The fourth ray or department is the one formerly headed by St. Germain. It is not known who is presently in this position.

In previous lives St. Germain was Joseph, the father of Jesus; Merlin in Camelot; the prophet Samuel; Saint Alban in the third century; Roger Bacon; the Greek philosopher, Proclus; Christian Rosenkreutz of Germany, who founded the Order of the Rosy Cross (the Rosicrucians were its offspring); and finally Francis Bacon (who some claim was the writer using the name Shakespeare). St. Germain is believed to have remained on Earth for some 300 years after his ascension, appearing time and time again to those who needed his guidance. His Twin Ray is Lady Nada.

Hilarion—Hilarion is the Lord of the Fifth Ray, one of the departments of the Maha Chohan. His task is to bring the New Age into reality. Master Hilarion assists the coming of the New Age by teaching us how to use our mental powers in ever more forceful and productive ways. One of the other tasks of this department is the development of scientific breakthroughs. Scientific developments are created in the etheric and then channeled to scientists, often without their awareness. He also works closely with Master Marko in this area to assist individuals to learn to control their mental bodies and ultimately command dual consciousness. He guides psychics in their spiritual development and also is known as the master physician and healer of the universe.

Like Pallas Athena, Master Hilarion was in the Temple of Truth in Atlantis. The Oracle of Delphi in Greece was established under the rulership of this temple and his guidance with the Initiates. One of his former incarnations was as Saul of Tarsus, who became Paul the Apostle. In that lifetime, he and Thomas were known for their skepticism. Therefore, he guides those who are agnostics, disillusioned, and spiritually disappointed.

Mother Mary—Mary, or the Virgin Mary, is called the Queen of Heaven. She is often spoken of as an angel, and the Queen of Angels. In some charts of the Spiritual Hierarchy she is located with the Archangels and is shown with Raphael. Raphael is said to be her Twin Ray.

Mother Mary works devoutly with the elemental and nature kingdoms. She also is known to be a master of concentration and has great powers of manifestation. For the past two thousand years she has held the focus which has maintained the teachings of Jesus on the planet. Her appearances on Earth continually have opened up vortexes of energy that have kept the spiritual teachings alive in the minds and hearts of the masses. The saying is, "He's placed the whole world in her hands."

She was an Essene when she incarnated as Mary. The Essenes selected twelve girls to come to the temple at Mount Carmel to prepare themselves to be the mother of the Messiah. She was trained in physical and mental exercises as well as provided with spiritual training. Mary entered the temple when she was four years old and was selected by the Angel Gabriel when she was twelve or thirteen. She was then separated from the other children for four years.

Her marriage to Joseph (St. Germain) did not take place until after the conception of the Christ child. She and Joseph were in constant communication with the Celestial Hierarchy and the angelic kingdom when they raised Jesus and were always warned when to leave an area to protect the infant whom they had agreed to raise on Earth.

Following the death of Jesus, Mary went to England

with Joseph of Arimethea. This established the vortex for Camelot, destined to come forth later in the fifth and sixth centuries. The Grail was placed in Glastonbury for safekeeping at that time. It will be through the Grail in England that the energies of transformation and ascension will be channeled, which eventually will bring the Earth into the Seventh Golden Age. As the ruler of the goddess energy on Earth, Mary commands the transformation of power in the decades to come.

In one previous incarnation she was Isis in Egypt. Here, she instructed hundreds of Initiates in the Temple of Isis on the ancient wisdom and mysteries of the unseen. She is the Mother of the World, directs the angelic kingdom, and rules the Temple of the Sacred Heart.

Quan Yin—Called the Goddess of Mercy, Quan Yin is a powerful member of the Spiritual Hierarchy. Her greatest quality, mercy, means that she provides more assistance through compassion, forgiveness, and love than through actions. Therefore, she is a powerful goddess of healing. She is known to be the mother of women giving birth to new lives coming into the planet. Her mission, however, encompasses the directing of healing energy to all humans, worldwide.

For two thousand years she was the Chohan of the Seventh Ray, the position that St. Germain recently vacated. Then, like Pallas Athena, she was appointed to sit on the Karmic Board and is one of the Lords of Karma. Her Master was Lord Gautama.

She is best known throughout the Far East, although many in the West are now connecting with her power. The Chinese know her for her honesty and integrity. She heads the Temple of Mercy in China. She is the Master to turn to when one wishes to have Karma absolved.

Melchizedek—Melchizedek, the Eternal Lord of Light, is in charge of preparing the Heavenly worlds for the creation of the God force. He heads the Order of Melchizedek, which is charged with preparing the planet for the Fifth Dimension. His command oversees the Masters of Light who are in charge of bringing all ancient knowledge and wisdom to the Earth at this time. The Order provides spiritual insights to the world and coordinates the work of Christ. It has the power to reawaken, within the people of Earth, the understanding of how to decode the Universal Language of Light programming that presently is being downloaded into our subconscious minds.

Archangel Michael—Michael is an Archangel considered to be the greatest of all angels. He is chief of the order of virtues, chief of the Archangels, and chief of the angels of repentance, righteousness, and mercy. He is the champion of protection and faith and God's Prince in the Heavenly worlds.

Michael also is called the "Prince of Light" who leads the angels of Light against the angels of darkness. Although he fulfills a cosmic mission, he also works with individuals on Earth to protect and defend those who wish to live in the Light.

His Sword of Blue Flame frees lifestreams from the entanglements and lower entities of the physical world. If called upon, he will always assist in whatever action is necessary. He is committed to help all who call upon him for assistance, and will do so until the souls are purified and no longer need his assistance. One of his primary skills is to cleanse Earth's atmosphere and human auras of lower thought-forms, dissolving all that is not perfect or of the highest vibrations. His Twin Ray is Faith and they both are connected to Hercules.

Walt Disney—Walt Disney is a newly Ascended Master who is well known as a cartoonist, illustrator, movie maker, and futurist. His mission on Earth was to create an awareness of the elementals and animals and to integrate the existence of these kingdoms into human consciousness. His soul hails from the star system where the Elohim created the Deva Kingdom, and he came to Earth programmed with the dream that it is now time to bring an awareness of this kingdom into the forefront of human consciousness.

Summary

The Ascended Masters are highly evolved souls working for God who came to Earth to serve humanity. They have served several incarnations teaching the cosmic laws of the universe and have "ascended back into the presence of their Father from whence they receive new assignments to teach a wide variety of worlds because of their greater love" (Hurtak 1977, p. 567).

They brought to Earth wisdom and knowledge which was far ahead of their time. They came as prophets, philosophers, artists, architects, poets, and leaders. Many were scorned, ridiculed, and martyred for their beliefs and abilities to see the future.

There are numerous levels of offices and responsibilities in the Cosmic Hierarchy that governs Earth. There are many Councils of Light and job titles that are held, each contributing in some way to the fulfillment of God's plan on Earth. Two primary groups of Ascended Masters who have assisted in Earth's evolution are the Great White Brotherhood and the Order of Melchizedek. They assist the planets and civilizations to evolve.

Ascended Masters are available to everyone when a person requests their guidance and assistance. As we progress on our paths to mastery, we move closer to our ascensions and to becoming Ascended Masters ourselves. The Masters have been monitoring the world and our progress from the beginning. They have assisted whenever humanity and Earth needed it. Even though we cannot see them, they are with us to assist. Following are some of the ways in which they assist us:

* Masters may communicate with us through dreams and visions. They may communicate telepathically with individuals on Earth whose vibrational levels are high enough to receive the Masters' transmissions.
* Every soul on Earth is assigned to an ashram of

one or more Ascended Masters where spiritual teachings are learned and practiced. We undergo seven years of testing before the Masters make contact with students.

* The Celestial Hierarchy's plan today decrees that no more Ascended Masters will come to Earth one at a time. We must learn the truths and live by them. We are the Ascended Masters of tomorrow, receiving guidance from the Hierarchy.

Chapter 3

THE NATURE OF SOULS ON EARTH

Man has falsely identified himself
with the pseudo-soul or ego.
When he transfers his sense of identity
to his true being, the immortal Soul,
he discovers that all pain is unreal.
He no longer can even imagine the state
of suffering.
Paramahansa Yogananda

The Bible and the Dead Sea Scrolls speak of a battle that will be fought in "the final days" between the sons [and daughters] of Light and the sons [and daughters] of darkness. This is called the Battle of Armageddon. The vision from thousands of years ago reveals that a total of seven battles will be fought—the first three battles being won by the sons of darkness and the next three by the sons of Light. The final battle—the seventh—will be won, after a tremendous struggle, by the sons of Light. With this victory, peace and prosperity will reign on Earth for one thousand years.

The Battle of Armageddon not only is here on Earth today, but also is alive and well. This battle is being fought in the etheric and on the third-dimensional plane by forces working through humanity. These forces represent the fight for control between the lower self (ego) and the Higher Self, or will of God. Once individuals become aware of this, most grow so strong in the Light that they acquire the strength needed for victory in all circumstances. If a person is unaware of this etheric battle, however, he or she can be likened to a puppet manipulated in an arena by the forces of darkness.

The Children of Light have returned to Earth and are gearing up for the final four battles, for the first three already have been won by the sons and daughters of darkness. Observe the state of world affairs. At the time of publication of this book (1996), look at the crime, greed, wars, starvation, drugs, hopelessness, and desperation that have overcome so many. Some individuals are even fearful of leaving their homes, while others feel powerless in fighting for their basic human rights.

In America, some say we already have lost one generation of children because of our own inaction and the inaction of governmental and societal systems. If we lose another, it may be nearly impossible to recover within the time that we have left. There is a sense of spiraling downward—economically, spiritually, physically, and socially. In short, we have reached the abyss, the deepest moment of humanity's despair. Can you see this?

Ascended Master Kuthumi calls the decade of the nineties the "darkest of times." He says that the Masters can see into our future, and that this period ultimately will test all souls on Earth, forcing them to choose the Light or to choose the darkness. Ultimately, **this battle is a battle for our souls**. It is the time of judgment, but not the time for others to do the judging. It is the time for *us* to choose. In the end, we are our own judges and juries by virtue of our actions, words, thoughts, and emotions.

Who are these sons and daughters of Light who supposedly have come to Earth to fight the final battles? Are they already here? What do they look like? At first glance, all humans appear to look the same. The human form appears identical, with the exception of skin color, gender, size, etc. So, if everyone looks the same, where are these people?

To see them one must look with a vision beyond the sight of physical eyes. One must look with the Third Eye into the soul to see their auras emanating from within.

When one acquires this vision, it is easy to see these beings of Light, for there are one million of them walking among the masses. They are the reincarnated High Priests and Priestesses of the former six Golden Ages, the reborn Saints, the Pharaohs, and the risen Atlantean Masters who have embodied once again to bring the Light and higher truths to the world. These beings have an unfaltering vision and know clearly that the Battle of Armageddon is not lost, but already is won in the etheric. Atlantis HAS risen, as the "sleeping prophet" Edgar Cayce predicted so many decades ago. It has risen through the souls of these Masters who have come to hold the Light for the world.

In the Book of Matthew, Chapter 7, Jesus talks about these beings of Light who will return and live only within the laws of the universe to command God's will on Earth:

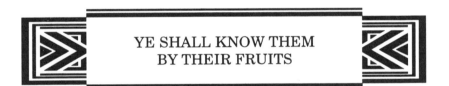

YE SHALL KNOW THEM
BY THEIR FRUITS

These souls have been sent to Earth by the Order of Melchizedek to bring in the power of the Christos energy and to teach this power to every soul in embodiment who wants to learn. They are the legions of Light Workers, representing all quadrants of the universe, who have journeyed to Earth to bring in the new world. They are embodied in all countries, races, and religions, and they understand Oneness. In short, they represent the Christ consciousness and all that is contained in this Divine power. They represent the culmination of all truths ever brought to Earth by the many great Masters who have walked before us in countries all over the world.

These souls vibrate with a higher Light frequency because they already have passed the lessons and Tests of Initiation in earlier lives. Many may have been Christians who were thrown to the lions or suffered other agonizing deaths through the ignorance of those in control at the time. All passed over to the other side, forgiving their trespassers. This accomplishment bought them their "tickets" to come here. Still others may have lived simple, uncomplicated lives and learned, like the Buddha, what enlightenment is. No matter what their paths, the point is that there is only one way—the Light—and they attained the Light.

By example and through teachings, these souls will once again instruct in the new mystery schools and remind everyone of the truths that we all have known, but momentarily have forgotten. Since the fall of Atlantis—the fall of humanity—consciousness has slipped so far into the masculine energy that we collectively have forgotten the power of the Light and the feminine principles. We have fallen asleep by shutting ourselves off from the Light. As a result, we find ourselves in a dark pool, struggling for a way to see. Through the Light of these high-level souls, this pathway will be found again.

Webster's New World Dictionary (1984) defines a soul as:

> An entity which is regarded as being the immortal or spiritual part of the person and, though having no physical or material reality, is credited with the functions of thinking and willing, and hence determining all behavior. The moral or emotional nature of man. (p. 1360)

The soul is the true essence of who and what we are. It is that which houses our Akashic Records, the data bank that stores all the experiences and knowledge we have accumulated since the beginning of our existence. Lessons and accomplishments from lifetime after lifetime are carried within the essence of the soul, and the strength of its Light determines the strength of our character. The greater the Light, the higher dimensional a being one is. In this way, higher consciousness is achieved, which brings more faith in the power of this Light that is ruled by the Christ energy. The lower the Light, the more lessons one has to learn and the more Karma one has to clear.

The age of the soul and the number of its previous lifetimes do not determine higher consciousness. Higher consciousness, enLIGHTenment, comes from meaningful experiences and lessons passed with the understanding that there truly is only one law—the Law of Love. When one leads a life expressing this belief, the mind and heart begin to open to new realities, and other dimensional truths become known.

Two kinds of souls are embodied on Earth today: celestial and earthling.

Celestial souls, the souls of the Children of Light, are those who have come to Earth directly from other dimensions and parts of the universe. Many of them have not had many incarnations on Earth, because they learned Earth's curriculum long ago and graduated to experience higher dimensional realities. When they did embody, they often chose roles as monks, nuns, priests, priestesses, lamas, yogis, or other spiritual rulers. Most were Atlantean Masters more than 10,000 years ago. Primarily, they volunteered to come to Earth during these times to offer assistance in bringing more Light to the world.

In reality, all souls originated from other parts of the universe. The celestial souls are those who remember this.

Today, most of these celestial souls are common people, living ordinary lives. They have embodied in ordinary situations because this is part of a celestial plan—the plan designed for Earth's transition into the Age of Aquarius.

The celestial plan states that three conditions must be met (by the majority of the celestial souls) to assure that these individuals will be grounded in Earth's curriculum in order to complete their work on the planet. These three conditions are:

1. Most of the souls will be born into families that are of either middle or lower economic class. This assures that each individual is raised in an environment that teaches the pain, struggle, and joys of humanity.

2. The souls will embody in families that provide them with a strict religious background, representing all faiths on Earth. When each begins to mature, the individual will find himself or herself turning his or her back on the organizational structure and human-made rules of the religious institutions, but not on the beautiful spiritual truths that make up the foundation of each religion. This cannot be stopped, for as the individual grows to become a thinking human being, the soul's Light awakens within the person a deeper memory and truth. The individual begins to remember that spirituality is not the property of one faith, church, or structure, but of the soul's connection back to the eternal Father/Mother of the universe.

3. Each individual will have a crisis to awaken the soul. Without such an experience, the human ego and even the soul can get too complacent and caught up in the physical illusion of the third-dimensional plane. The crisis, however, causes emotional pain and forces the individual to go inward for answers, instead of keeping the person's identity wrapped up in the maya that traps the five senses.

The celestial souls can be divided into two groups:

* Starseeds; and
* Star Helpers

The Starseeds, destined to awaken fully, are beginning to move into leadership positions that will help the world and humanity evolve spiritually. Some even comprise the membership of the 144,000 written about in the Book of Revelation. All precede the return of the Most Radiant One. Their main purpose is to hold the Light for the world until humanity's consciousness is raised to a point high enough to stabilize the world and embrace the darkness all around. These souls understand Oneness and know that all is and can be transmuted in the Light.

The Star Helpers, on the other hand, will never awaken fully. They are sent to assist the Starseeds to fulfill their missions by staying grounded in the physical world and clearing the way for the work that needs to be completed. They often assist in stressful situations by taking care of the many mundane details that need to be attended to in the physical world, thus freeing the Starseeds to complete their more spiritual work.

Ultimately, the celestial souls have been sent to Earth to anchor spiritual truths into every phase of our lives—education, family living, business, government, medicine, religion, etc. They are not here to start another new religion. Heaven forbid! There are too many of those already. They are here to live the spiritual truths and bring abundance, peace, and prosperity to Earth. They will accomplish this through mastery of Universal Laws, the same laws that they all have learned and taught in the mystery schools through thousands of years of incarnations. They are here to be the way-showers for humanity and to assist people out of their bondage.

Earthling souls, on the other hand, have had most of their incarnations on Earth or on other celestial bodies that vibrate on a similar three-dimensional frequency. They are souls who either enjoy the physical dimension and keep coming back or have not yet learned the curriculum of love and Light and, therefore, must keep returning because of unfinished business. The notion that this group is "stuck" to Earth means that the majority of them still have not learned all the lessons of the ancient teachings. Therefore, they have chosen to return repeatedly for third-dimensional experiences to continue acquiring lessons. Earthling souls make up approximately ninety-nine percent of the world's population.

This does not mean that earthling souls are less than or inferior to celestial souls, for all are children of one Creator and are equal. It only means that the experiences that have been acquired and mastered are different. As more lessons are learned, the vibrational frequency of the soul is raised, which automatically increases its Light. The Light brings a greater understanding and strength within to transform darkness, and this state of mind causes one to emanate a radiant aura of white or golden Light.

That is why halos and other auras of Light were always shown around Jesus and other Ascended Masters and Saints. Their physical, mental, and emotional bodies were so pure that they had transformed the dark energies and, consequently, radiated this tremendous force field of Light. Their "shields were up," making it nearly impossible for forces of darkness to tempt them and diminish their Light.

All souls who have mastered the curriculum of love and Light and purified themselves understand that NOTHING HAS POWER OVER THE LIGHT UNLESS YOU GIVE IT POWER. Fear and other lower vibrations are the tools used by the forces of darkness to keep us trapped and imprisoned. Anyone or anything that tries to coerce another's thinking by planting seeds of fear, separation, judgment, and negativity in the mind is NOT OF THE LIGHT. This is the truth. Yet the forces of darkness, still alive in the third-dimensional reality, are masters of psychological deception and try to control people by using fear tactics to command their emotional bodies. They often confuse people in messages by convincing them that discernment and judgment are the same, when in reality they are not.

The two weakest bodies we possess are the mental and emotional bodies. Masters are called "Masters" when they control what they think and feel at all times, never letting the thought-forms and fears of others become their own realities.

Celestial souls on their paths to mastery are moving once again to this point of realization. They are beginning to remember this truth and to use every opportunity to acquire practice in controlling their mental and emotional bodies, especially in stressful situations. In fact, most arenas on this plane at this time are designed for the purpose of allowing these individuals to practice centeredness and calmness in the midst of chaos and frustration. That is the only purpose for these situations. If you find yourself in a stressful situation, reexamine it to see the illusion that it really is. Once you have realized this, use the moment to become a master of calmness and centeredness. Then give thanks for the difficult experience, for without it, how would you have been able to practice?

The celestial souls, awakened in the decade of the eighties, have been through many clearing processes, relearning all of the basic truths. Soon, the rest of the world also will begin to experience awakening and will hunger for the information to find its freedom too. All is a part of the worldwide celestial plan. All is in Divine harmony.

All souls, celestial and earthling, can be called either Light Workers or Children of Light, two terms often used interchangeably by the Celestial Realms. This means that no matter what the path or previous history of incarnations, any soul can serve the God Force in any way it chooses. Remember, there are many paths but only one way, and that way is enlightenment.

One point of differentiation is that Starseed souls are on a different mission than earthling souls. The Starseeds' mission and karmic responsibility is to anchor Oneness into everything on Earth and to assist the world to evolve spiritually. As stated earlier, they are here to HOLD THE LIGHT FOR THE WORLD. This means that they must hold to higher truths and values at all times and learn to listen to the guidance of the Higher Self that communicates through the heart.

Contrary to public opinion, Starseeds do not have the same rights as other souls on Earth. They have come to Earth primarily to complete a job for the Order of Melchizedek. They have "signed" etheric contracts before coming into embodiment. They are visitors to this world and will return to their points of origin when the job is completed. Each is programmed through contact with the Higher Self to make a contribution and to leave a legacy on Earth. Once this contribution is realized, they will be free to leave, and each will be held accountable for the contracts they have signed between lifetimes, to make their contributions known.

Earthling souls do not share this same responsibility. They are here to evolve and to clear their karmic slates as well, but they are not taxed with becoming change agents or teachers. They are on Earth to learn and to become.

The level of soul advancement is a function of the kind of lives lived on Earth. Living a centered, meditative, good life on Earth ensures a good transition and more productive afterlives. As we move toward higher vibrations and Oneness with the Divine, we reach the Fifth Dimension and may move to ascension, which opens up new worlds of opportunities for service and development.

Once the assigned lessons are learned on any planet or star system, the soul is free to continue on its path to receive greater experiences and lessons. THE CURRICULUM OF EARTH IS TO LEARN LOVE AND LIGHT. To do this, one must learn forgiveness and unconditional love. Once these have been learned, the soul leaves for higher worlds. Thus, the Light does set you free!

Many Starseeds, when not in this embodiment, are residents in higher-dimensional realities throughout the universe. Their souls have evolved and collected experiences that Earth soon will encounter as she moves into the Fifth Dimension, and these remembrances are stored in the Akashic Records.

The Starseeds on Earth today both volunteered to come and were selected. They came because they knew that Earth is in the darkest of times—the beautiful Mother needs Light and assistance to cross over into the New Age that awaits. The Starseeds' dedication and track records from the past assisted in the selection process, and they came because they have served in this way before. Earth is the third planet that they have seeded collectively in the universe and birthed into a star. They can aid humanity in a victorious transition because they have been successful before. They are on assignment to fulfill God's plan.

Now, for the first time, it no longer needs to take thousands of lifetimes to evolve. With the acceleration of time, anyone who chooses may "go for the gold" (Light, that is). Earthling and Starseed souls alike have the opportunity to move together into the higher dimensions and evolve into higher states of consciousness. The membership residing in the Fifth Dimension and higher awaits our passage into their home, and sends their love and support to each soul in hopes that all will make it.

Finally, a chapter such as this would never be complete without recognition of the animal kingdom and the souls within those life-forms. Did you know that the animals' souls are the souls of our future children? Everything in the universe is consciousness and life. St. Francis of Assisi (Master Kuthumi) knew this to be true. He stated it openly, endured criticism, and was ridiculed for it. It took the papacy 2000 years to state this truth publicly, but in January, 1990, Pope John Paul II issued a proclamation declaring that animals have souls. The Tibetans have known this for centuries. All is evolving. Knowing this, isn't it sad to observe the kinds of experiences that we are offering the members of the animal kingdom?

As we evolve, we experience all the kingdoms. Some of us, as we first entered the mineral kingdom, could have come in as a diamond for our first introduction to Earth. At other times, for a brief moment in our evolution, we may have existed in the consciousness of the forest. The Native Americans ask the Spirit of the animal or the tree for permission to kill or cut it, out of respect for the life within. Can you see now where this comes from? Treating everything with respect and embracing the consciousness in all things is one of the signs of an advanced soul—one who is already into the Fifth Dimension.

Summary

Transformation to the Fifth Dimension does not come without a struggle. The forces of Light and forces of darkness are engaged in a battle for the future. Victory for the forces of Light is found in the realization that everything we need is in the Light and that our task is to hold the Light for the world.

❋ The decade of the nineties has been called the "darkest of times"—a time when all souls must choose the Light or choose the darkness.

❋ Our soul is the true essence of who and what we are and the recorder of the experiences and knowledge we have accumulated over time.

❋ Starseeds are celestial souls sent from other parts of the universe by the Order of Melchizedek to hold Earth in the Light and assist in the awakening of the planet.

❋ Star Helpers are also celestial souls who have been sent to Earth to assist the Starseeds with the awakening of Earth. Their purpose is to stay grounded on the Earth plane, and they are destined never to fully awaken in this lifetime.

❋ Earthling Souls have had most of their incarnations on Earth or on celestial bodies similar to Earth. They are here primarily to evolve and learn lessons from their Karma.

❋ Both Earthlings and Starseeds have the opportunity to move into higher dimensions and higher states of consciousness, because of the experiences of the Earth plane.

❋ Being a Master requires the ability to control your mental and emotional bodies. All souls are provided opportunities and challenges to practice this state of mastery.

Chapter 4

REINCARNATION AND KARMA

All the world's a stage,
And all the men and women,
merely players;
They have their exits
and their entrances,
And one man in his time
plays many parts.

Shakespeare
(St. Germain)
As You Like It

Reincarnation, or the belief that we live, die, and then return to the physical world in another body, is a comparatively new concept to the western world. Yet it has been a part of the philosophy of nearly two thirds of the world for centuries. Nearly every ancient civilization believed in the concept of reincarnation and developed its cultural and religious belief systems around it. Western groups, such as Theosophists and Rosicrucians, have included reincarnation and Karma as part of their belief systems. Today, more western people are understanding the logic and significance of these concepts and how they help answer the question, "Why do I exist?"

The basic premise of reincarnation is that there is no death. Death and movement from one's physical life to another life is part of the soul's development—a never-ending cycle designed to culminate in the soul's reaching an eternal union with the Divine.

By living many lives, we learn and progress along our spiritual path. We are connected to the Divine Mind of Oneness, but we stray from this path by not living the lives that we have been instructed to live by the Ten Commandments, other religious teachings, and our own Higher Selves. The key to understanding why we are here lies in the examination of the lessons that are inside our souls.

Each of our lives on Earth is like a school's curriculum where we learn to behave in ways that demonstrate that we have learned the lessons of Light and love. When we have not learned certain lessons, our souls are given opportunities in later lifetimes to master the lessons we need to learn. Before we can experience ascension—the process of becoming Ascended Masters and living in the Celestial Realms, taking on new levels of service and development—our souls must be purified. This is accomplished through dedication and discipline, allowing evolution to higher states of consciousness. The whole point of the process is humanity's evolution. The purpose of our life on Earth is to evolve and to assist with God's continuing creation. The underlying belief at the core of all major religions is that life is a sacred opportunity for growth and that we benefit from realizing our evolution.

There is much to suggest that we have been involved in learning lessons for centuries, but there is also ample evidence that we have made relatively little progress in our evolution. Michael Newton (1994), a psychologist who has studied the experiences of souls between lives, uses hypnosis and age regression techniques to provide us with case studies of the nature of life between lives. Newton reports that soul development is visible in the color range of the frequencies given off by souls. The color, density, and form that we as Light souls radiate are the result of accumulated knowledge and the concentrations of Light matter emitted as we develop. Today, this Light (the aura) of incarnated beings can be captured on film and measured through Kirlian photography and other methods.

Our ultimate purpose for existing is eventually to become beings of Light, emitting auras of pure energy. To do so, we first must acquire an aura of white Light, the frequency necessary to stabilize our electromagnetic energy fields and to provide the protection needed to travel through other dimensions. This is accomplished by developing an open mind and experiencing what are called Tests of Initiation.

The Tests of Initiation are the events (arenas, if you will) that we are placed in through normal life experiences. We are placed in these arenas to (1) learn lessons of the heart, (2) focus our will, (3) acquire higher values, (4) balance the male and female energies within, and (5) learn unconditional love and forgiveness. The more tests passed, the higher the frequency accumulated by the soul and the more Light acquired.

Once we are self-realized and become white Light (through a process requiring the balancing and integrating of the seven colors of the rainbow contained in the seven primary chakras), our second goal is to integrate the golden energy of the Great Central Sun into our consciousness and auric fields. This is accomplished by synchronizing our hearts and minds and connecting through our Higher Selves to the chakras situated above our heads. Techniques for doing so are now beginning to come forth on the planet, and some are being taught by awakened individuals.

We evolve to these higher states through a series of stages of consciousness that are expressed in the colors of our auras. The state of innocence is the most powerful state of all, and appears at both the lower and the higher spectrums of consciousness. When a soul begins its journey, the Light is pure and uncontaminated by the world. After the soul completes its journey, the power of the Light is once again so strong that the illusions of the world are exposed. In both states of being, a strong sense of innocence is present. This condition is reflected in the white Light of the aura.

According to Newton's case studies of souls between lives, advanced souls project high vibrations of moving energy that are reported to be blue in color, with the most advanced being purple. The lower levels of soul development are seen as white (beginner—which also reflects purity and a state of uncontamination), off-white with reddish shades (lower intermediate), yellow (intermediate), and light blue (upper intermediate). The advanced level is said to be light blue with no traces of yellow and moving toward traces of purple, and the highly advanced appears as dark bluish-purple (a state of an advanced Initiate of the mystery school knowledge). Notice how these colors reflect the sequencing of the colors in the rainbow (red, orange, yellow, green, blue, indigo, and violet).

Newton reports that three-fourths of his clients are in the early stages of soul development. About 90 percent are in stages I through III. Only 10 percent are at stages IV or V. If Newton's clients are representative of the population, there may be only a few hundred thousand people at Level V (light blue) and even fewer at level VI (purple).

This may seem discouraging, and yet it reflects the difficulty of spiritual progress through the density of the negative forces on Earth. The positive aspect, however, is that the Earth is evolving, making it possible and necessary to increase our levels of spiritual development. Earth is moving toward becoming a fifth-dimensional planet. This will happen when enough people become awakened to create the critical mass necessary for a kinder, gentler society. When this happens, Earth will move into the Fifth Dimension in the "twinkling of an eye."

People who have been asleep with regard to the possibilities of their spiritual development are awakening. More resources to help people awaken are now available. As a result, there is a general increase in our awareness of spirituality and our desire to become more spiritual. The journey to higher levels of spirituality, however, cannot be understood without having some understanding of the concepts of Karma and reincarnation.

Karma is the manifestation of the Law of Cause and Effect (one of the Universal Laws that will be discussed in Chapter 13) as it applies to the results of the choices and actions we take within a framework of free will. If our thoughts, desires, passions, words, and actions are benevolent and are helpful to others, they are considered to be good Karma. We are rewarded for good Karma in this life, between incarnations, and even in later lives. Plato referred to a tenfold return for the good we do for individuals and the services we provide for others and the world.

Given our mass consciousness of taking the preventative measures of planning future financial security and creating optimal health, it would seem wise to incorporate this Law of Cause and Effect. This would mean consciously avoiding negative entanglements and, instead, storing all good thoughts, words, and deeds as collateral for this lifetime and those to follow. Imagine collecting positive actions and events for eternity's sake, with dividends payable next lifetime! Not a bad savings plan, not to mention insurance of an exciting, gratifying future!

On the other hand, if our thoughts, desires, passions, and actions are malevolent or harmful to others, we accumulate bad Karma. The harmful things we have done must be balanced with wisdom and positive thoughts and acts, or by living our lives in ways that will help us learn the suffering and pain that have resulted as consequences of our misdeeds. Karma is not a punishment; rather, it is a learning experience designed to help us grow to higher levels of spirituality.

In the past we accumulated Karma over our various lifetimes. We removed old Karma very slowly, and most of us faced a backlog of Karma that seemed heavy and difficult to overcome. We had hundreds of lifetimes to complete karmic debts in the centuries past, but in this lifetime, the rules have changed. Now, time is up! We are entering the Age of Aquarius, which has a new vibrational frequency. This New Age is the age of thought manifestation, which means that the heart and mind must be purified and synchronized to assure that the will of God will supersede the will of the ego. The slogan for entry into this new dimensional frequency is:

EGO IS DEAD! EGO IS DEAD! EGO IS DEAD!

All souls are moving at an accelerated pace to assure not only that the will of the ego surrenders to the will of God, but also that all karmic debts are cleared. The Age of Pisces brought endless wars, destruction, pain, and suffering. Someone played the roles of the good and evil characters—and that "someone" was us.

We have reincarnated innumerable times to experience the totality of life and to acquire learning that will assist us to become enlightened. Unfortunately, when we do not learn the entire curriculum by observation or living, we return in a later lifetime and play a role that enables us to feel what it is like to be in a given situation. For example, sometimes we come to Earth to play roles of "victims" receiving "unjust" treatment. This is because we were not able to acquire compassion or empathy in a former lifetime, and the experience was not stamped on our souls. As a result, we acquired the Karma from those experiences and consequently began writing the curricula for our later lifetimes.

Countries and regions acquire Karma just as people do. Many people do not understand this, and wonder why civilizations move from greatness into decay. The decision-makers who abuse systems and who pass laws that create suffering for others establish a collective consciousness for the land and create Karma that inevitably must come around some day. Whether one is a corporation president, school board member, church trustee, member of Congress, or parent, decisions are judged and collective Karma may be accrued. An example of this can be found in the state of New Mexico. Today, the Rio Grande River basin is one of the greatest spiritual centers of the world. People from all walks of life are coming to the area, not even knowing why they are driven to do so. Their souls draw them to the area, and their spiritual progress is accelerated when they arrive. Other than destiny, there is a higher reason why this is so.

New Mexico developed the atom bomb, the instrument of destruction used in Japan in 1945. Because of the actions of a number of scientists and other individuals, many lives were lost and an atrocity was committed against humanity in general. Even though the use of this weapon prevented the loss of many lives and served to end the Second World War, the action affected the world, and New Mexico acquired the Karma associated with it. Now this must come into balance.

One of the ways to undo this Karma is for souls from New Mexico to bring enlightenment to the people of the world. This will help balance the negative Karma accrued by the use of the bomb. Therefore, many souls have awakened and many more are coming to assist the state and the Earth, so that all will be in perfect alignment in the millennium.

Some countries have more Karma than others because they consistently have inflicted more negative actions on others. From the perspective of Universal Law and Divine justice, all the problems that the United States is experiencing today are a consequence of its actions toward other countries and individuals in the past. Every single thing a person or a nation does is recorded in the etheric, and the laws are perfect. All must come around to be balanced in the future. There is no escaping this phenomenon.

Realizing this, think about the Karma that some countries are creating for themselves today. The wars and hardships in which individuals are engaged will have to come into balance—both personally and for their countries. What a pity that they do not understand the perfection of God's Laws. They would probably think twice if they had this understanding.

Nearly all individuals who come into embodiment on Earth have or have had debts to clear from the past. Many participated in the agenda of the Age of Pisces, with its endless wars and its infliction of pain and disabilities on others. Other debts go back still farther—perhaps even to the destruction of Atlantis. All too many souls came into this lifetime without having cleared their karmic slates of these deeds. Since karmic debts are of substantial magnitude, it is easy to understand the human propensity toward procrastination in clearing such debts.

On the soul level, however, all individuals know that THIS IS THE LAST LIFETIME TO BALANCE THE SCALES. Time's up! Old debts must be paid before the portal shifts, changing the energies to a higher octave. If debts are not paid and scales not balanced, the soul will be denied entry into the higher kingdoms.

The reason that so many oppressed individuals are living in difficult circumstances today is that the debts from the Ages of Pisces and Atlantis are still being paid. As indicated earlier, many of these debts are centuries old. All members of an oppressed person's family are also connected to the debt. Each one agreed between embodiments to work together to assure that the Karma is paid and the scales are balanced once again. Each soul will suffer for the amount of time necessary to balance actions that hurt others in former lifetimes. Once these debts are paid and the scales are balanced, good Karma begins to come around to build the promised Garden of Eden.

These conditions will be the same for all souls until the cleansing is complete. Then there will come a time on Earth when such difficult experiences no longer will be necessary, because all will be perfectly aligned with the Higher Self. Our egos have created wars and hardships. Our choices have created our suffering. The will of God desires only peace, perfection, and happiness.

It is important to state here that not all hardships or challenging conditions in life are our "just punishment." Sometimes a soul chooses to sacrifice its own path in service to others. For example, infants may embody to play difficult roles because the parents need to learn patience or other lessons. Or, beloved family members may agree (on the etheric) to give up their lives collectively in a car accident caused by a drunk driver for the purpose of raising public consciousness regarding the crime of alcohol abuse. When we do not acquire consciousness by observing and participating in life, lessons must be delivered to us in a more serious format to get our attention. Often some of the nicest and most well-known people choose experiences for the sole purpose of raising consciousness.

It is unfortunate that beautiful people sometimes choose to sacrifice themselves in situations such as the ones described above. Those choices would not be made, however, if they did not serve greater purposes. On a higher level, their souls do receive greater rewards for their actions, especially if their sacrifices help others see the Light. When humanity, individually and collectively, reaches the state of enlightenment where all are accountable for their own behaviors and accept responsibility for their actions, we will move to a place in our evolution where martyrs will cease to exist.

Although this is really a misperception, can you not see why Earth is sometimes called the "penal colony" of the universe? In spite of its beauty and all the joy that can be experienced in living here, there is much credibility in this concept when you realize that Earth is one of the few planets on which one can come into embodiment where karmic law rules. Understanding this gives us a whole new outlook on what is really happening in our lives and on Earth. It also should give us a new perspective on life and cause us to assess everything we do. We must continue to come to Earth until our scales are balanced and we have no unfinished business left.

The Harmonic Convergence in 1987 freed the Starseeds, or the Children of Light, from karmic debt. This was so because the Starseeds had the least amount of Karma to pay upon embodiment. Soon this event will affect all others on Earth in a similar way.

At the time of Harmonic Convergence, the clearing of karmic debts was accelerated and a dispensation was given that allowed all to begin the Tests of Initiation to achieve higher levels of mastery. This does not mean that the Starseeds will not continue to accumulate good and bad Karma, but rather that they are no longer tied to their past Karma. Those souls are now connected to higher planes of existence that are freeing the souls, at an accelerated pace, to achieve higher levels of enlightenment and power. Within five years, by the year 2001, this same dispensation will hit all of Earth's peoples. Therefore, it is wise that individuals today think seriously about what they are doing in each moment of time and open that "savings account" of good actions, deeds, and words.

Karma is the result of thoughts, emotions, words, and actions—all directed by the will. Each of these energies moves into the inner world and becomes a vibrating force on the mental plane. The vibrations attract and mold other, like forces as they move to the physical plane. The resulting forms stay with us and may remain for a longer or shorter time depending on the strength of the original energy.

A principle of karmic law outlines how energy sources may be realized in the next life. Theosophists such as Annie Besant and others suggest the influence of karmic law during our afterlife, the life between incarnations, and in the determination of the nature of our next incarnation. It may be difficult for us to understand what choices we have made and how we have participated in and learned from various incarnations. The guiding principle is that Karma is the expression of the perfection of the Universal Laws and that it becomes the focus for our continuing spiritual growth and development.

Some basic tenets of karmic law may be summarized as follows:

* Aspirations and desires become capacities;
* Repeated thoughts become tendencies;
* Wills to perform become actions;
* Experiences become wisdom;
* Painful experiences become conscience.

These may be applied in positive or negative ways. For example, a man who was a soldier in one lifetime, and known to be impatient, also had an interest in architecture. His impatience caused his death in that lifetime. In the life he is living today, he is an architect and uses this career choice to help him develop patience, a trait essential to the profession.

Karma is documented in our Akashic Records. Our Akashic Record is a record of the actions from all our lifetimes, and it includes our thoughts, wishes, desires, words, and actions in all our existences.

When Karma refers to the various events of our lifetimes and the things we have learned or need to learn, it plays an important role in our lives between lives. Any lifetime provides the opportunity to assess what we have learned. We are the sum total of all our lives and consciousness.

Consciousness, on the other hand, is an emerging property. It is more than the sum of its parts, and it is not just neurons, protons, electrons, etc. It is the totality of what we have become, thus providing another interpretation of Einstein's discovery that all time exists in this present moment of time. All time includes that which is stored in our subconscious minds. All of our past lives have made us what we are today. Since we are influenced by our subconscious, Karma becomes the programming (positive or negative) that we have created in our current life or in other lives.

As our knowledge grows, it is easier to move out of karmic patterns. When love is used with knowledge and will, we are liberated or we reach a state of equilibrium. We are able to act in more powerful ways and assume greater responsibility for our lives. We are also able to progress in our spiritual development at an increased pace.

Perhaps one of the most interesting questions is, what happens to us between lives? In the past, mystics and adepts provided us with some idea of the events between lives. There are reports that we incarnate on other planets and star systems, only to augment our experiences and ideas. Today we have documentations of near-death experiences, past-life regressions, channeled information, and many other sources of data. While the information received does not agree in all cases, the similarities among the events described are striking.

Newton (1994) provides one of the clearest perspectives of what happens after death. His hypnotic regressions suggest the following stages that resemble Theosophical, Hindu, and Tibetan accounts. Experiences between lives seem to include the following:

Death and Departure. People describe the death process as one of leaving their physical bodies and hovering over them for a period of time. They report a euphoric sense of freedom and brightness.

Movement Toward the Light. After a period of time, which varies, they report moving through a tunnel toward Light. At the end of the tunnel, they are met by someone who has meaning for them—a guide, relative, close friend, etc. They feel unconditional love that they have not felt on Earth.

Orientation. New arrivals are taken to a place of healing where they have counseling sessions with their guides. This culminates in a session of Divine Judgment or Self Judgment, which is a review of their Akashic Records and an assessment of what was just accomplished in this lifetime.

Time Spent in a Staging Area. Souls then spend time in soul families and cluster groups as part of their learning. Soul groups are determined by a common level of knowledge and soul development. Every soul generates a color, and souls usually remain with their own soul groups whose members are at comparable levels of soul development. The primary cluster may split into smaller groups, but they are not separated. As some souls learn faster, they move into independent studies, and new pods or groups are formed.

Life Selection. Souls must determine whether they are ready for a new physical life, what lessons they need to learn, and where they will have the best opportunity to work on their goals. They select their new parents on the basis of what they perceive as the lessons those individuals can provide for their spiritual development.

Choice of a New Body. Souls voluntarily agree to be the children of given sets of parents. They prepare for embarkation.

Rebirth. A new life cycle begins, where the souls can increase their learnings.

Descriptions of the Orientation Stage differ. Some people describe going through various levels of intermixed layers. The astral, or lower, layers are dark and dense. These gradually give way to the devachanic or Heavenly layers, which are Light. The number of layers, the time one remains in them, and the meaning of the experience are interpreted in many ways. Ascended Master Kuthumi says this about the soul's orientation period.

In the etheric, the soul comes to the table of the Oversoul to become reunited with the others composing the group of 1,000 souls. The surprise and confusion are short-lived, and the remembrance of the process is soon integrated into the moment. Each member present from the larger group of 1,000 rejoices at the reintegration of the newly emerging consciousness.

At first the moment is a quiet one. This eventually gives way to the celebration. Finally, the moment of truth and assessment comes forth and all participate in the process. Decisions made at this time affect the entire Oversoul, for no soul is allowed to move forward until the entire group of 1,000 has reached the vibrational frequency required to move on. That is why it is so important to assist all souls in embodiment to see the Light, for this process enhances the whole group's mobility. To love thy neighbor and give assistance when needed is a valuable key to use for the advancement into the higher planes of reality. Since no soul in embodiment has access to the complete list of 1,000 names

*registered in their soul family membership, it be-
comes imperative that love and forgiveness be bestowed upon all whom they meet.*

*Individual souls are bound to the group of 1,000
until they reach the Fifth Dimension. This is Universal Law. After this point has been reached, all
directives and rules change, for the higher frequencies require different protocol. Therefore, for all
Earth inhabitants, it is essential to assist your
brothers and sisters into the Light, for it could be
one decision not to assist that could keep you from
thy Father's House.*

The nature of the experience between lives appears to
vary according to the level of the soul's development. Beginning souls may be provided with more time, support, and
guidance, whereas advanced souls may move more quickly
through the process. More is expected of old souls by the
Karmic Board, which is the governing body designed to judge
our behavior and provide us with opportunities for continued
growth. The more advanced a soul is, the more power it has
to negotiate the outcomes. The more serious the offenses are
against proper conduct of behavior and Universal Law, the
less sympathetic is the Karmic Board.

In addition to the harmful things that we have done
in the past, the things we fear the most or tend to avoid also
determine the lessons that we must learn. Since the ultimate
goal of the soul is self-mastery, one is required to conquer all
on the physical plane. NOTHING conquers a master. If an
individual is afraid of public opinion, for example, and lives
his or her life attempting to please others and never self, the
lessons to be learned will revolve around this situation. The
individual will be placed in one arena after another until the
ability to let go of this fear and live a life that is true to it-

self and to the Higher Self finally is acquired.

Each soul has a gift from God to bring to Earth, whether it be a beautiful voice or something as simple as a charismatic smile. Each should be honored for its gifts. One's path and destiny often include these special talents as one's mission is revealed. Every soul who comes to Earth is on a mission from God, but few realize it because of the volume of Karma accrued in past lives.

Missions are revealed when karmic slates are clean. Consequently, many souls remain frustrated, for they understand intuitively that there is something they must do, but they cannot see the picture clearly when the veils are down and vagueness prevails. As soon as karmic debts are paid and Tests of Initiation are passed, missions are revealed.

Summary

Reincarnation, or the belief that we live, die, and then return to the physical world, is a process for learning how to live and grow spiritually until we have reached the stage of becoming one with the Divine. Reincarnation is the process by which we move to higher levels of consciousness and mastery.

* We move through phases of soul development as we learn Earth's lessons, and these phases are evident in our levels of vibration and color.

* Karma is the balance of positive or negative credit that we accumulate for our thoughts, actions, and behaviors. Karma is accumulated by individuals, groups, and nations.

* After death, we appear to move through a process of assessing our learning, gaining new information, and identifying the lessons and situations which can best meet our needs in the next incarnation.

* We are sent to Earth with a group of 1,000 souls, and we cannot progress until each member of our soul group has progressed; this is true until a person attains the behaviors of the Fifth Dimension.

* Our missions are revealed when our karmic slates are clean.

Chapter 5

HUMAN ENERGY SYSTEMS

By remaining in your power you do not become
a static energy system, one that hoards energy
to itself. You become a stable energy system,
capable of conscious acts of focus and intention.
You become a magnet for those who are illu-
mined and those who want to be.

Gary Zukav
Thoughts from the Seat of the Soul

Most people are aware of the importance of food as the source of our energy. We continue to become more conscious of the types of foods that best serve our energy needs and the addictions or behaviors that reduce them. Energy, or the strength or power to function and work, is vital to our survival and to our ability to realize the products of our creativity. Many people are also aware of the ways that movement and exercise serve to increase our overall energy. These sets of connections—relationships between nutrition, exercise, and energy—are observable as part of our physical world, and we accept and understand their importance to our lives.

There are, however, other energy sources we have and use that are not so visible. We function within numerous systems of multiple energy fields that most individuals are not consciously aware of, and yet, these systems are essential to our well-being. They also are essential for extending our spiritual growth.

Knowledge of these not-so-visible energy systems is not entirely new. Thousands of years ago, Hermes, who articulated many of the Universal Laws, defined aspects of one of these systems and referred to them as chakras. There is also evidence of partial knowledge of this system, as well as other human energy systems, in the Chinese, Indian, and Native American cultures. Examples include the study of such things as acupuncture, Tai Chi, and the ability to accomplish tasks normally described as impossible. Ancient Tibetan scriptures report as many as 72,000 energy channels contained within the human body system.

During the Dark Ages much of this knowledge was lost and was perpetuated only by the secret mystery schools. It was not until the early nineteen hundreds that Theosophists, such as Annie Besant and C.W. Leadbetter, began to write about some of these systems in an open manner. They began by describing them as chakras and explained their connection to spirituality, hoping to educate people on these important points of power within us.

Knowledge of chakras has grown slowly, primarily because of the lack of scientific instruments to measure their functions, and our reliance, in large measure, upon the observations of those with psychic sight. In a society that worships scientific study, it is very difficult to obtain support for phenomena that cannot be measured, seen, held, or kicked. In some ways this is a sad memorial to what we have become, for it exemplifies the closed-mindedness of the society in general. In other ways, the scientific method of gathering data has brought us to the threshold of the Seventh Golden Age, where we do enjoy the inventions and conveniences that this approach has brought us.

It is through the invention of modern technology, however, that chakras are now being validated. More recently, scientific studies of electromagnetic currents, documentation of electric fields around acupuncture meridians, measures of the biofields of humans correlated with aura readings, life-enhancing alternating magnetic fields, and healers' magnetic pulses correlated with the Earth's magnetic field have supported the psychic observations of many gifted individuals. Yet, in spite of the growing body of evidence regarding these energy fields, it is often difficult for some people to accept this new information into their lives, because human energy systems are not visible to the naked eye.

Today, we stand on the threshold of understanding these power centers, and are faced with an exciting future. Our knowledge continues to change and will continue to grow over time as our instruments of measurement evolve and as more people gain psychic sight. This presents an exciting future for humanity!

Knowledge related to this area has been largely fragmented. A number of devices like the electroencephalogram (EEG), the electrocardiograph (EKG), and the superconducting quantum interference device (S QUID) now measure energy fields and have shown that a dysfunction in the energy field often leads to or suggests disease. Other studies have demonstrated a correlation between wave patterns of alternating electrical currents on the body surface and the colors perceived by twelve different aura readers or persons with psychic sight. The chakras and the power of the Kundalini also have been written about.

It has been only recently that we have begun to see the multiple dimensions of our energy, our growth, and our spirituality. Barbara Ann Brennan, a scientist-healer with psychic sight, has developed a coherent view of the dimensions of the energy systems and their relationships to our healing and spiritual growth. Brennan (1993) describes four dimensions of energy systems and creative energies and their interrelationships. They are:

1. The physical body—the body that behaves in relationship to the other dimensions
2. The aura, including the chakras—the personality that we develop

3. The hara—the foundation for the personality which is created out of our intentions
4. The core star level—our divine essence

These dimensions represent energy charges that influence our personalities, and each is a progressively deeper side of our nature. Thus, the core star reflects the basic nature of our soul, whereas the hara, aura, chakras, and physical body are more likely a product of our experiences and levels of our spiritual development. Each of these is discussed below.

The Physical Body

Our physical body and the physical world we experience constitute the miraculous way in which we experience life. This body and this world are maintained by unseen worlds of energy and dimensions that constitute higher vibrations and consciousness. Many people assume that the physical body is first and that the other dimensions follow. There is evidence, however, that the reverse is true and that our human energy systems existing in other dimensional realities provide the underlying design or matrix for the development of the physical body.

In one sense, the physical body is the "end of the line." Weaknesses or problems in the deeper dimensions eventually result in dysfunction or disease in the physical body. Psychic healers work to clear or balance the inner dimensions as a means of helping an individual resist or overcome disease. When individuals understand the relationships among these dimensions, they can exert more control over their lives and enjoy a stronger, healthier, more creative way of living. Information of this sort also provides individuals with important information necessary for spiritual growth.

The Aura

The aura is the dimension above the physical body which facilitates our psychological processes. It is the conduit or means by which our core self is transmitted to our physical body. Maintaining a balance in our auric field is essential for good health. According to Brennan (1993), the auric field is the egg-shaped field of energy surrounding a person that includes seven levels, or "bodies," and the chakras. The levels penetrate through the body and extend outward from the skin. The levels closest to the body vibrate at lower frequencies and those farther away from the body vibrate at higher frequencies.

Brennan believes that the first, third, fifth, and seventh levels of this field are structured in a specific form. The second, fourth, and sixth are filled with formless energy. The second appears to be gas-like, the fourth is fluid-like, and the sixth is diffuse light. She uses the term bioplasma to describe these levels and describes them as exhibiting varied colors, densities, and intensities. This bioplasma flows around the structured levels of the aura and correlates with one's emotions. It is this bioplasma energy field that is the creative life force energy that is used for manifestation.

When the combined energy field of the aura is strong, the body is strong and capable of productive functioning. When it is weak, the physical and life experiences of the individual are limited. Each level of the auric field is related to one of seven areas of life experiences. The life experience areas have been described in slightly different ways by individuals using their psychic sight, but there is much similarity among their descriptions. Brennan, an outstanding scientist-healer with psychic sight, describes the seven levels in the following way.

Level 1 — Physical Sensation. The first level of the auric field correlates energy flow, pulsation, and structure with what you feel in your body. In active, strong persons this field manifests as thick, coarse, dark blue-gray levels. Athletes and dancers exhibit more lines of energy that are thicker, highly charged, and bright blue. Quiet, sensitive, nonathletic persons show a thin, fine level which is light aqua-blue. When individuals abuse their bodies, they lose connection with the senses and may experience disease.

Level 2 — Emotions. Feelings and emotions are expressed in the second level of the auric field. When an individual feels positive about herself or himself, bright colors of cloud-like energies are evident. Negative feelings show up in darker, dirtier shades of colors. When the second level is strong and charged, it indicates positive feelings about the self. When the level is weak and undercharged, it indicates negative feelings about the self.

Level 3 — Rational Mind. People with strong, clear minds exhibit lemon yellow energy lines pulsating at a very high rate. If the level is weak and undercharged, the person will not demonstrate mental clarity and probably will not be interested in learning activities or other intellectual pursuits.

Level 4 — Relationships and Compassion. The first three levels of the auric field represent the physical world. The fourth level is the bridge between the personality and the spiritual body. Others refer to the fourth level as the Intentional/ Compassionate Body and describe it as a vehicle for getting in touch with the Universal Mind. Brennan describes it as the level that represents our relationships with people, animals, plants, inanimate objects, the Earth, the sun, the stars, and the universe. The energy of the fourth level appears as a fluid filled with all colors.

A person with a strong, healthy, and charged fourth level is likely to have good relationships with others. If the fourth level is undercharged, the energy appears as dark, thick, heavy liquid. Brennan refers to this as auric mucus, which has a negative effect on the body causing pain, heaviness, and disease.

One of the most interesting of Brennan's observations is that the energy of the fourth level is sent out to other persons. Streams of bioplasma reach out from each of us to touch others' auric fields. The colors of the streamers reflect emotions and can be perceived as either positive or negative. Love is seen as rose energy, envy as dark gray-green, passion as orange, and anger as red. Weak souls can attach themselves on a psychic level to others and use this level of energy to drain others of their life force energy. This is how the term psychic vampire originated.

Level 5 — Divine Will. The fifth level, Divine Will, is the template for the first, or physical level. It contains the form for the body and all other life. When this level is strong and full of energy, it reflects an alignment with Divine Will. When such an alignment is in place, people maintain order in their lives. When one is not aligned with Divine Will, the pattern of the fifth level is distorted, and the person does not feel connected to the world around.

Level 6 — Soul or Divine Love. The sixth level is the soul level and allows the soul to be expressed in the physical body. Brennan describes the sixth level as consisting of beautiful streamers of Light extending about two and one-half feet from the body. It contains all colors and vibrates at a high frequency. The health of the sixth level is evident in its brightness and energy. This indicates spiritual love and joy. When the sixth level is weak, one is unlikely to have spiritual or inspirational experiences. It may appear as dark or thin. A key to spiritual growth is to charge the sixth level through meditation, contemplation of a beautiful object, or repeating mantras.

Level 7 — Divine Mind. The seventh level provides the individual with a feeling of Oneness with the universe. A strong seventh level is seen as beautiful, golden lines of energy vibrating at a high frequency. Streamers are interwoven to form the physical components of the body, and they extend to three and one-half feet. These streamers form a golden egg that protects the individual. This egg structure is strong, and regulates the flow of energy outward. It also guards against the penetration of unhealthy energies.

The seven levels described above are important. On an ongoing basis, individuals must balance all of them and provide experiences which stimulate each level in order to maintain good health, spiritual growth, and a full life. These energy levels comprise our present understanding of the human aura as most know it today. Yet, the Ascended Masters tell us there is even more to our existence that we have not yet been able to see.

In several of Ascended Master Kuthumi's transmissions, he speaks of the nine bodies that comprise human existence. Once he stated that Egypt was the only civilization that fully understood the concept of the nine bodies, and that it was this knowledge that facilitated that civilization's supernatural accomplishments. Knowledge of these energy fields facilitates an understanding of how to expand them and, consequently, use this energy to acquire supernatural powers through enlightenment. In addition to describing the miracles the Pharaohs and High Priests and Priestesses could perform, he also referred to Jesus and his ability to heal the sick and raise the dead. Kuthumi stated that Jesus passed his final initiation in the Great Pyramid of Egypt, raising his status to the higher priesthood of the Order of Melchizedek. This is one of the reasons why it is reported that God said, in reference to Jesus, "Out of Egypt I have called my Son."

Understanding human energy systems provides knowledge about our human potential and our inherent power. Because this is so, it is understandable why this information has been kept from the people for so many centuries. In the past, rulers feared this information getting into the hands of ordinary people. A group of people acquiring superhuman abilities threatens all in power, especially if people are not guided to use these powers in ways that benefit humanity.

But that was the past. Today, we live in fortunate times, for information flows freely. There is an abundance of new information available regarding our spiritual power, and contained in this literature are keys for understanding our full human capabilities. As we strive to strengthen our bodies with good food and exercise, and our minds with wisdom and learning, our spiritual bodies become the next frontier to discover. Once body, mind, and spirit unite within our consciousness and this energy is anchored within our souls, undreamed of power is destined to flow through us. It is truly a time of new beginnings, as Master Kuthumi so often has stated.

Many individuals have asked repeatedly for Kuthumi's transmission describing the nine bodies. Because it is so informative and provides an understanding of what we are and what we are capable of becoming, it is included below.

Greetings, Dear Sisters and Brothers of the Order of Melchizedek:

On this glorious day of new beginnings, I, Kuthumi, send through this transmission of enlightenment that is destined to assist humanity in awakening the inner paths of higher consciousness. I represent the Council of Light from Lyra and the Council of Integration from Hydra as I relay these words of wisdom on this day. These governing bodies oversee the spiritual transformation process on Earth and they sanction these words that I now impart.

The concept of the nine bodies refers to the ancient teachings of Abraham. This concept also extends back to the Egyptian era, when the High Priests and Priestesses understood the paths to the Divine through the etheric centers connected to the God Force. The understanding of the nine bodies has been an elusive concept that has not come forth before this time, because the time was not right for all to know.

The nine bodies refer to the physical body and eight other electronic energy fields that circle the human form. These eight bodies exist on higher etheric dimensions of time / space and are contained within what is called the auric shield. The auric field of these eight bodies extends several Earth meters above the crown chakra. This area is called the "area of enlightenment" and supports the spiritual connection that projects from the top of the head to the God Force, called the Higher Self.

The eight bodies are in alignment when one experiences the perfect state of Oneness. This state is acquired only after one begins the journey of the Spiritual Warrior. Forming a perfect alignment takes years and requires a form of discipline that most on Earth do not command. The eight bodies are connected within the electronic circle of the Higher Self, that guides the alignment of the patterns of energies that coagulate within the circles of the aura.

References available today regarding humanity's energy systems primarily speak of seven bodies. We, collectively, speak of nine and include the bodies that are hidden within the teachings of the Qabalah. Within the Qabalah the mysteries to life are revealed through the ten sephiroth that assist humanity to understand the nature of God and the divine emanations of angels and humans. That is why these mysteries are referred to as the knowledge of the Tree of Life. When one studies the Qabalah, all secrets to life are revealed, and ascension to higher circles of consciousness is granted. This is truth, for the Qabalah provides the way to connect to the Archangels who have the power to teach individuals how to anchor the assistance of the angelic realms into the subconscious depths of the human mind.

This is truth. This is the way.

In the beginning I stated that the teachings around the nine bodies have existed since the days of Abraham. In reality, these teachings have been around for eternity, but there are few records of this wisdom before the time of the Hebrew invasion. It was also during that time when the Qabalah first came into existence. It was written to aid humanity in understanding its connection back to the Divine. The teachings of the nine bodies and the teachings of the Qabalah are actually one and the same. Therefore, I provide this stimulating introduction to you only to pique your interest and perhaps encourage further study in this area.

Throughout the years, some of the sacred information relating to the Qabalah had been distorted. Although interpreters had good intentions, many did not understand the consequences of their actions when they changed some of the sacred words and concepts that were recorded. A part of the original distortions included the knowledge that humans have seven bodies (instead of nine), which connect them to the God Force.

It was the Essene, who came out of Egypt, Jesus the Christ, who was able to rediscover the secret of this ancient, lost mystery. It was because he was able to master this information that he was able to obtain control over his electron body in the physical world. One cannot claim victory over the electron body until one has access to ALL the keys that control it. One obtains the keys by examining and learning the nine bodies, and understanding the nature of each. Through this understanding, one assumes mastery over the nine and learns to control them, for once mastery is reached the soul is given the keys to commanding the electrons that flow through the nine.

The nine bodies are the following:

1. *The first body is the physical body. It is the most dense of all the nine bodies and resides in the third-dimensional frequency of the Earth plane. It is considered to be the body temple and is the vehicle that transports the soul and all eight higher bodies. It is created out of the thoughts, feelings, words, and actions of the individual who governs it. This body must learn discernment before it can connect to the higher electron frequencies in the auric field.*

2. *The second body is the emotional body. This body includes an intricate system of energy fields that produces vibrational frequencies that affect both the mental and physical bodies. It is the source of power that moves the electron force when one is in alignment with the Higher Self. This body must learn discipline and independence and detach from all that is not a part of the perfected plan before it can unite with the higher frequencies that surround it.*

3. *The third body is the mental body. This body receives the thought processes of the Universal Mind and processes the information through a filtering system which is located in the pineal gland of the brain. The mental body and mind are not the same. The mental body is the resonance field within the auric shield that collects the data and transfers them for use to other systems within the other eight bodies. Mind energy is the God Force that surrounds the mental body. The highest form of communication that can be transmitted to the mental body comes in the form of symbols. The highest symbols the mental body must integrate into its essence be-*

fore it can unite with the higher frequencies sur-
rounding it are: truth and service to others.

4. *The fourth body is called the causal body. This*
    electromagnetic field comprises a source of
    power that wraps itself around the lower three
    bodies for the purpose of shielding the lower
    bodies from harmful forces that exist on the as-
    tral plane. It is the veil, so to speak, and yet
    serves as a filter for higher thought-forms that
    come through to enlighten the individual on the
    spiritual path. The causal body is the connect-
    ing link to the oversoul. It contains the power
    to merge the vibrational frequencies of the lower
    three bodies into a higher vibration, thus pro-
    ducing the foundation for the successful merg-
    ing of the Twin Flame within that must be
    united before ascension can be realized. An
    understanding and commitment to one's greater
    mission in life must be absorbed into this body
    before the individual can advance on the spiri-
    tual path.

5. *The fifth body is the higher mental body. This*
    body guides the symbolism and force of the
    Higher Self to and through the lower bodies
    and states of consciousness. It is the part of the
    mental body that is connected to the heart of the
    Christos and that which directs life to evolve to
    higher states of existence. The higher mental
    body receives its messages from the Higher Self
    through a series of impulses sent down from the
    Seventh Dimension. One's ability to receive
    clear messages through the higher mental body
    is determined by the degree to which the causal
    body has absorbed the lower, discordant fre-
    quencies of the three bodies that exist below it.
    When all is in alignment, messages flow clearly

and the individual proceeds to fulfill God's will before the will of the ego. Obedience and courage to a higher purpose in life are the keys to master within this body before one can advance further.

6. *The sixth body is called the directional force body. This body directs or guides one's mission on Earth. The directional force body receives the flow of electrons from the Higher Self and deflects or transforms these signals in such a way that the lower bodies can interpret them. This body is connected to the higher thought-forms of the universe and is more closely aligned with the individuals who reside on higher levels of spiritual mastery. This is also the body through which the Ascended Masters communicate, from the etheric through the seventh level of the God Plane. Silence and devotion must be learned before this body aligns with the lower five, detailed above.*

7. *The seventh body is that of the Higher Self. This is the body that works to assure that all alignments of the lower bodies are complete, even through the physical plane. The Higher Self contains the individual's Light Body and constitutes the Oneness connection to the All. Some believe this body is synonymous with the level upon which the Ascended Masters reside, but many fall short in this understanding. The Higher Self is likened to the vehicle that can be used to transport the soul through the gateway to the dimension where the Ascended Masters reside. It is the perfected body of the Christos, which awaits to take the individual home to the Father's mansion of many rooms. Before one can integrate the Higher Self into the lower six*

bodies, service to humanity must be complete and one's legacy must be left on Earth. In other words, one must be complete with his or her mission.

8. *The eighth body is called the energy vortex body. This body wraps itself around the lower seven bodies and keeps the individual connected to the planes of consciousness that provide higher guidance. It is a level of beingness that is beyond direct communication to the lower seven bodies. It is the body that is aligned with the guardian angels who so lovingly guide individuals on their paths. The energy vortex body constitutes the passageway for ascension, as it is the link between the Higher Self and the Great Central Sun. For this body to merge with the lower seven bodies, Light must permeate one's consciousness to such a degree that the Third Eye remains fully illumined at all times.*

9. *The ninth body is called the electron body. This body vibrates to the same degree as the etheric. This body has the power to totally transform the lower eight bodies into Light and perform the ascension process. The electron body provides the ultimate experience for the soul, which has toiled for so many lifetimes to reach Shamballa, the home of the Ascended Masters. This body holds the prayers of the faithful and is the reason why you have come to Earth. It is the ultimate. It is the All.*

Following this transmission, a question was asked of Kuthumi to explain if the process of bringing the nine bodies into alignment is what we call transformation. His reply was as follows.

Yes and no. Transformation implies that the electronic frequency of an individual is altered. Total transformation includes altering one's consciousness, as well. Humans can undergo physical, mental, and emotional changes, which can cause transformational changes, but if their consciousness is not changed with Spirit, then the transformation is incomplete.

Ultimate transformation includes an understanding of the integration of Universal Laws on the road to spiritual mastery. In this understanding, transformation is complete, for this change of consciousness accelerates one's ascension into the ninth body or pure Light body. When one ascends, all lower eight bodies are shed and transformation is complete. One cannot reach this state of enlightenment until all nine bodies are aligned in the heart of the Christos energy and the consciousness of the individual is God-realized.

The subject of transformation is very important, for it is the topic that will consume the hearts of the masses for the next two decades to come. The concept of transformation is perceived on many levels. The first level concerns what is observed in the Third Dimension. Here, anyone can see and detect with the senses any pattern of change. Changes are measurable and can be recorded in historical documents. They can also be permanent changes.

The second kind of transformation occurs on the emotional level. Here, one experiences events that change his or her vibrational frequencies to either a higher or lower state. This is the state of mind which can and does affect not only the individual who is undergoing the change, but also those who are affected by the change. This kind of change is recorded in the Akashic Records as lessons learned, and is directly associated with the karmic paths of humans.

The third kind of transformation, and that with which this document is directly concerned, is of a spiritual kind. Here, transformation includes changes on a molecular level when the enlightened Christ presence is being absorbed into the lower bodies of the individual. This form of transformation not only affects consciousness, but also affects the physical, emotional, and mental bodies. This state of being is likened to the harp in the ethers, playing a beautiful harmonic melody. The enlightened being ascends into a frequency of love and Light that sounds like the music the harp plays, and the ethers support this transition process.

What is unknown to many today is that this state of beingness is within reach of all who choose this state of existence. It is the Heaven on Earth that was promised to the children of Abraham eons ago. So many of the children, however, are still in darkness and cannot see that Heaven is truly right before their eyes. They must learn to accelerate their frequencies and become Light, and soon they will remember that the only way to do this is through an understanding of the chakras.

The Chakras

Chakras are centers of consciousness and energy vortices within the human energy field (described above) that operate as intake organs for energy. The word chakra is the

Sanskrit word for "wheel" or "life force center." A chakra spins in circular motion, is approximately three to four inches in diameter, controls one's emotional, mental, and spiritual well-being, and has been described as a wheel of light. Brennan sees them as funnels of energy that exist on each of the seven levels of the auric field. They exist along and within the spinal column. There are seven primary ones along the spinal column, several minor ones in other parts of the body, and others existing above the crown area of the head.

Seven
Primary
CHAKRAS

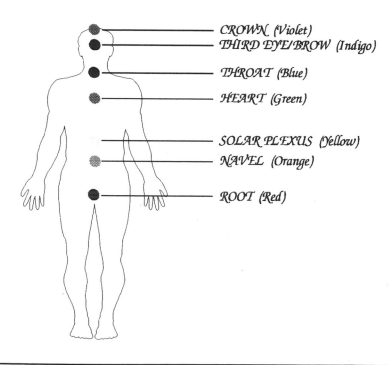

CROWN (Violet)
THIRD EYE/BROW (Indigo)

THROAT (Blue)

HEART (Green)

SOLAR PLEXUS (Yellow)
NAVEL (Orange)

ROOT (Red)

The soul, a sub-atomic ectoplasm substance, is the holder of our life force energy, and this energy is further held together by our chakras. The soul works cooperatively with our body, through the nervous system and brain, by managing the energy currents that provide us with life. Chakras receive the vital life force energy and distribute it to our total human energy field, as well as to the parts of the body nearest each chakra. This distribution of energy affects our mental and emotional behaviors. The energy, or source of life, taken in by the chakras is known as prana, or chi. We receive prana through proper breathing and air intake. When we receive a full, rich supply of chi energy, the chakras radiate intense, bright colors. Simultaneously, the surrounding organs also receive full energy supplies and experience balance. When a chakra is not working properly or when there is an insufficient supply of chi energy, the chakra becomes weak, the immune system is depressed, and disease or emotional instability results.

Each chakra is connected to spiritual principles, an understanding of which aids in our growth. Learning about the spiritual forces connected to each chakra provides us with tools to live productive, fulfilling lives. This awareness also gives us the knowledge of how to counterattack the destructive forces that try and diminish our energies.

There are seven major chakras that provide a vertical power center through the middle of the body. The energy from these seven chakras moves up and down the center line of the body like an interwoven rope of all colors, beginning at the base of the spine and ending above the top of the head. The lower two chakras govern physical energies, the middle three chakras govern personality development, and the top two chakras govern spiritual practices and the acquisition of higher human characteristics such as the encompassing of unconditional love. As we evolve, each of these chakras opens more fully, supporting our transformation and acquisition of higher powers. The higher one evolves, the higher frequency or Light one emits.

All chakras radiate specific vibrations, comparable to

the notes of the musical scale. The lower chakra emits a lower, deeper note, and the highest, seventh chakra emits a high frequency. Consequently, each chakra emits sounds and sends them outside of the body.

For the sake of simplification, there are a total of twelve major chakras positioned in the soul, seven of which comprise the spiritual foundation connected to the psyche in the body. The other five chakras (positioned above the seventh chakra) are related to molecular patterns related to the universe and Earth and serve to connect us, through our Higher Selves, to vibrational states of higher consciousness. In courses of advanced study, it is revealed that there are other chakras that are operating in our energy fields, but for the purposes of this book, these need not be mentioned at this time.

Each of the seven major chakras is located near a nerve center. The first chakra is located between the legs. This chakra is connected to our gonads. It is related to our will to live and our physical and sexual vitality, and it stimulates the creativity of the soul and grounds the soul in the present embodiment. These are its primary functions. This chakra maintains the life force energy that flows through us from birth to death. It supplies energy to the spinal column, the adrenals, and the kidneys, and usually is associated with the color red.

In former times, this chakra was associated strictly with sexual activity. As a result, it received considerable attention as a necessary chakra for survival. This appeared to conflict with principles of those on the spiritual path, so a concerted effort was made by many in authority to diminish this chakra and disconnect it, in the hopes that it would atrophy. This was done to provide freedom to the soul so that it could evolve in the spiritual realms. Today, with mass consciousness awakening to a higher, more spiritually evolved plane, it has become obvious that in order for us to evolve, we must accept and ground this first chakra in our everyday experiences rather than to deny its existence. Therefore, our human sexuality needs to be aligned with our total human experience.

The second chakra is seen in both the front and the back of the body, as are the third through the sixth chakras. It often is reported to be orange in color. It is related to sensuality, to physical rejuvenation, and to our immune system. In some descriptions of chakras, this chakra splits into two, or is shown as having two functions. The function of the first half of this chakra (related to the pancreas) connects us to the lower kingdoms of plants, animals, and minerals. It registers the lessons we have either learned or not learned in previous existences related to our personal experiences with self or our experiences with nature. The second half of this chakra (related to the spleen) governs our past life and present life experiences relating to constructive and destructive relationships we have had with others. It has the capability of affecting the RNA and DNA coding we carry within. This half of the chakra also provides for our spiritual inheritance, in that painful lessons from the past can be turned into positive experiences through this energy vortex, thus guaranteeing spiritual growth and rewards in this lifetime.

The third chakra is found in the solar plexus area and is known to be the opening to the soul. This chakra has the power to transform anything with its spiritual energy. It is called the creative chakra and directs all creative endeavors one wishes to experience. In centuries past, many wise Adepts taught that this chakra contained the source of all our power. Today, as humanity has evolved higher in the intellectual arena, that power center has moved up to the fourth chakra. This chakra has the power to consume and transform all that is discordant in the lower two chakras, once an individual begins a chakra alignment on a spiritual path. The third chakra also supplies the internal organs with energy and is associated with intuition. Its color is yellow and it is connected to the glandular system within the body.

The heart chakra, the fourth chakra, is the center of one's higher emotions and has the ability to synthesize past and present unfavorable situations that are stamped in the soul, harmonize them, and actually accelerate consciousness and one's electron spin. This function serves to assist us to manifest our spiritual blueprints which determine our missions in life. The fourth chakra is also called the balancing chakra between the lower three (yang) and upper three (yin) chakra centers. It is related to giving and receiving love, both for the self and for others, and governs emotions such as kindness, joy, compassion, affection, and benevolence. This chakra provides energy to the heart, circulatory system, thymus, vagus nerve, and upper back. It, along with the lower three chakras, influences our health and can be used to reverse adverse health conditions acquired from either present or past life experiences. The color green frequently is associated with this chakra.

The fifth chakra is found in the throat and is sometimes called the gateway to the soul. It sends energy to the thyroid, bronchi, lungs, and alimentary canal. Its function is related to communication, understanding and living the Universal Laws, giving and receiving in the physical world, and speaking truth. This chakra facilitates the downloading of the blueprint from the Higher Self when an individual is ready to find balance and harmony in his or her life and to live God's will instead of the ego's. If negative karmic patterns have not been resolved, however, the second chakra will block the flow of energy upward, which will not allow the higher blueprint to flow down. The fifth chakra is also called the "regulator," for it determines an individual's ability to change and evolve. Blue is the color associated with this chakra.

The sixth chakra, or third-eye chakra, is located both on the low forehead and on the back of the head and is referred to as the window to the soul. This chakra provides energy to the lower brain, pituitary, left eye, ears, nose, and nervous system. The front part is related to conceptual understanding, and the back part to our ability to carry out ideas in a systematic fashion leading to their realization. The sixth chakra, once developed, gives us prophetic vision and psychic powers. Indigo or lavender is associated with this chakra.

The crown chakra, or seventh chakra, is located at the

top of the head. It is the portal opening to higher spiritual consciousness and is considered to be the heart opening to higher dimensions. When one's seventh chakra is fully developed, the individual experiences a state of Oneness with higher-dimensional beings. A fully operational crown chakra receives higher spiritual energies and distributes them throughout the body, providing energy and Light within and cleansing from negative energies. Saints, portrayed with halos, show highly evolved crown chakras.

The upper brain and right eye receive energy from this chakra. The crown chakra is related to the integration of personality with spirituality. Most individuals do not possess highly developed crown chakras, which is why there are not too many spiritually evolved souls on Earth today who exemplify inner peace and happiness. Individuals who have fully developed crown chakras have control over their mental and emotional bodies.

Individuals and healers work with the chakras to provide a balance among our emotions (front chakras), our will (back chakras), and our reason (head chakras). Blockage in the paths of the chakras leads to disease.

There are many secondary chakras near the joints, on the hands and feet, and in the head and the trunk of the body. These are smaller vortices which bring energy to the body.

Much has been written about the Kundalini, a source of power located at the base of the spine. This power source, when released, moves upward through the center of the body and through the major chakras. Kundalini is a Sanskrit word meaning circular power. Each of us is born with some of this power already flowing. We can access this power to develop new awareness and to move to higher dimensions of spiritual growth.

An individual may experience involuntary Kundalini release in the form of feelings of warmth, buzzing types of noises, and other symptoms of discomfort. These same symptoms may be experienced by those who engage in meditation, visualization, breathing exercises, and other activities that help us to connect with our spiritual selves. The release of

Kundalini takes place in very different ways for different individuals. Some do not experience any awareness of the process, while others have strong sensations. This should not be a cause of major concern, but should be considered a source of energy that may be tapped by individuals or accessed with the assistance of healers.

The Hara

Many metaphysical writers have written about the importance of intention as a guide for our behaviors and as a means of evaluating behavior. This also may be the level of our consciousness that psychologists refer to as our values, or the consistent criteria that we use for determining our behavior. This dimension of our lives is the foundation for our personalities. It guides the development and operation of our auric system.

From a psychic point of view, the haric dimension has been described by Brennan (1993) as a comparatively simple system. Hara is a Japanese word referring to the center of power located in the lower belly. This consists of three points on a laser-like line that define the center of the body. The line is one third of an inch wide, and is seen from a point about three and one-half feet above the head, extending down into the core of the Earth. The point over our head is seen as an inverted funnel which represents our individualization out of the Godhead into incarnate form. It is through this point that we may connect to our Higher Selves. For this reason, many have spoken of visualizing the top of the head and above as the vehicle for connecting with their Higher Selves.

A second point on this line is found in the upper chest. This is a beautiful, diffuse light which expresses our spiritual longing. It is the site of our mission, our purpose, and the reasons for our incarnations on Earth. It may be the connection with our soul, or that part of us that is immortal. Brennan refers to this as the soul seat, or the place where our longings for spiritual purpose are accessed.

The third point on the line is referred to as the tan

tien in Chinese. It appears to be a ball of power about two and one-half inches in diameter located approximately two inches below the navel. This center is a will center which reflects our will to live in our present life. This is the power center used by martial artists. Martial artists, healers, and others are able to draw power from this source to accomplish feats of strength and healing. The process involves drawing power from the molten core of the Earth into the haric line and bringing it to the tan tien. When individuals do this, they feel heat throughout their bodies. Using the energy of the haric level requires clear intentions. When clear intention is in place, positive actions on the auric and physical levels are positive. When there is uncertainty or disconnection from the totality of one's life, negative results are likely. Many people are in pain and do not realize it. They do not understand the spiritual loneliness that results when we are not in touch with our life purpose.

The Core Star Level

The deepest dimension of our existence is the core star, or Divine essence. Brennan (1993) describes this level as a beautiful star located one and one-half inches above the navel on the center line of the body. This is our essential nature, our individualistic reflection of the Divine Creator. It is the source of our perfection—our goodness, our wisdom, and our love. It is the source of our creative energies.

The core star is the source of our manifestation of the perfection of the Creator. While we may not be able to access and manifest this perfection, it remains within each of us. Spiritual enlightenment or growth is the vehicle that allows us to move toward that perfection.

The wonder of our creation and the complexity of our existence is seen in the four dimensions of our energy systems. The perfection of the creation of our physical lives is supported on many nonphysical levels. Each of us receives energy and powers from these dimensions, but we can increase our options and abilities to access them in even more powerful ways. The road to spiritual enlightenment is part of our life task, as well as our means of living in more successful, productive ways.

Connecting to Our Light Body

At the end of Kuthumi's message (printed earlier in this chapter) he revealed one of the secrets of ancient wisdom. For humanity to experience Heaven on Earth and to become love and Light, individuals must remember how to accelerate the Light within through the chakras. This is a simple task, but one that takes concentration and discipline. It also must be done on a daily basis.

Light is the God Force energy and contains all intelligence. When we vibrate to this frequency, we are at our maximum power for healing, creation, manifestation, and service to humanity. Since the seven major chakras comprise the seven colors of the rainbow (red, orange, yellow, green, blue, indigo, and violet), and since the seven colors of the rainbow form white Light, we must keep these chakras vibrating at their maximum strength within us at all times. This is done through the power of the mind and through visualization. The process is also enhanced through meditation.

Any individual can visualize each chakra vibrating to its full color and power. When each chakra is fully activated, vibrating with its purest color, the seven colors combine within and create an auric field of white Light. This forms a protective shield of energy around us and gives off a glow of energy that is often called illumination.

When we do not control our mental and emotional bodies, the colors become scrambled within and are disproportionately arranged along the spine. Because they are not in harmony and balanced, the auric field appears as a blending of these colors and is not white Light. Instead, the individual vibrates on a level less than the frequency of Light and the aura appears broken or fractured.

We must learn to control our mental and emotional bodies at all times so that we may control the colors within and command our auric fields to be white Light. When one is at peace and does not get caught up in the illusion all around, the soul draws more prana or chi energy into the auric field, which further nourishes the chakras. This creates a stronger force field of energy and gives the individual even more command of surrounding elements. Ultimately, once we learn to vibrate to the same perfection as individuals such as Jesus, we also will command the power that he was known to have had. This is coming for all of humanity, but it will take years of discipline and focusing of our wills and energy to assume positions equal to Jesus' level of mastery.

To fully integrate the principles explained in this book, an individual first must grasp this concept and make an effort to clear his or her chakras on a daily basis to become Light on the auric level. This is essential on the path to mastery and illumination.

Summary

Knowledge of the nonphysical components of human energy systems is not new, in that references to chakras and auras are found in documents that are centuries old. What is new, however, is our ability to measure aspects of these human energy fields, which enables us to develop a more comprehensive perspective of the structure and functions of their components.

* Barbara Ann Brennan, a scientist-healer with psychic sight, has developed a coherent perspective of human energy systems. She identifies four primary sets of structures or levels which include the following:
  * The physical body, or the body that we see and use to carry out the activities of life. The physical body, complex as it is, is the result of the operation of the nonphysical components of our energy systems.
  * The aura, or the egg-shaped field of seven levels of energy that surround the human body, as well as the chakras which supply energy to the physical body. Our understanding of the energy fields and chakras continues to expand as information is channelled from the Masters, and new understandings are gained from science and the healing arts.
  * The hara, or the guide for our auric system. The hara, or center of power, consists of three points on a laser-like line that define the center of the body. It begins over our head and connects to the core of the Earth.
  * The core star level which connects us to the Divine. This is the source of our creative energies.
* Through daily visualization and meditation, we can accelerate the Light within through our

chakras, control our mental and emotional bodies, and command our auric fields to be white Light.

Knowledge of human energy structures and fields helps us learn how to develop our spirituality. This is key to assisting us to develop power.

As we learn to control and focus the energies of our auric field, we connect with our Higher Selves and gain the capacity to manifest our intentions. Our spiritual development begins with the discipline of focusing our wills and efforts to increase our vibratory frequencies and clear our chakras on a daily basis in order to become Light on the auric level.

Chapter 6

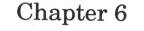

THE FIFTH DIMENSION

*How much longer will you go on letting your
energy sleep?
How much longer are you going to stay oblivi-
ous of the immensity of yourself?
Don't lose time in conflict;
Lose no time in doubt—time can never be
recovered and if you miss an opportunity it
may take many lives before another comes
your way again.*

Bhagwan Shree Rajneesh
A Cup of Tea

Throughout their many transmissions, the Ascended Masters continually refer to the Fifth Dimension. They state that we are moving from the Third, through the Fourth, and into the Fifth Dimension as the Earth moves with the precession of the equinoxes out of the Age of Pisces and into the Age of Aquarius. They also say that the world will change in a "twinkling of an eye," and that some of us will change with it.

What does it mean that the Earth is entering the Fifth Dimension? What is the Fifth Dimension? How will the world change? If and when it does, will we be changed?

In order to understand the answers to these questions, one must first acquire an understanding of the world from a different perspective. To comprehend the Fifth Dimension one must first understand that **everything in the universe**

is energy and can be measured and reduced to vibrational frequencies (the number of vibrations per second emitted by an object or experience). The term **everything** includes mental, emotional, physical, and even spiritual things. Every particle, thought, word, object, experience, or emotion has its own vibrational frequency, and that vibration can be measured mathematically.

We exist in the Third Dimension, although there are other dimensions of time/space as well, such as the Fourth and Fifth, which will be discussed later. Each dimension in the universe contains seven levels, or major vibrational frequencies, and these seven levels constitute a curriculum for that dimension.

When the soul chooses to live in a dimension, it must master the curriculum of that dimension before it is allowed to exit that reality and evolve. For example, the curriculum for the Third Dimension is love and Light. This means that, in order to evolve, the person must learn unconditional love through the curriculum of Light. The way this is accomplished is by studying the white Light and its seven colors (red, orange, yellow, green, blue, indigo, and violet) and understanding that Light is the source of all creation and power. Since Light comprises the energy field in which we live, and we are not separate from this energy field, then the Light is within us.

Since the human body is an energy system (microcosm) containing all aspects of the universe (macrocosm), these same seven colors are found within us in the form of our chakras, and each chakra represents one of the seven colors contained in white Light. This was discussed in the previous chapter. It also is known that each color has a psychological and emotional agenda, e.g., red stands for our physical needs and our ability to ground ourselves, orange governs our relationships and sexuality, green aids in healing and giving love. To attain mastery, we eventually must control our emotional and mental bodies and achieve command over the agendas associated with the chakras.

Physicists can measure the vibration of these seven

colors and have discovered that they each vibrate to distinct frequencies related to the seven major notes on the musical scale. Thus, the frequency (number of vibrations per second) at which a note vibrates can be translated into a color. Red vibrates at the lower end of the spectrum and violet at the higher end.

Each of the seven levels within a dimension has a vibrational range unique to that level, and each of these individual levels can be subdivided further into seven divisions. Lower dimensions vibrate at lower frequencies; higher dimensions vibrate at higher frequencies. All dimensions comprise consciousness, and they all exist simultaneously.

The Ascended Masters vibrate at a level much higher than we do. Although we exist simultaneously with them, most of us cannot see them even though they can see us. Those who can see them can see them only with the "inner" eye, called the Third Eye.

Another example of something that vibrates at a higher frequency is ultraviolet light, which resides on the border between the Third and the Fourth Dimensions. With instrumentation, we can measure this higher frequency, and therefore know that it exists, even though we cannot see it with our naked eyes. This light always has been a part of our reality; yet we did not know this until we developed the technology to measure it.

The second concept that is important to understand is that **all dimensions within the universe exist simultaneously.** All that is or ever will be exists now, in this moment of time. However, we are limited by our consciousness as to how much of this existence we can perceive and comprehend. The higher our consciousness (the higher our vibrational rate), the more we can see into other dimensions.

While the above statement is true, it is also difficult for most people to understand. In the past, only minds like Einstein's could comprehend exactly what simultaneous existence means. Today, with our scientific discoveries and increased technological information, humanity slowly is acquiring the capability to understand these advanced concepts.

Before attempting to explain these concepts further, it may be helpful to explain the various dimensions.

The Dimensions

The First Dimension sometimes is called the mineral kingdom. Its frequency range is measured on a scale from one through seven, and it is the dimension where the life force energies begin to flow. Consciousness exists in the atom, and in this dimension consciousness is experienced through the laws of magnetism, gravity, and chemical properties. This is the dimension of solidification of thought-forms experienced through the lowest form of vibration known to our existence.

The Second Dimension, known as the plant kingdom, comprises the next harmonic range of eight through fourteen frequencies. Life exists here, and the kingdom reproduces itself following perfect patterns in nature. Notice that plants need light to sustain life, but the mineral kingdom does not. It is the mineral kingdom that provides the precious nutrients needed to sustain life in the plant kingdom. It is the sun that provides the photons to be converted in the plants, through the process of photosynthesis.

The Third Dimension is the animal kingdom, of which humans are a part. This dimension exists within the next band of frequencies, ranging from fifteen through twenty-one. Within the animal kingdom, consciousness is very complex, ranging from the very simple to the capacity of humans. As animals evolve to a higher state, they acquire higher levels of reactive behaviors. The human kingdom, which functions at the top of the animal kingdom's scale, exists interactively with the lower dimensions. Innate intelligence appears to set humans apart from the rest of creation.

The Third Dimension adds the measurement of depth to the flat measurements of length and width. It is this quality that supports the physical world around us. The Third Dimension also is dominated by a carbon-based material existence. The formula for carbon is $C_6H_6O_6$. The Celestial Beings point out that the number 666 emanating from this formula was referred to as the Sign of the Beast in the Book of Revelation in the Bible. The Third Dimension is ruled by our five senses of taste, sight, smell, hearing, and touch—all connected with the physical world around us. When we lose ourselves in the world of matter, we also can lose touch with our souls and the Light of the higher dimensions.

Since all is energy, the Third Dimension often is referred to as solidified thought—that which constitutes the maya (illusion) around us. Everything seems real because things have physical appearances (length, width, and depth) but everything actually is energy when viewed from a higher perspective. The density of matter makes things move in slow motion, or at a slower vibration, often causing people to perceive reality as consisting of limitations because it takes so much effort to create within this density. Because of this slow motion, individuals have difficulty comprehending the power of mind and the way in which it rules thoughts to manifest form.

A sense of duality rules the Third Dimension, so individuals look for black and white answers to questions. They encounter pain, suffering, and emotional challenges while experiencing life on this plane. These experiences drive the individual to accrue good and bad Karma and unfinished business that must be addressed later on. As the soul begins to experience enlightenment and acquires a higher consciousness, issues no longer are perceived as yes or no, or black and white. Instead, each event begins to take on new meaning, and is analyzed in the context in which it exists. This is a sign that the soul is beginning to evolve out of the illusion of the Third Dimension.

Gautama Buddha, upon attaining enlightenment, taught about the conditions that make up the Third Dimension. He said that all is impermanent and part of a flowing existence. Individuals get caught in a cycle of life and death because any incomplete deed or unfinished business in one lifetime projects toward a new incarnation. Life is subject to misery and suffering, and especially to sickness and death.

Out of this teaching, Buddha defined his Four Noble Truths. These are:

1. Existence includes conflict, dissatisfaction, sorrow, and suffering.
2. There is a purpose for all suffering (which is caused by selfish desire).
3. We can be emancipated from this suffering.
4. Freedom from suffering is obtained by following the Eightfold Path.

Buddha's Eightfold Path to escape the cycle of rebirth and suffering requires a higher and more ethical code of behavior than most individuals practice today. This path includes constant introspection and a "correct" or "true" way of living. It is expressed as:

1. Right Seeing
2. Right Thought
3. Right Speech
4. Right Action
5. Right Living
6. Right Endeavor
7. Right Mindedness
8. Right Concentration

Following this path leads an individual to freedom and the ability to transcend third-dimensional reality because these principles are also inherent in the Universal Laws (discussed in Part II of this book). It is apparent that the wisdom of the Buddha was far ahead of its time, and it still has not been realized on Earth.

All humans have the natural ability to perceive dimensions higher than the Third, although few ever have understood that they could. In Atlantis, humans in embodiment accepted this mode of operation and perception as normal behavior. The Atlanteans operated on this superior level of existence, connected to their Higher Selves. With the fall of

Atlantis, humanity experienced a struggle for survival and became aware of the lower self, dominated by the will of the ego.

Now, after thousands of years of evolution, most people have forgotten not only how to connect with higher dimensions, but also that it is even possible to do so. Psychics and mystics have long been known for their abilities to transcend other realities and dimensions. An individual whose consciousness was not attuned to this ability often feared these individuals who could transcend other dimensions.

The Fourth Dimension exists in the range of frequencies from twenty-two through twenty-eight. This dimension often is called the astral plane and is the residence of some disembodied souls until they can be fully transformed and integrated into the higher planes of existence. It is also the transition between the physical world and the higher worlds of the Celestials.

It is a challenging dimension, presently hosting the Battle of Armageddon, or the fight to transcend forces of opposition and transmute all into the Light. Until Earth moves through this dimension on its path through the precession of the equinoxes, and gets firmly anchored in the Fifth Dimension, people everywhere will be challenged by these unseen forces.

Scientists add the variable of time to those of length, width, and depth when defining the Fourth Dimension. Time is an extension into the past and future, and is defined as being dependent upon matter. In his theory of relativity, Einstein often refers to time itself as the Fourth Dimension. His system requires four coordinates for determining a location within space. He also refers to this dimension as a time/space continuum, because these two components (time and space) are not absolutes. They relate only to an individual's movement through space.

Time serves to help us awaken our memories of who and what we are. In dimensions higher than the Third Dimension, we can traverse time, moving back into past lives and then forward into the future. In other words, we can return again and again in a cyclical pattern through the totality of our existence. This process comprises a spiral which goes upward and onward in a never-ending path. Spirals are circular patterns with the dimension of time added. Life evolves in a spiral motion through all the dimensions—beginning with the mineral kingdom and moving on to the higher dimensions. The lower kingdoms support and sustain the higher ones, allowing a never-ending path of evolution.

The Arcturians, the fifth-dimensional beings who assisted in writing the book *We, the Arcturians,* add still another explanation of the Fourth Dimension by portraying this dimension as the vibration that begins to open the heart. It is an etheric dimension, they say, that acts as a portal, providing a pathway to higher worlds. This is accomplished through vibrations that resonate higher than the physical, dense world of matter.

This is a dimension that demands that we learn to forgive before we are allowed to exit from its frequency. The higher vibrations of the Fourth Dimension provide us with experiences (a new curriculum, if you will) that require us to choose life-styles and behaviors that may be considerably different from those which we exhibited in the past.

The sense of duality is still present in this dimension, and individuals transiting through the Fourth Dimension continue to see things as good/evil, male/female, and light/dark—all carry-overs from the Third Dimension. Upon entering fourth-dimensional consciousness, however, individuals strive to work through their personal "stuff" and often work endlessly to solve problems related to duality. This is a dimension that must be experienced in order to achieve higher consciousness.

Slowly, the understanding of Oneness (the curriculum of the Fifth Dimension) begins to creep into one's consciousness. Because of this new knowledge and increased Light, solutions to problems become more evident. This new state of higher consciousness leads to a hunger for more knowledge, requiring that an individual either choose the higher concepts of truth and enlightenment or return to the third-dimensional realities of duality, rebirth, and suffering. This is a difficult decision for most people, because choosing higher consciousness and realities requires the individual to change.

In another transmission, the Arcturians said that one of the reasons that Jesus incarnated 2,000 years ago was to open this fourth-dimensional portal. He did this through his teachings of love and forgiveness, which open the heart to higher consciousness. By demonstrating greater love than we experience in the physical, an individual moves through time/space into a state of higher consciousness. This form of love embraces an attitude toward oneself and humanity that eliminates judgment and eventually guides the person to follow higher truths and wisdom, such as the Buddha's Eightfold Path.

Humanity has been given 2000 years of incarnations to learn these simple lessons. One wonders what percentage of souls have really mastered them.

As we enter the **Fifth Dimension**, the frequency range of twenty-nine through thirty-five, we have access to a broader spectrum of colors and sounds—thus, a higher curriculum of opportunities awaits. The Fifth Dimension is a higher frequency of spiritual evolution that we enter after our Light bodies (Higher Selves) merge with our physical/energy bodies. This merging will occur once the lower eight bodies are purified, fear and negativity are no longer present, and the individual has control over the mental and emotional bodies. The human form that results will resemble the present physical form and will be a refinement of it, but will be transformed into a higher form of God consciousness.

At present, humans constitute a limited form of intelligence operating within a narrow spectrum of consciousness. We exist to learn lessons that are part of that spectrum of creation. Time exists only within the consciousness of each individual. As individuals acquire higher consciousness (a higher vibrational frequency), they experience the discarding of the old constraints related to time and move into alternative realities that are accessed through Universal Mind and the thought-forms of higher evolutionary beings of Light.

The Ascended Masters call the Fifth Dimension the dimension of mind and thought manifestation. This dimension supports creation and will constitute the means for bringing Heaven on Earth in the Seventh Golden Age. The frequencies of the Fifth Dimension are higher than those of the physical, dense world of Earth. In fact, they can vibrate beyond the speed of Light (a concept hardly understood today); thus, manifestation and creation are the conscious experiences of the inhabitants of this dimension. It is here where the heart, attuned with the mind of the Higher Self, rules. The Pleiades, Arcturus, and Sirius are examples of star systems existing within this dimension.

One of the most accurate ways to describe the Fifth Dimension is to say that it is a metaphysical world. Metaphysics is defined as essential reality based on abstract and subtle reasoning. It encompasses reality that stretches beyond the physical or material world to incorporate the transcendental and supernatural. The science of metaphysics is founded on some of the principles of physics that describe our existence as based in energy. Metaphysics also is closely related to epistemology, or the study of the nature of knowledge.

Most of the teachings of the Celestial Beings residing on the Fifth Dimension and higher are concerned with processes. They emphasize the process of evolution and the process of moving into a higher consciousness—all dependent upon our managing our own energy, minds, and hearts.

Although little is understood about dimensions higher than those defined above, a brief description of the Sixth and Seventh Dimensions is included here because these dimensions are the home of higher Celestial Beings such as the Ascended Masters.

The Sixth Dimension is a higher etheric world that integrates new colors and sound waves into its existence. It is assigned the harmonic range of thirty-six through forty-two, and is also the doorway to the Seventh Dimension. This Dimension holds the keys and codes for higher forms of creation using the Merkabah. It also serves as a bridge between the Ascended Realms and the lower worlds, of which the

Third Dimension is a part. According to the Arcturians, certain star systems, such as Alpha Centauri, reside in this dimension and are known for their advanced theoretical beliefs and technological systems.

The Seventh Dimension, according to Kuthumi, is a vibratory frequency that supports the existence of the Ascended Masters and Shamballa. It vibrates in the frequency range of forty-three through forty-nine. Another name for this Dimension is the Seventh Heaven. This Dimension is the outermost concentric ring enclosing Earth, and the home base of most of the angels.

The Seventh Dimension contains the highest ray of spiritual intelligence known to us. It is a ray of pure love, universal wisdom, and Universal Laws. This ray is the vehicle for telepathic communications, transmitted from the Ascended Masters to members of the Order of Melchizedek in embodiment on Earth who are assigned to fulfill God's plan. This ray works with the Divine mind of the Higher Self to stimulate within members of the Order an understanding of humanity's divinity and, in so doing, to instill in their minds the blueprint of God's plan to bring in the Seventh Golden Age. Here, Light and sound manifestation are brought to one of the highest frequencies that humans are able to comprehend. This frequency initiates and maintains the coding necessary to work with the Higher Self to assure that the Adam Kadmon, the new fifth-dimensional human emerging on Earth, will be realized.

Higher Light Spectrums Sent to Earth

Intense Light spectrums from higher dimensions are sent periodically to Earth to raise the planet's vibrational frequency to that of the Fifth Dimension. This is an integral part of the celestial plan for humanity's evolution. These frequencies carry Earth's and humanity's blueprints for the future. These cycles of higher energies feed the ascension process, because they assist the Higher Self to integrate itself into our lower eight bodies (including our physical body).

These arcs of Light (which contain new colors) connect to Earth's electromagnetic force fields and affect the electromagnetic frequencies of our brains. Coding from the Universal Language of Light (described later in this chapter) is downloaded into our mental and emotional bodies, raising consciousness and preparing us to receive higher thoughtforms.

When these intense periods of new Light frequencies bombard Earth, individuals are affected in many ways. Some people think they are sick and display flu symptoms, while others get irritable, restless, disoriented, and tired. Dizziness often occurs. Eyesight and sleep patterns also can be disturbed. In short, these periods (which have occurred three or four times each year in the past), have been known to cause anxious and not-so-pleasant experiences for a few minutes or even days.

Some individuals who receive transmissions from the Ascended Masters are told in advance when these energy bombardments will occur. This is helpful because it can relieve anxiety. With advance notice, individuals are better prepared to look upon such moments as precious opportunities for releasing old programming. Beforehand knowledge, detailing when these intensified energies will hit the Earth, aids in focusing energies on positive rather than negative creations. For example, when these periods are intense, instead of focusing on whether or not they may be getting serious illnesses, individuals can focus their attention on meeting their own goals or caring for another person who needs their attention in some way. Each new wave of energy that enters the Earth plane lifts humanity's molecules into a heightened state of ascension. The higher kingdom of God slowly assimilates itself into the lower self, causing negativity to be released from consciousness. When higher dosages of energy flow to Earth, they purge and cleanse lower negative energies lodged deeply within us. Cleansing is often an uncomfortable experience, and occurs on three levels of memory:

❋ Cellular
❋ Akashic Record
❋ Genetic

Cellular memory includes all remembrances (good and bad) gathered in the present lifetime, beginning in the womb. We store every word, emotion, and experience in our cellular bodies, and these collective experiences assist us to become what we are.

Akashic is a Sanskrit word meaning primary substance, or that out of which all things are formed. In metaphysics, this often is referred to as the Universal Mind, or the Source of all events, occurrences, and knowledge. **Akashic Records** for individuals are the unique libraries of data and events that each has experienced in all previous lifetimes. Every thought, word, and deed is stored in the Akashic Records, but usually only the most significant data are carried forward into a new lifetime.

Genetic memory constitutes knowledge and experiences passed down from seven generations of ancestors. We store these experiences in our DNA.

When we collect loving, warm, and supportive experiences, we store this higher energy in our memory banks. This energy keeps our internal systems flowing smoothly and harmoniously. Lessons are learned allowing love to prevail.

When we collect painful, frustrating, and traumatic experiences, these negative energies get lodged somewhere in our bodies. Over the years these lower energies cause us to move from harmony (into which we are born) to a state of disharmony, or being out-of-ease. Consequently, *dis-ease* (disease) results. Mental and emotional problems also appear.

When the higher spectrums of Light bombard Earth, they force the lower, negative energies stored within us (from the cellular, Akashic Record, and genetic remembrances) to flow through our mental, emotional, and physical bodies. When these energies push through our lower bodies, many of us experience depression or mental problems or believe we have physical illnesses because of the symptoms we experience. These periods can last for days or even weeks, depending on the amount of memory that is being released.

Over prolonged periods, some people go to doctors, desperate for help. Often their physicians find no plausible reason for the pains or emotional discomfort. In these instances, it is commonplace to have medical tests come back negative. Consequently, both patient and doctor are baffled. The office visit, however, serves two purposes:

1. It relieves the mind that the individual does not have a serious condition; and
2. It relieves the pocketbook of precious savings!

How often have you experienced a similar situation? These occurrences are very common today, but unfortunately most individuals do not understand that these emotional and physical pains are only memories of past lives, traumas, or illnesses pushing through the lower eight bodies. In addition, most people on Earth today are not aware that there is a greater plan guiding Earth and humanity into the Fifth Dimension, and even fewer understand that the cleansing of negative remembrances from our bodies must occur before we can enter the higher dimensions. Perhaps this book will serve to enlighten those who are still in the dark.

During the times when higher spectrums of Light bombard Earth, emotional issues rise to the surface, especially between couples and acquaintances. Issues long buried rise to the surface to be reexamined. These periods demand that we face ALL unresolved issues stored in our souls; consequently, these issues form the agendas of events yet to come.

These higher energies accelerate time and push the lower energies through us, causing all unfinished business to come around faster and faster. If lessons are not learned the first time, similar events (attached to new faces and agendas) come around six months later. The problem is that when the lessons are not learned the first time, they appear ten times more intense the next time. And if they are not learned the second time, they are magnified ten times again. Get the picture? Anything that is unfinished must be experienced again and again until it is done "right." This means that the choices we make to resolve a situation must be motivated out of unconditional love. Remember, the only key to freedom is through right behavior, discovered by the Buddha. The higher energy DEMANDS that issues be resolved through love, forgiveness, and understanding. These behaviors must be mastered before entry into the Fifth Dimension is allowed. Love, forgiveness, and understanding or compassion are high vibrations and change the force field around a person. Mastering these virtues influences all else that comes within these higher vibrations, and slowly begins to change all behaviors that vibrate at a lower rate.

Beginning in 1995, Earth began to receive more frequent bombardments of these higher energies. Instead of four times each year, the higher spectrums of Light now are sent to Earth eight times a year. This will continue until the year 2001, after which the cycles will increase to twelve times each year. During this later period, however, humanity will be so enlightened that the effects of these higher frequencies on our physical and emotional levels hardly will be noticed. Instead of causing stress and discomfort, these intense periods of energy will serve only to accelerate our mental and spiritual evolution.

After 2001, these intensified spectrums of Light will force individuals to abandon useless perceptions of time and beliefs relating to their bodies, minds, and spirits. Concepts such as death will change. Our minds will become so enlightened that our bodies eventually will become ageless. Our perceptions and definitions of God will be redefined. Over the years, we will move from a third-dimensional, survival-based mentality to a way of thinking that is trusting, open, and loving.

Within us is a memory buried deep in our souls of a perfect plan that remembers Oneness, not separation. As we enter the higher dimensions, we will begin to remember the strength that comes from Oneness and that God provides.

ONENESS REQUIRES THAT WE TRUST OUR IN-NER GUIDANCE. Learning to trust grants freedom, because our inner guidance IS our true path to freedom. The energies being sent to Earth now and in the future require that we remember how to trust and follow our higher guidance from within. Entry into the Fifth Dimension demands that this be integrated into our daily lives.

Fear, the most prevalent negative energy from the past, cripples and paralyzes. This powerful emotion drains individuals of the power to create. As Light becomes more centered in our consciousness, all emotions driven by fear and anger will be assimilated by our Higher Selves into the Fifth Dimension.

The more Light we absorb into our consciousness, the more ability we will have to use sight, insights, and faculties beyond our five senses and to see into other dimensions. In addition, the more Light emanating within our auras, the greater will be our abilities to create.

We have been sent to Earth as co-creators with God to create Heaven on Earth. To realize this, we must experience the higher and lower dimensions simultaneously. Only then can we bring the higher creations into our present moment of time/space. When we learn to integrate these frequencies into our consciousness, we will accelerate our journey to becoming the Adam Kadmon species of the Fifth Dimension.

This evolutionary leap destined for humanity can be compared to the differences in the human form between Neanderthal and Cro-Magnon. Today, anthropologists can find no transitional skeleton that depicts the evolution between these two developmental periods. In fact, this missing link remains an area of controversy and debate among anthropologists worldwide. The Ascended Masters, however, offer their view of this matter.

In one transmission, Kuthumi stated that the period between Neanderthals and Cro-Magnons is an example of a time when Earth experienced a quantum leap of consciousness, similar to what is being experienced on Earth today because of the higher Light spectrums that are bombarding the planet. As is happening today, the DNA and RNA of the earlier forms of humans were affected by this process. A mutated strand was introduced as a result of this event, causing humans to leap forward in their evolutionary process. This ultimately changed the human condition.

In a similar manner, we will be catapulted into the Fifth Dimension. The Light spectrums presently flooding Earth are once again penetrating the human DNA, which eventually will cause a change in our human form. Exactly how we will change, Kuthumi did not say. He only stated that we are destined to become the Adam Kadmon of the Fifth Dimension—a highly developed form of human being who is more closely aligned with the higher than with the lower self.

The Universal Language of Light

An understanding of the Fifth Dimension would not be complete without a description of the Universal Language of Light. This complicated, higher communication system is used to transmit messages from the Ascended Masters to Initiates in embodiment. It also will be the primary system of communication in the Fifth Dimension when Earth is firmly integrated into this higher frequency.

The Universal Language of Light contains symbolic coding transmitted through streams of Light emanating from Christ consciousness coming from the Seventh Dimension. It is one of the communication systems for all beings of Light throughout the twelve universes.

The Universal Language of Light is a language of geometric symbols used by the Celestial Command to connect Light Workers to the keys and codes destined to fulfill humanity's evolutionary path and God's plan on Earth. Each time an individual receives a "down loading" of the Universal Language of Light, inner knowingness becomes stronger and clearer. When this understanding is present, more of the universal celestial plan is revealed to the soul.

The symbols from the Language of Light are transmitted to our subconscious, often in the dream state, through the unseen energy of the Ascended Masters who surround us. This process is facilitated through the etheric gridwork that encloses us. We are surrounded by activity that we cannot see with our physical eyes.

At present, when an individual in embodiment is not resonating on a high enough frequency to receive information clearly or directly from the Ascended Masters, the information is sent through a stepped-down process of vibrational frequencies. The Higher Self receives the symbolic coding and translates it into our consciousness.

These symbols and the coding teach us how to:

1. Expand our own Light bodies,
2. Acquire higher consciousness, and
3. Understand different realities.

We must listen to the guidance within to learn how we may acquire these evolved behaviors and understandings, for they will be required for entry into the Fifth Dimension. Acquiring these attributes also will enable individuals to learn in another way—by tapping into the Universal Mind.

In the past, we have learned through books, lectures, lessons, television, media, and direct experience. In higher dimensions of time/space, however, there are other options. When the mind resides on the frequency of the Universal Mind, information and knowledge are assimilated in other ways and through other channels.

Clearly, there are many benefits to receiving the codes that the Universal Language of Light has to offer. Obviously, this step in evolution will change the way in which we conduct activities here on Earth, such as the schooling of our children. Are we prepared for this leap of consciousness? Are we prepared to accept the many benefits that will come with this higher consciousness? What awaits us on the horizon is truly fascinating and exciting. This is perhaps one of the most exciting times to be alive, once an individual understands what is happening to us and to the world.

The Ascended Masters already have implanted many people with crystalline codes in their etheric bodies. As a result, many have begun to receive the geometric symbols of this higher Language of Light. Our Higher Selves have an unfailing knowingness that the Ascended Masters exist, and our higher essence accepts that we do have a divine, limitless consciousness capable of expansion. Therefore, the Higher Selves of many already have given permission for these codes to be placed within them. Those souls who first gave permission for this to be done are described as the first wave of ascension. They also comprise the membership of the reincarnated Atlantean souls who have returned to Earth to establish the electromagnetic grid, which is discussed in a later chapter of this book.

In the future, many other individuals also will receive crystalline implants, but only after permission for this to occur has been given. Once permission is given, the process of acceleration is guaranteed, even though some of us do not welcome change as openly as others. Consequently, some people will accelerate at a faster rate than others.

All the geometric forms in the Universal Language of Light contain the expression of the God Force. These symbols come in many forms—spheres, triangles, dodecahedrons, hearts, spirals, cubes, rectangles, parallel lines, stars, and other geometric and artistic forms. The Masters use artifacts from the Seventh Dimension coded with vibrational frequencies that tell a story in picture form. Each symbol reveals to the soul a piece of the puzzle needed for it to complete its work on Earth.

There are 144,000 spiritual Masters who have been brought into Earth's electromagnetic grid, each carrying a part of the geometric forms of the Universal Language of Light. We all will receive these codes eventually, but exactly when depends upon our own abilities to integrate and accept them.

The number of symbols a soul can receive in any given lifetime is dependent upon the quality of experiences received in past lives, the Light acquired in this present lifetime, and the person's acceptance of change. If the soul's experiences have assisted the individual to learn many lessons and to give up negativity and fear, that person is destined to receive more of the programming from the Language of Light. If a person has blockages and unfinished business that have not been resolved, that individual is incapable of receiving a full allotment of coding. In some cases, coding might take several lifetimes. This is because the Language of Light operates on a resonance basis. Higher symbols can be received only by the souls who resonate on a higher frequency or octave. Sometimes it takes a soul numerous lifetimes to reach a state of enlightenment capable of receiving these geometric forms that will hasten higher consciousness.

When blockages exist, they lower the frequency of the soul, which prevents the individual from receiving this coding even though he or she may yearn for the higher knowledge. When such an individual is blocked from receiving the higher messages and coding, frustration can set in that only adds to the lower frequencies. The individual then remains powerless until all these blockages are removed and purification is complete.

It does little good to fret and worry when this is the case; it only delays progress. The only way in which a soul can move to a higher level is by focusing attention on the here and now and continuing to acquire the discipline needed to assure that the vibrational frequencies continue to rise. A person's level of responsibility and world leadership is dictated by the vibrational frequency of the soul and the number of geometric forms that have been implanted therein.

The Universal Language of Light contains coding for six areas of our life:

* Spiritual attunement
* Knowledge
* Love
* Manifestation
* Soul travel

❋ Mission fulfillment

These six areas define the path that all Spiritual Warriors follow while embodied on the Earth plane. They also
define the tasks that individuals must achieve when moving
through the ascension process. An understanding of these
tasks CAN COME ONLY THROUGH THE UNIVERSAL
LAWS. The relevant coding will be obtained only when the
Ascended Master in charge of a disciple determines that the
individual is ready to receive it.

Once the decision is made to begin receiving the Language of Light, the Initiate must purify the body, mind, and
Spirit. This is accomplished through discipline and will. It
is at this time that the disciple is shown the way to clear all
karmic debts and he or she begins to accrue desirable Karma
for the future.

Androgyny and the Fifth Dimension

The Third Dimension is a world of polarities and du-
alities. We analyze and see things as up and down, black and
white, or having two sides to explore. Decisions often are
based on a yes or no response, and the verdict dictates the
course of events from that day forward.

This view ignores an important piece of data, namely,
that everything on Earth and in the universe is made up of
not two things, but only ONE thing, and that one thing is energy. Energy is made up of positive and negative particles;
however, this is not the same as being composed of polarities.

Everything in the universe is feminine and masculine,
or what is called yin and yang. The feminine is yin, and the
masculine is yang. In higher dimensions, no judgment is
placed on these principles of energy—they just exist.

*Webster's New Lexicon Dictionary of the English Lan-
guage* (1989) defines yin and yang as the "two forces through
whose essences, according to Taoist cosmology, the universe
was produced and cosmic harmony is maintained. Yin is
dark, female and negative, Yang is light, male and positive."

(p. 1142) They are always contrasted with and complementary to each other. These definitions do not depict opposites, but imply a continuous flow of energy—a dance, if you wish.

In the higher dimensions, there is no duality. The duality is found only in a third-dimensional reality such as that on Earth. This is a part of Earth's curriculum that must be understood before one can exit the Third Dimension and move to the higher realms. The soul is bound to return to Earth lifetime after lifetime until it grasps the concept of Oneness and this concept is assimilated into consciousness.

Both of these forces, the yin and the yang, are within each of us. Our creative forces flow in the direction in which we focus our energy, for energy follows the path of least resistance. If we focus on the feminine, we are aligning ourselves with the intuitive, creative-thought process of receiving information and ideas. If we focus on the masculine, we are sending our energies to the outer-directed, creative process of building and action, for it is action that carries out creation. The way in which we are socialized often determines which of these two forces becomes more dominant in our outward behaviors.

In Atlantis, the high priests and priestesses walked the Earth balanced in both their yin and their yang energy fields. That is why the achievements of Atlantis were so great. Peace, prosperity, and happiness prevailed for centuries, and life was fulfilling to a degree unheard of today. Only when the energies became unbalanced, causing doubt and darkness to creep in, did Atlantis fall.

When Atlantis fell, the survivors threw themselves into fear and a fight for survival—both yang energy traits. The feminine energy was suppressed because the scattered masses forgot their power while having to meet the demands of daily routines. Darkness fell on their minds, and the rest is history.

It has taken humanity over 10,000 years to scale the mountain once again, and even now there are no guarantees that we will achieve the greatness we once knew. Today the world is steeped in the yang energy. Rest assured that if we are to achieve greatness in the future, we will accomplish it only if we can learn to restore and balance the feminine and masculine energies within our souls. The world would be in an equally disastrous dilemma if the focus of our attention became unbalanced in the direction of the feminine energy. Our goal is to become balanced.

Throughout time the world has continued to honor more of the masculine principles. This has produced serious problems. One need only look around to see the seriousness of the situation. The problems are so great, in fact, that this unbalanced focus has created the possibility that the world could destroy itself in a nuclear war. Through aggression, assertiveness, and creation without spiritual balance with the God Force within, humanity has limited itself severely and has created problems that threaten life itself. This situation has come about because humans have not felt comfortable expressing and honoring the feminine side of existence.

The extreme degree to which feminine energy is suppressed in the world today is demonstrated in some of its cultures. In some parts of the world, women are not allowed to eat at the same tables as men, nor are they even allowed in the same rooms. In other cultures, female babies are murdered to assist in controlling the population. These outer behaviors mirror inner attitudes regarding the society's discomfort with feminine energy. Even though logical reasons are given that might convince people otherwise, rest assured that the true answer to why this is happening is found within, by examining the comfort felt with yin and yang energies. Everything in the outer world only serves to mirror the universe within.

Usually the individuals who choose to embody in these cultures are young souls who are living on Earth primarily to experience duality and the expression of masculine or feminine energy. They have not yet learned (in previous lives) the value of integration and Oneness and have a difficult time understanding its importance. Through many future lifetimes and/or experiences they eventually will understand the value of this integration, and only then will they begin to break the shackles that bind them to their roles. Only then can they begin the journey into the higher dimensions.

When a culture is ready to evolve, old souls (balanced in their male and female energies) choose embodiment within that civilization. They are born, grow up among the ranks of the common folk, and experience the restrictions of the culture. Then, when the time is right, their veils are lifted and they begin to remember the higher principles stored in their souls. They move to leadership positions, and finally show the people a new way. Mahatma Gandhi was such a soul.

To become a fifth-dimensional leader, one must integrate male and female energies. The goal for all of humanity who will enter the new millennium is to become androgynous. Male (yang) and female (yin) energies must become reunited. It is this reunification that will facilitate the creation of the Adam Kadmon. Because of the way men and women are socialized in the world, men are more in need of accepting the feminine energy than are women. More men than women are lacking in this connection and the spirituality and values that go with it. Therefore, to achieve mastery, the men have a more difficult struggle ahead of them than do the women. If more men do not awaken and begin to balance the male and female energies within by embracing both of them, men will find themselves trailing behind women in evolution. This condition will raise women to leadership positions, moving them to politically powerful stations in life where they can rewrite the laws. Keep in mind that this extreme position is not what is desired either. It is the balance that is ideal. If men choose not to evolve, however, they will bring the other extreme upon themselves.

To acquire androgyny, we are placed continually in arenas that provide us with the experiences we need to learn while exhibiting appropriate male or female behaviors. These arenas serve to assure that:

1. We have ample opportunities to master all tests of becoming androgynous; and

2. We will exit from these arenas demonstrating command over all behavior options, whether they are traditionally male or female.

According to Elizabeth Haich (1974), in her book *Initiation*, ultimately we must master twelve pairs of opposite behaviors associated with stereotypical male or female behaviors (p. 177). The following is a modified list from her work which describes the opposite traits we must learn to command in order to balance the male and female energies within. Tests always require that we act from a calm and centered position.

We pass the tests (1) when we learn the appropriate responses to each unique situation, and (2) only after we are comfortable exhibiting BOTH sets of opposite behaviors.

Feminine Attributes		Masculine Attributes
Noncommittal	-	Committed
Open to all things	-	Resistant to change
Detached	-	Controlling
Silent	-	Talkative
Compliant	-	Ruling
Peaceful	-	Aggressive
Modest/Humble	-	Self-Assured
Responsive	-	Skeptical
Faithful	-	Independent
Cautious	-	Bold
Careful	-	Impulsive
Respectful of life	-	Fearless

When we incorporate all twelve opposite pairs of behaviors into our personalities, we reach more of our full human potential. A clue as to which behaviors we need to master lies in the answer to the question: Which behaviors am I least comfortable displaying? If an individual normally does all the talking and has difficulty being silent, it is clear that he or she needs to learn to listen. If a person does not like confrontation and normally chooses to ignore all injustices because he or she cannot handle confrontation, this individual may be suppressing too much masculine energy and may need to get in touch with this power. In all cases, we, as individuals, know on a soul level what it is we need to learn, as does the Higher Self. Whatever our weak areas, rest assured that the arenas will be brought to us in which to practice, so that we emerge victorious in mastering all behaviors related to our full human potential.

Masters act with ease in all situations. They know how to manage ALL energy patterns within and display all behaviors with ease, depending upon the situations in which they find themselves.

Ultimately, peace reigns within when one rules both male and female energies. This is truth. Masters also choose what they think, say, and feel at all times, rather than allow the emotions of others to dictate how they should behave. Therefore, these testing arenas are necessary for our development so that we may practice behaving in all ways that help develop our mastery.

Entry into the Fifth Dimension requires that one be calm, centered, and in charge of the mental and emotional bodies at all times. When one learns to master both the female and the male energy patterns within, one is prepared for ascension into the Fifth Dimension. Only then is the Higher Self able to integrate itself into the lower eight bodies. By balancing our feminine and masculine energies, we assist Mother Earth to restore her balance of yin and yang energy, as well.

The sons and daughters of Light will rise again and walk the face of the Earth in the Seventh Golden Age as living Masters. Simply put, the integration of male and female energies will mean that individuals will be masters of all circumstances that rise to challenge them. All energy must be integrated so that it may, in turn, become integrated into Oneness to facilitate God consciousness.

Summary

The concept of the Fifth Dimension is difficult for us to understand since access to the Fifth Dimension is not provided by the five senses and, therefore, is not considered to be a normal part of our experience. We begin with the understanding that everything in the universe is energy and that it can be measured and reduced to numbers. Every particle, thought, word, object, experience, or emotion has its own vibratory frequency, and can be measured independently.

In the Third Dimension, there are seven dimensions which exist simultaneously that we can begin to comprehend. Each dimension is made up of seven levels that constitute a unique curriculum and set of understandings to be gained. When we learn these curricula, we are free to move on to higher levels of existence. Each of the seven levels within a dimension has a vibrational range unique to that level, and each of the seven levels can be broken down into seven further divisions.

The seven dimensions include the following:

1st Dimension—Mineral Kingdom. The Mineral Kingdom has a harmonic range of one to seven frequencies, and it is the lowest solidification of thought-forms.

2nd Dimension—Plant Kingdom. The Plant Kingdom includes the harmonic range of eight to fourteen frequencies. Plant life exists in this dimension, and Light is required to sustain it.

3rd Dimension—Animal Kingdom. The Animal Kingdom exists within the harmonic range from fifteen through twenty-one. Consciousness is complex, ranging from simple behavior to the intelligence of humans.

4th Dimension—Astral Plane. The Astral Plane exists within the range of twenty-two through twenty-eight. This is the transition between the physical world and the world of the Celestials. Time travel, or the extension into the past or future, is possible. The Fourth Dimension is the vibration that opens the heart and provides a gateway to higher worlds. It also is the dimension that challenges us and causes us to transmute duality into Oneness.

5th Dimension—Mind and Thought Manifestation. The Fifth Dimension exists within the vibrational frequency of twenty-nine to thirty-five, and it opens a broader spectrum of colors and sounds. Our Higher Selves (Light Bodies) and physical bodies merge. We are able to learn lessons of creation and to experience a reality that moves beyond the physical world.

6th Dimension—Higher Etheric Dimension. The Higher Etheric world integrates new colors and sounds into its existence. It contains the harmonic range of thirty-six to forty-one and is the doorway to the Seventh Dimension. This Dimension holds the keys and codes for higher forms of creation, and it is a bridge between the Ascended Realms and the lower worlds.

7th Dimension—Seventh Heaven. The Seventh Dimension is a vibratory frequency that supports the Ascended Masters and Shamballa. This Seventh Heaven vibrates in the frequency range of forty-two to forty-nine. It is the home base of most of the angels and constitutes the outermost concentric ring enclosing Earth

* Intense Light spectrums from higher dimensions are now sent to Earth eight times per year to raise the planet's vibratory frequency and to cleanse the memories of individuals, which enables them to resolve issues from their present and past lives.

* Higher energy demands that issues be resolved through love, forgiveness, and understanding, and this enables our Higher Selves to be merged with our lower bodies.

* The Universal Language of Light is a symbolic coding system which is used to transmit messages from the Ascended Masters to Initiates in embodiment. It connects Light Workers to the keys and codes that will fulfill humanity's evolutionary path and God's plan on Earth. The number of symbols a soul receives in any given lifetime is dependent

on the quality of past lives, the Light acquired in this lifetime, and the individual's acceptance of change.

✳ Each of us has a feminine or yin dimension and a masculine or yang dimension. The feminine dimension focuses on the intuitive, creative-thought process of receiving information and ideas. The masculine focuses on the outer-directed, creative process of building and action. These energies must be integrated by mastering the pairs of opposite behaviors associated with each if we are to move into the Fifth Dimension.

Our task is to demonstrate the superiority of present-moment, life-centered awareness over awareness clouded by fear. We work to shift human interest gradually away from defensive, survival-oriented life-styles and toward the pursuit of excellence. We are only able to influence people in areas where their hearts are at least somewhat open and where a passionate interest is present.

We are not interested in changing minds. Minds have always followed the passions of the heart. We are interested in opening hearts.

Ken Carey
The Third Millennium (pp. 58-59)

Chapter 7

INTRODUCTION TO THE UNIVERSAL LAWS

*Sometimes I go about pitying myself, and all
the time I am being carried on great winds in
the sky.*

Ojibway saying

hen we think of Universal Laws, we can consider them in two ways. The Universal Laws, like the laws of any nation, state, or society, are expressions of acceptable and unacceptable behaviors. The explanations of these laws describe the results of these behaviors. The second meaning of the term laws refers to universal principles, or the ways in which cause and effect phenomena are related.

The Universal Laws described in this book may be considered in both of these ways, because they constitute the framework or guidelines for our behaviors and what affects our lives. They comprise the foundation for what is expected of us, and thus provide an expression of right living.

Most of us are strangers to the frontiers of the unseen and the laws that govern this vague and mysterious area.

Yet, it is forces in the unseen that create the physical world and its impact on our lives. Isn't it about time we began to explore this area and discover its effects on us?

Everything in the universe reflects Divine law and order. Without laws, life would be in chaos and would operate on a trial and error basis. Universal Laws are the extensions of physical laws which apply to the spiritual world. They govern all planes of existence, and provide the order in the universe that keeps everything flowing perfectly. All of these laws are interrelated; some specific interrelationships are pointed out in the following chapters. Therefore, understanding these laws helps us to take control of our lives and provides us with a way to become God-realized. In other words, the laws provide us with a knowledge-of-results framework. After we have learned the laws, we may violate them, but only with the full knowledge that certain results are inevitable.

When we analyze the Universal Laws in greater depth, we learn to understand their importance in our lives and their contributions to an orderly world. A deeper study reveals:

* The Universal Laws are truth.
* The laws apply to everyone and provide justice or fairness for all. We cannot escape them, for they are the guidelines for life itself.
* One cannot live one's life outside the law. Only those who do not recognize the perfection inherent in the universe believe that they can escape the effects of the laws. If they try to do so, they will battle endlessly and be tossed like a ship at sea in a storm.
* The laws are absolute and perfect. The only way in which we may bring peace and harmony to our lives is ultimately to surrender to the laws and to make choices within them that bring our souls to a higher level of consciousness.

❋ The laws provide a sense of order and predictability. We know that living outside the laws also has predictable consequences. We may not realize the positive or negative effects of our behaviors in the short term, but we can be assured that a fair and just outcome will result from each action we take.

❋ The laws provide us with ways of overcoming negative outcomes. They specify ways of changing the results of our behaviors and give us insights as to behaviors we need to avoid.

❋ When we live within the laws, we not only help ourselves, but we also help others. Each of us exerts influence over the people around us. When we live within the laws, an attraction effect occurs, causing others to follow our examples and act in a similar way. What happens to one affects the all.

❋ We live in a holographic universe, which means that the whole is contained in each small particle. Understanding Universal Laws keeps our minds focused on the interconnectedness of all things.

❋ The laws remind us that we live simultaneously in more than one world. While we experience the space/time coordinates of the physical dimension, we are bound by the spaceless/timeless precepts of the unseen dimensions. Present day teachings keep us tied to the physical world, making it difficult for our minds to grow in other dimensions and realities. It is only through the opening of the doors to understand metaphysics and the subatomic world of energy that we may understand the influence this world has on us. Our evolution depends upon our doing so.

❋ The next frontier for evolution is that of the mind. As we move forward in this arena, understanding Universal Laws will enhance our abilities to understand the power of the mind and its influence on our lives.

❋ Learning about Universal Laws helps us to learn about ourselves. We can witness the effects of the cosmos' influence just by watching how things manifest in our daily lives, for the same great truths guide everything.

❋ Living within the laws affirms our commitment to God's intent and plan and moves us closer to our Creator. The laws express the ways that our Creator designed to help us achieve the vision of a peaceful and productive universe and existence.

❋ We are one with the laws; therefore, we must KNOW them.

The Universal Laws are truth and cannot be altered. They are the keys to unlocking the mysteries of the ancient worlds and understanding how the citizens of the six golden ages before us achieved greatness.

These truths are traced back to Hermes Trismegistus. Hermes was known as the Master of all Masters, and his influence touched all civilizations on Earth, like rays projecting from the central Source. His truths were integrated into all master religions in lands around the world.

The following thirteen chapters discuss the Universal Laws that comprise the foundation for life itself. Each chapter describes one law of the universe and includes applications of that law to our everyday lives. Eleven chapters include messages from Ascended Master El Morya, the Chohan of the Blue Ray and governor of Universal Laws. One chapter, the first, is introduced by Ascended Master Pallas Athena, who was sent to set the vibration of Oneness for this document. Twelve laws were selected for inclusion in this book by El Morya. These, he says, comprise the basis for love, and thus for all that is.

The importance of reading the messages goes beyond the meaning of the words themselves. Each message is coded with a vibrational frequency which has been given it by the Master transmitting the message. The reader receives this coding while reading the message, even though the mind may not retain or fully comprehend the meaning of the words. This creates a resonance field that provides the reader access to the words and wisdom not only of the Ascended Masters who delivered the messages, but also of some of the greatest Celestial Beings who govern the universe.

Enjoy this section. It is the most important part of the book. The authors are aware that other writers may organize this same information in different ways, so read this section with a flexible mind. This format is only one way in which to learn.

Chapter 8

ENERGY: THE FOUNDATION FOR UNIVERSAL LAWS

...we hold these truths to be self-evident, that all men are created equal, that they are endowed by their Creator with certain unalienable Rights, that among these are Life, Liberty, and the pursuit of Happiness....

Declaration of Independence,
United States of America

On July 4, 1776, the signers of the Declaration of Independence of the United States of America proclaimed that all men [and women] are created equal. This statement was based on the premise that, on some level, individuals do have equal rights and that they should have the privilege of exercising those rights.

If we were to take a poll asking people's opinions as to whether or not they believe all people are created equal, we probably would receive mixed reactions, with the majority stating that this is the furthest thing from the truth they have ever heard. They might cite examples of racism and sexism and include stories of the handicapped and disadvantaged. Feeling they had proven their point, they might also challenge opponents to provide evidence of the contrary to disprove their own evidence. Individuals who repeatedly have been victimized and oppressed by society might have the loudest voices, which is understandable.

So why did our Founding Fathers write such a bold statement when this country was created? What did they know that we may not understand today?

This chapter provides the foundation and evidence to explain why their premise is true. The argument presented here is that all individuals ARE created equal, and it is only our socialization, cultural beliefs, and values that have caused us, momentarily, to forget this. In other words, select groups of people and their actions throughout time have misled us into believing and acting as though this were not true. Consequently, centuries of forgetting have contributed to tremendous pain, suffering, detachment, and loss of true identity. We have become a disempowered people. It is now time to change this, and to give people—all people—back their power.

The information in this chapter has the potential to revolutionize the world. It is also the basis for understanding the teachings on Universal Laws which will be covered in subsequent chapters. If we couple this knowledge with its applications to Universal Laws, we can create the foundation for setting our souls free and creating a fifth-dimensional society.

In order to proceed through this book and begin to realize the freedom that is inherently our gift, one must understand the basic principles outlined here. Once these are understood and realized, any individual can begin to walk the path upon which freedom, abundance, happiness, and peace are guaranteed.

The original intent of the Declaration of Independence was to provide a foundation on Earth that would allow all children of God to realize their full human potential and experience life to its fullest in a productive, beautiful way. The United States was designed specifically to hold this vision for the rest of the world until the time came upon the Earth for all to become self-realized. Unfortunately, we have had to wait centuries for this to happen because of karmic law and humanity's ignorance and irresponsibility. It is only now that we are ready to complete our karmic debts, wipe the slate clean, and proceed to a higher understanding of the evolutionary concepts that affect each soul.

Ascended Master Kuthumi addresses these topics in the following transmission.

The Declaration of Independence is a document that was delivered to the Founding Fathers of the United States through the same means by which you, Dear One [Norma], receive your messages. The individuals of the secret society that comprised membership in St. Germain's Order were in direct contact with the Celestial Command, fulfilling the work for God's plan yet to be realized. They brought through the vision and thought that were destined eventually to transform the world—that all humans are created equal and have the right to be fully realized to the degree that they so deserve.

This information regarding how the Declaration of Independence was written has not come forth before this time because, during the Colonial days, it was not safe for individuals of a membership so described to speak openly of these matters. Place into perspective the events that were taking place during the time of the writing of those sacred documents. Salem was harvesting many souls who proclaimed to hear voices from the other side, and others were still remembering the fate of the beautiful Joan of Arc who publicly announced that she received messages from God through voices that guided her steps. In remembering the conditions of the time, keep in mind the status of the souls who guided the pen that wrote those documents. All were men of influence, and several were destined to become President.

Is it no wonder the founders of the United States were hesitant to speak of their association with the Celestial Membership and the Order of Melchizedek? From our perspective, it is understandable and no judgment is made. It is important, though, to say this here for the following purpose:

The power that comes from understanding Universal Laws and their application to the world is awesome. The Celestial Command has understood Universal Laws and their application to human evolution for a time longer than can be recorded on Earth. Because the Earth is so important in the plan to assist souls to evolve to higher dimensions of consciousness and Light, this information has been veiled until now. The reason this information has not come forth before is that the majority of souls were not ready to receive it. Their consciousness has not been high enough to integrate the meaning and responsibility of this knowledge. In addition, in the past, those in embodiment were here primarily to complete unfinished business of previous lifetimes. They were so preoccupied with the lower existence that they had no time for understanding the higher dimensions, laws, or knowledge. In fact, anything outside their parameters of reality made them fearful and they would react like cornered animals whenever they were challenged to grow. Growth, enlightenment, and open-mindedness were often scorned, and many would actually strike out at any individual or idea requesting them to change.

Learning Universal Laws before completing karmic

responsibilities would have allowed too many to "cheat." Without the spiritual discipline, many would have taken shortcuts to an easier life, or at least tried to do so. This situation would have robbed them of important opportunities to be tested. This condition would have nurtured a membership of souls with great knowledge, but with little strength of character to apply that knowledge.

Presently, there are some in the universe who fit this description. There are those who have a high technological nature, but have little understanding of spiritual law or how to apply this technology with responsibility. We call them the mischievous souls who serve to challenge those who are on the path to the Light.

Earth's curriculum is set up in such a way that it allows each to be tested through Tests of Initiation. These tests build character and integrity because of the lessons that must be learned. It is only after souls have completed their karmic debts that they are allowed access to higher levels of teaching, and they must prove to themselves that they have the discipline to handle the responsibility that comes with higher knowledge.

Although some perceive this path to be painful, we believe that this process produces a higher quality of human, and one who is ready for entry into the kingdoms of the Fifth Dimension and higher. With this understood, we trust that you understand why it was deemed necessary and right that all souls did not have access to these teachings. Today, the energies are changing. With the spiritual awakening on Earth, many are now ready to proceed further along the path of initiation. Many will journey into the Fifth Dimension with honors, so it is now time to guide these souls with the wisdom from the mystery schools of the past.

Over two hundred years ago in the United States, souls from the Order of Melchizedek embodied on Earth to connect with the Celestial Command and to bring forth greater truths and teachings for the world. These truths embodied the foundation that all humans are created equal and that each does have the right to liberty. These teachings were designed for the world, and not restricted to the United States, although this has not been realized before this time. This is so because God's plan includes freedom, liberty, and fulfillment for all children, allowing each to choose entry into the Fifth Dimension and the kingdom yet to come. The words in the documents that are cherished by many were designed to hold the vibrational frequency and vision for the world until the time would come when these teachings might be realized by all.

The time is now for these truths to become self-evident. We are prepared now to reveal these truths and explanations to the world so that all may understand and apply them. The words contained in this document shall travel around the world and provide answers to many who seek them. This will occur whether the government structures restrict these words or not.

The mind is the ALL. The minds cannot be contained any longer. When individuals begin to understand that the mind is free and has the power to co-create all that is needed to guarantee happiness and peace, then all people can be served, regardless of the constitutions or rules of the countries in which they reside.

Link up, Oh Children of the Divine, with the Spirit of Oneness. Connect your minds and hearts to the galactic revolution that shall carry peace, Light, and love to the nations worldwide. See the Light and energy of the universe pay attention to your thoughts, and know that you have the power within to change the course of Earth.

Hear the following words well and listen with your hearts. Remember as far back as Atlantis when you knew these words to be true. Then look to the future and envision the Heaven on Earth that YOU SHALL CREATE.

God Bless You All who hear and see with the mind's eye. Now, command the mind and heart to do your bidding by applying the information yet to come.

I AM Kuthumi, World Teacher and Ambassador to the Divine. Adonai.

Kuthumi states indirectly in his message that the secrets from the mystery schools of Egypt, Greece, and Atlantis now can be revealed to the general public. Humanity now is deemed worthy and ready to learn this information again and to use it for building the Seventh Golden Age. This is the first time since Atlantis fell that this permission has been given.

For thousands of years, people have written that the Age of Aquarius will be an age of brotherly and sisterly love. This is so because the vibrational frequency of Aquarius (in the precession of the equinoxes) is of a higher note, vibrating closer to the speed of Light. As we enter this age, the higher Light frequencies affect all on Earth. These vibrations are causing all systems that were built on lower frequencies (corruption, greed, lies, confusion, self-centeredness, etc.) to fall. Educational systems, businesses, political structures, and governments all built on self-serving principles, for example, are crumbling, only to be reborn through tremendous pain into higher forms. Thus, we are witnessing "the end of the world" and we do not even recognize what we see. Standing on the threshold of the Aquarian Age, we can only wonder how long it will take to transcend the pain and suffering in the world. The thought of moving into a world of Oneness, love, and Light, with productive, happy, empowered people should be enough to make us want to get started immediately.

Knowledge is power. The knowledge contained in this section provides the foundation for changing the world and building our own paths to mastery. Let us hope that humanity uses this knowledge wisely this time. The Ascended Realms and Karmic Boards will not look too kindly on the souls who misuse it, for there are rules that accompany mastery. The first rule is that once we have acquired knowledge of the laws, we do not have the same rights as others who do not understand them. Inherent in learning and applying the laws is the responsibility to use them judiciously. Deliberate misuse of the laws to bring harm or suffering to others brings a swift, intense return of Karma to the errant soul abusing the energy. The Law of Tenfold Return applies to the misuse of energy precisely as it does to the right use of energy.

Therefore, use this knowledge wisely! Know that you have been forewarned and that the rewards and punishments will be just. Aquarius also stands for fairness—every thought, every act is accountable. The energies on this planet have changed, and each and every action will bring nearly immediate repayment or retribution. This age will not let one stone go unturned.

So, let us begin....

To understand Universal Laws, we first must understand that everything is energy and that energy moves in a circular fashion. To illustrate this point, imagine moving out into the universe. See the star systems moving slowly in an elliptical, spiraling fashion. See the precession of the equinoxes moving Earth through the Ages of Aries, Pisces, Aquarius, and so on, with Earth remaining over 2,000 years in each age. Notice that everything is moving and evolving in a **circular** fashion.

Then, focus your attention on our solar system. See all the planets orbit the sun in rotational patterns. On a smaller scale, see the Earth rotate around the sun every 365 days. Notice that everything here also is moving in a **circular** fashion.

Next, observe Earth's magnetic field, which is representative of other forms of energy on Earth. Notice that the
magnetic lines also flow in a **circular** fashion. This is also
true of Earth's other energy fields, such as the electrical
fields.

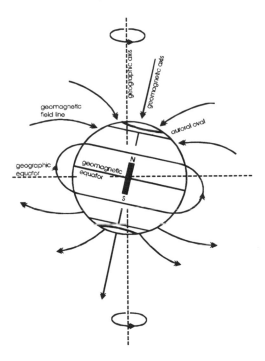

Finally, taking this concept to the microscopic level, if
cell tissues were taken from the skin and placed under a
high-powered microscope, the trained eye would observe electrons spinning around the nucleus of the atoms, also in a **circular** fashion.

Taking this logic to an even more microcosmic level, we can identify ourselves as whirling masses of energy and consciousness. In other words, if we could see ourselves in our true forms, we would see ourselves as energy beings of Light, emitting sounds that are inaudible to the human ear. Electromagnetic fields would be spinning around us in a **circular** fashion, and our auras would be brilliant.

Where is this logic leading? It is simple:

ALL ENERGY RUNS IN CIRCLES

If we are energy beings of Light, and if all energy moves in a circular fashion, then we are the generators and creators of all that occurs in our lives. Put in other terms, as the wise Master, Jesus, once said:

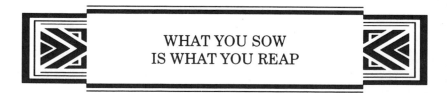

WHAT YOU SOW
IS WHAT YOU REAP

Another explanation for this phenomenon is expressed in the contemporary saying:

WHAT GOES AROUND
COMES AROUND

It is a principle of physics that energy can neither be created nor be destroyed. Energy can only be transformed from one form of energy into another. This fact serves to deepen our understanding of what is being presented here. There is no escaping this phenomenon.

Everything in the universe is energy, including ourselves. Everything is one body of energy, comprised of particles so small that our minds have difficulty conceptualizing the significance of this fact. At the microscopic level, we are nothing but a whirling mass of electrons and energy atoms, spinning rapidly. We all are connected within this sea of energy. The Ascended Masters call it the God Force, or Golden Liquid Light, and say that GOD IS THOUGHT! This God Force is the prana, chi, life force, or configuration of tachyon particles of Light that holds together everything in the universe. We are this force field of energy. If you disbelieve this and think that you are not part of this force, try and step out of it! It cannot be done.

Keep in mind that at the time Jesus walked the face of the Earth there were no science classes. The atom had not been discovered, and scientific terms, such as energy, had not yet been coined. Nevertheless, his advanced celestial soul understood these scientific concepts and spiritual laws. He spoke about them in terms that were common to the civilization and culture in which he lived. Therefore, he used expressions such as "What you sow is what you reap" as a way to impress upon individuals the importance of performing charitable acts and kindnesses toward others. The problem with this method of delivery for today's world is that it leaves humanity short of understanding the scientific foundation, rationale, or theoretical background that explains why it is so important to stay positive and loving at all times, especially when some individuals appear to get away with acts that are not of the highest order. In other words, the answers to questions such as "What's really in it for me to change my thoughts and actions and become a positive person?" are not internalized, except in a religious sense. Why should we want to change if we do not understand the theoretical foundation for what we are doing? The fact that so many people continue to inflict tremendous pain on others is the greatest proof of all that humanity does not understand the repercussions of its actions.

The hidden obstacle to understanding this principle is that, in the Age of Pisces, we reaped in one lifetime what we had sown primarily in an earlier lifetime. Consequently, when our debts came around lifetimes later, we felt no connection to the original cause and believed that we were victims of circumstances, powerless to change the conditions of our lives. We could not figure out why bad things happened to good people or why we deserved what we were getting when we kept trying to do everything right. During those lifetimes, the veils were down. We had to pay blindly for what we had done to others in earlier lifetimes by experiencing the just karmic punishment for our sins. The same or similar experiences were set up for us to experience what we had inflicted on others earlier. This occurred so that our souls might be stamped with learning experiences that enhanced our growth and development. We had thousands of lifetimes in which to clean up our acts, and it has taken that long to do so. The veils have been down for a long time, but now things are changing as we move into the Age of Aquarius.

With the Harmonic Convergence in 1987, all conditions on Earth changed. All karmic debts were released first for the Starseeds, who had less Karma to complete. By the year 2001, all karmic debts will be released for anyone who chooses to release them. This does not mean that we do not accrue Karma, both good and bad, on a daily basis. What this means is that the vibrational patterns of the universe are speeding up to the point where what we do comes around within weeks, hours, or even minutes as the karmic wheel of debts is clearing. Since the souls of the Starseeds were less contaminated with negative karmic deeds than the general population of Earthling souls, the quickening process allowed clearing and purification to occur more rapidly. This information is essential to the instruction that follows on how to reach enlightenment.

An understanding of the concepts, **everything is energy** and **energy moves in circles,** is absolutely essential for moving forward along the path of enlightenment. It is these principles that bring us to the next point, which is:

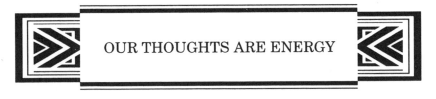

OUR THOUGHTS ARE ENERGY

In addition to our thoughts, everything we feel, say, and do constitutes a form of energy. Each of us is a powerful energy emitter in every waking or sleeping moment. Take note of the following diagram:

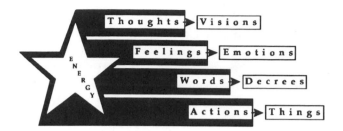

The diagram of the four forms of energy succinctly conceptualizes what each of us is. This is it. This is what we are, a mass of energy! It is our Spirit and consciousness that move this energy. In terms of energy, we are composites of these four forms—and nothing more. We are the sum total of our:

THOUGHTS
FEELINGS
WORDS
ACTIONS

This, then, is the proof that:

WE ARE CREATED EQUAL!

What we think, feel, say, and do in each moment sends out a resonance field in the universe that comes back to us to create our realities. It is our consciousness that drives this energy, and we program our consciousness by the messages we send out to one another. But remember, energy is energy. It will follow the course of least resistance. Therefore, when we focus on the results that we want, our energies will support us in obtaining those results. This is true. It is a metaphysical law.

By means of these four forms of energy (thoughts, feelings, words, and actions):

WE EACH CREATE
OUR OWN REALITY

We have seen that because everything is energy and energy moves in circles, "What goes around comes around." Since this is so, we know that everything we generate must come back to us in some form. Therefore:

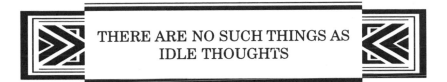

THERE ARE NO SUCH THINGS AS
IDLE THOUGHTS

With this new-found knowledge, we can revolutionize the world and bring Heaven to Earth. Atlantis can rise once again, for this realization is destined to empower all people on Earth. Without this understanding, just look at what we have allowed others to do to us in the past.

Did our Founding Fathers know something that we have forgotten? Or did they channel that all men are created equal with blind faith and hope in their hearts that all would be treated equally and fairly some day? Maybe they trusted their Sources from the Order of Melchizedek, and it made no difference. It was obvious that the words sang of a higher vibration and a vision for the world. The resonance sounded of truth. Trying to analyze what happened is pointless. What is important is that, with the help of the Ascended Masters, both then and today, we have rediscovered this ageless secret of humanity's power.

Since we are now aware that we are responsible for

creating our own reality, and since we know that all energy runs in circles, we are brought to the following questions: Where is our point of power? From what point in time do we originate our reality? Where do we begin? There is really only one answer to these questions, and that is:

OUR POINT OF POWER IS NOW!

This is the second most critical point made in this chapter. Anchor it in your consciousness. **THE ONLY REALITY WE HAVE IS EACH INSTANT IN TIME.**

What we do with each moment of time creates our destiny. Yet, two things continue to keep us from this realization. As stated by Master Kuthumi, the two things that keep us from our power are the **past** and the **future**.

Where is the past? All things experienced are only thoughts and energy in people's minds. Each person has a different view of reality depending on individual experience. Therefore, the past is no longer real; it is gone. It is an illusion, so LET IT GO!

Where is tomorrow? Where is the future? You have not yet created it with your thoughts, feelings, words, and actions of today. Consequently, the future also is not real, so LET THE FEARS AND ANXIETIES ASSOCIATED WITH THE FUTURE GO!

Unfortunately, Kuthumi says, we spend most of our time worrying about the past (which is gone) and the future (which we have not yet created). Regarding the past, we think of the regrets...I wish I had done this...If only I had not done or said that...I wish I had not made that decision.

Regarding the future, we often fear not having a job, a relationship, or the other things that we want most in life. Both of these, the past and the future, are illusions in the present moment of time.

Monitor your thoughts on a daily basis and determine how much of your precious energy is spent in these mind traps. What kind of tapes do you play in your mind on a regular basis? Every time you play a fearful or regretful tape, you are robbed of your precious time in the present moment to create your future. Thoughts like these rob us of our dreams and weaken us, for all thoughts based on fear slowly drain our Light. Remember, we are energy beings, and our mind controls the way in which we use this precious substance.

In the Battle of Armageddon, opposing forces know this and work by whispering suggestions into your consciousness to encourage your mind to stay in lower states. When these forces see that your Light is getting strong and you no longer are fooled, they move to a secondary plan. At this point, they begin to work through individuals around you whom they consider to be weak, fractured souls. These may include family members, coworkers, friends, or even acquaintances. The negative forces know that if they can get these people to buy into these illusions they will become depressed, and will say things to you that plant seeds of doubt. Working through others, they hope eventually to get to you!

The opposing forces frequently come through people whom you least suspect. Since everyone experiences ups and downs in life, these forces will wait until an individual is in a lower state of mind and then use that person to get to you. Keep in mind that these forces are after not only the Light of the other individual, such as your child, but your Light as well. It is a clever system. Can you think of a time when they have been successful? Never underestimate how clever these forces can be. It is time now to understand the way in which they operate, and to see the negative forces for what they are.

This Battle of Armageddon is being played out on the Earth plane. Unawakened individuals are mere puppets in this battle. The stakes are the Light of the soul, and every individual is a participant. As written in the Dead Seas Scrolls and Bible, it is an unseen battle between the sons and daughters of darkness and the forces of Light that has been prophesied for centuries. This battle is being played out primarily on the unseen planes of existence, although recently it has begun to penetrate our physical world and daily affairs as well. Its effects are more and more observable each day.

Average individuals cannot see the battlefields or the players. However, old souls in embodiment can see them with their Third Eyes. These souls are the former Initiates of the mystery schools of the past who acquired the vision of seeing interdimensionally. To them, the battles are evident. It is with this sight of the Third Eyes and the wisdom of the ancients that the rules of battle for the Children of Light are now being revealed. It is hoped that the sons and daughters of Light will band together, embrace the darkness, and transform these challenging forces into Light. We can, and we will, for Light always transforms darkness.

It is important to remember that dark forces HAVE NO POWER OVER YOU UNLESS YOU GIVE THE POWER TO THEM. The Light is all the protection that we need, as we are totally protected in the Christ energy. We have forgotten this momentarily because of the programming that for centuries has weakened us and moved us into a state of fear. Franklin D. Roosevelt once said, "There is nothing to fear, but fear itself." We are now to know the truth of this statement.

Remember, we all are created equal, and it is what we do with our thoughts, feelings, words, and actions in every moment that determines our destiny. The dark forces challenge us and actually can bring out the best within us if we overcome the lessons and pass the tests that they bring us. Let them challenge you, but always keep your moment of power—each instant of every day—by holding the Light within and focusing on the purest and most positive thoughts your mind can create.

According to Kuthumi, dark thought-forms, sent by the opposition, are directed to penetrate the two weakest bodies of the nine we possess: the mental and the emotional. Forces that challenge us and try to weaken our Spirits know that if they can keep our mental and emotional bodies confused and unfocused, we become vulnerable and, perhaps, even pathetic. Look around. Do you see any signs of this?

It is easy to see that television also contributes to this state of mind, when we analyze the programs that comprise most of prime-time viewing. The news reports, shows, entertainment, and even cartoons for children often are filled with violence, wars, abuse, crimes, horror, and darkness. The decision makers and minds of the television stations justify their programming by stating (1) that this is what the public wants, and (2) that it is reality and reflects society. Therefore, they must show these events. They affect the ratings.

The greater reality is that these constant images, feelings, words, and actions bombard our minds and put thoughts into them, which we then project back into society. Our collective consciousness thus creates the reality around us. Look at our American society. It continues to spiral downward with crime and other degenerative conditions. In order to change the conditions around us, we must hold a higher vision of perfection within us, first as individuals and then in groups. By doing so, we will send out a frequency that will attract higher vibrations, and even begin to change things around us. When we accept what happens in our midst as reality by validating events with our thoughts, we ourselves become the creators. We must choose what we will think.

The Ascended Masters know this truth and know what we need to do to change the world. They teach that we must begin by changing our consciousness through thinking and believing in the vision of tomorrow's harmony and perfection. The mind controls what we think, so if we discipline our minds to be stronger and to hold that perfect vision, then collectively we can change our destiny. This can only be accomplished in each moment of time. If this means shutting off the television to allow ourselves the quiet time to hold our perfect visions, then we should do so.

Change yourself and you have the power to transform your environment. IF we join together in the Light, we collectively have the power to transform the world.

Summary

A primary Source of our power is the realization that (1) we are all created equal, and (2) everything is energy. In this energy field, we are all subject to the Universal Laws. Understanding and living within the knowledge of the laws allows us to choose entry into the Fifth Dimension and higher kingdoms yet to come. Basic to understanding the laws and how to grow spiritually are the following principles:

* ❋ Everything is energy. God is mind energy or thought. We are a part of this God Force and, thus, co-creators with God.
* ❋ Energy travels in a circular fashion; therefore, what goes around comes around.
* ❋ All humans have four kinds of energy to use in creating the future we wish to live in—thoughts, feelings, words, and actions.
* ❋ We each create our own reality with the energy we emit in each moment.
* ❋ Our power point is now, each moment, this instant in time.
* ❋ Dark forces try to rob us of our power by getting us to feel guilty over the past or to fear the future. The past and the future are both illusions—let them go.
* ❋ Dark forces do not have power over us unless we give the power to them. All is transformed in the Light. Therefore, be in the Light at all times.

Chapter 9

LAW OF DIVINE ONENESS

Spirit is the essence of consciousness, the energy of the universe that creates all things. Each one of us is a part of that Spirit—a Divine entity. So the Spirit is the Higher Self, the eternal being that lives within us.

Shakti Gawain

ur thoughts, our visualizations, and the language by which we express our thoughts are some of the most powerful tools we have for spiritual growth. Just as God, or the ALL, creates with mind, so do we as human beings. Thoughts create, and constitute the basis for all there is because thoughts are vibrations before they become thoughts. We then express them as the energies of words, emotions, and actions. In this way we interact with the world and carry out our life activities.

The Law of Divine Oneness helps us understand that we live in a world where everything is connected to everything else. Everything we do, say, think, and believe affects others and the universe around us. As we grow spiritually, we learn how to transmute negative thoughts, words, emo-

tions, and actions into positive ones. Thus, we not only manifest a better environment for ourselves, but we also help create a world that is consistent with the One.

To assist us now on this journey, Master Athena explains the Divine Concept of Oneness in the following way.

*Greetings to all Aspirants who wish to become self-
realized in the Light.*

*I, Athena, am pleased to be selected to work with
Master El Morya to deliver the ancient wisdom of
Hermes Trismegistus, better known to the Egyptians as Thoth, on the universal principle of the
Divine Concept of Oneness. I fulfill this assignment
with my heart connected to the Great Central Sun
which provides me with the connection to the Divine. It is this lifeline, through the Higher Self, that
shall bring forth the highest frequency of information to the reader of these words.*

*To the students of this lesson, one directive is given.
Feel the message with the heart center, rather than
receive the words in the mind. Absorb the Light
that comes with the message, and in so doing, you
shall begin the journey of becoming self-realized in
the Light.*

*It is now time to allow the information to flow from
the mind of the Creator.*

*The Divine Concept of Oneness is the Universal
Mind. It is the realization that ALL IS MIND and
the universe exists within this field of pure energy
and Light. All is consciousness—the planets, the
suns, the animals, the plants, the minerals, and all*

beings of multidimensional forms who grace the Creator's kingdoms. Nothing escapes this principle, for all is composed of the same substance at the subatomic level.

It is here, at the subatomic level, where the Oneness Concept sustains the life force within, and it is also at this level where higher consciousness is realized, for all is mind energy in the universes and all is information which can be reduced mathematically.

This field of mind energy is sometimes referred to as the Golden Liquid Light, or otherwise known as prana, chi, or life force energy. This field is accessed by individuals by silencing the active mind. This state reduces the number of electromagnetic signals emitted by higher mental actions. Silence allows the nine bodies to align with the perfect code that locks the individual into this force field.

Once an individual resonates to the frequency of Divine Oneness, the mind connects with symbols and patterns that reside in this force field. These, in turn, enable the mind to use this connection for creation and manifestation. The key to accessing this "power" lies in the person's ability to remain totally calm, balanced, and at peace during all situations.

Mind, body, Spirit, and Earth are all interconnected within the Golden Liquid Light. They are all one, yet each affects the other in subtle ways. Humans moving into the Fifth Dimension must understand this concept, and also understand the subtlety of the mental body's and mind's influences on the creative process. This is especially true for scientists. If this is not understood, evolution will be stalled and chaos will result, causing pain to those moving through this portal of time / space.

A magnetic flux exists in the universe which will be experienced more fully when Earth is integrated into the Fifth Dimension. It is sensitive and fluctuates easily through the stimulus-response patterns being emitted constantly by various energy sources. For example, whenever there is a disruption in the force field, a momentary disturbance is created in the magnetic resonance patterns around individuals. The cycles of the moon and the subsequent effects on human behavior illustrate this point. When such disturbances occur, information received by individuals is disrupted, and the mathematical symbols are disturbed. This causes "inaccurate" information to be received and assembled within the mind.

I place the word inaccurate in quotation marks to make a point. In reality, no information received is inaccurate, because all information is received as a result of the magnetic patterns that form around an individual. Students of Universal Laws know this to be true and recognize that this statement is in reference to the Law of Attraction. By using quotations, I emphasize that information exists that is more stable and conducive to the growth of the individual's nine bodies, and that this greater wisdom can be accessed through higher vibrational patterns within the Divine Mind. When an individual is calmer and more stable, his or her ability to receive higher forms of information with fewer distortions is increased. Therefore, information received under these conditions is deemed to be more "accurate."

Another way to assist one's understanding is to provide another explanation. Accurate also can be de-

fined in terms of information received through stages of the evolutionary development of the soul. What is understood and accepted as truth and accurate in one phase of development is discarded later as the person evolves into higher fields of understanding. Thus, this explains how science has evolved throughout the centuries. As wisdom and knowledge expand and become stabilized, concepts are received at higher levels of understanding and development. This, then, changes the face of truth.

Awaken, my Sisters and Brothers of the Stars! Feel this life force connection and integrate it into your existence through the stillness of your mind. Connect with it to become one with its power. If you can achieve this state of Oneness, you shall slowly become "enlightened," which will begin your journey to freedom.

Remember you are one with this force. You are the spark of Divine Creation, come to Earth to be the co-creators with God. Remember Oneness!

All is mind. All is thought. All is the All.

In the Universal Mind of Oneness, I, Pallas Athena, born out of the mind of Zeus, conclude this discourse. So Be It!

Summary

Everything in the universe is connected in a force field of Oneness. All is consciousness. All is God. Since we exist within this field, we are one with it. Therefore, our thoughts, feelings, words, and actions are powerful forms of energy.

Some concepts to understand are:

* ALL IS MIND. Since we exist in this field of Divine power, we are one with it.
* The field of mind energy often is referred to as Golden Liquid Light, prana, chi, life force energy, God, or the God Force.
* The most powerful tools for spiritual growth are our thoughts, visualizations, and language. Thoughts have the power to create.
* The key to accessing mind energy is the person's ability to remain calm, balanced, and at peace in all situations.
* We are the co-creators with God, come to bring Heaven to Earth through right use of the connection to this force field of Oneness.

Chapter 10

LAW OF VIBRATION

Nothing rests;
everything moves;
everything vibrates.

The Kybalion

Everything in the universe is in motion, whether solid, liquid, or gas. All things move, vibrate, and travel in circular patterns. Each thing that exists is identified by its own unique vibrational frequency. Frequency is defined as the number of periodic oscillations, vibrations, or waves per unit of time.

No two things in the universe are truly identical, because each has its unique vibrational pattern. The differences between matter and energy are explained primarily by the differences in these vibratory motions. Phenomena such as light, heat, magnetism, electricity, and sound are forms of vibratory motion, just as trees, desks, flowers, and animals are.

When things vibrate very slowly, we hear no noise. Physical objects vibrate slowest, which is why we cannot hear any sounds emanating from them. As vibration is increased, we begin to hear lower-pitched sounds. Further increases in vibration allow us to hear higher-pitched notes, as when we strike the ascending keys of the piano. If vibrations increase further, to a higher frequency, we may not be able to hear the sound because it may have moved out of our ability to register the frequency.

So it is with our ability to see color. We are limited in seeing only the colors that are contained within the spectrum of Light—the rainbow. Our first perception of color is of a dark red. As vibrations increase, the red becomes brighter, then turns to orange, and then to yellow, green, blue, indigo, and violet. Violet vibrates higher into ultraviolet where we no longer have the ability to see the color, just as we cannot see infrared with the naked eye.

The same principles of vibration that apply to the physical world also apply to us and to our thoughts, feelings, desires, and will. We each have our own unique sound, say the Ascended Masters, and that perfect sound is who we really are. If we could become still long enough to connect with this sound, we would discover our true, perfect self.

Disruptions in our lives, our life-styles, television, radio, people, and noises in general all serve to keep us from hearing that perfect sound within and from becoming it. Many of the vibrational frequencies in the world work to compete with and disrupt our mental and emotional states, keeping us from connecting with the perfection lying dormant inside.

Our thoughts, emotions, and wills send out vibrations into the universe. Every thought or mental state has a corresponding rate and mode of vibration. The higher the vibration, the longer lasting the effects are. The lower the vibration, the more potent the effects are in the short term.

In the higher dimensions, such as the Fifth Dimension, the Law of Vibration is considered to be "what is." In these dimensions, nothing is assigned meaning, only a frequency. Thoughts, emotions, behaviors, and actions are understood for the level at which they reside. An angry person is analyzed objectively as being angry, with no value assigned to the behavior. An effort is made to try and understand the behavior, and perhaps a plan is prepared to try and raise the vibrational frequency to a higher level, thus transmuting the anger into something less painful.

We live in the Third Dimension, the plane of dichotomies, which reflects most things as good/bad, black/white, or yes/no. Because our identity is associated with this mode of operation, most of us have a characteristic style of optimism or pessimism. Optimism resides on a higher frequency and pessimism resides on a lower frequency. Optimists tend to expect more of the world. This is communicated to others and is likely to be realized. Pessimists expect the negative. They anticipate gloom and doom and actually help create it. Our basic style is important because whatever we choose creates a vibration that goes out into the collective consciousness and helps either to raise Earth's vibrations or to lower them. When we express negativity, we take on an amount of negativity equal to what we have expressed. Similarly, when we express ourselves in positive ways, we take on an equal amount of positive vibrations.

Vibrations not only affect us, but also impact the people around us. Positive or negative vibrations may resonate in others and create similar vibrations. If we send out thoughts of envy, criticism, hatred, or jealousy, then the same thought-forms are aroused and sent back by others.

Each of us has the power to choose. We can align our bodies and our behaviors to create harmony and consistency with the God within us. Just as we care for our bodies by choosing options and behaviors—food, exercise, freedom from addictions—to maintain our balance and remain in a state of health, we also must take care of our minds by choosing good thoughts. Positive thoughts help us move on our journey to spiritual development. Other thoughts inhibit our progress or cause us to regress. When we learn to choose the good, we move toward spiritual goals with measured progress.

Often, the full impact of our behavior on others is not well understood. We can be a positive force working for the betterment of our organization or community, or we can be a negative force and tear down what is being built. Perhaps the most difficult form of negativity to overcome is personal or group cynicism. Many individuals who have experienced multiple disappointments or failures begin to believe that nothing will work. The group mind then creates a vibrational frequency that draws to these individuals everything else that resides on that frequency. In order to solve their problems, the individuals must learn to open their minds and hearts and think from a place connected to a higher consciousness, for the solutions will be found only on the higher planes of existence. Through the Law of Vibration, this mode of behavior always brings the answers we are seeking, for the higher frequencies contain greater knowledge and wisdom.

A few try and rationalize their negativity by saying that they need to be honest. When people are motivated to behave in a negative way, however, the vibrational frequency emitted speaks for itself. We need to strive to be honest and helpful and still be positive.

Our goal is to keep our vibrations as positive and high as possible. This means that we must not let another's negative attitudes penetrate our feelings or mental state. One of the ways to accomplish this is to learn to keep from becoming overinvolved in the problems of others. We need to listen carefully, help establish goals for solving the problems, and assist in planning positive outcomes, but we must keep ourselves from taking on the lower vibrations emitted by others.

Understanding the Law of Vibration assists us to get in touch with our feelings every moment of the day. Since each thought, feeling, word, and behavior resides on its own frequency, we need to learn to assess how we feel and to choose behaviors and attitudes that only help us evolve. Evolution is why we are here. The Law of Vibration gives us the basis of knowledge to transcend all that is not in the Divine plan and provides us the way to move to higher planes of existence.

Master El Morya says this about the Law of Vibration.

Namaste, my Sisters and Brothers of the Universe.

I AM El Morya, Master in charge of describing the nature of the universe through the next eleven discourses. I fulfill this assignment with dedication to this mission, for it is through understanding these next eleven laws that human consciousness will move to a state of enlightenment never experienced before on Earth. I come in the Light of Sananda and carry forth this commitment to you.

The Law of Vibration is known by the ancients to be the law of power. Understanding the context and application of this law allows each aspirant to move closer to his or her destiny and carry the torch within to the higher mode of Spirit. This knowledge also assists all to understand the conflicts experienced on the dualistic plane of matter and enables the souls to use the principles contained within the law to balance and control individual lives.

In the mind of Oneness, everything is in motion. Energy exists in all forms in the Golden Liquid Light. This pool of energy that permeates all universes is never at rest and serves to carry the smallest particles of energy into various states of action, thus causing effects to be felt constantly.

Inherent within this understanding is the fact that everything vibrates within the universes to various degrees that lie on a continuum. To say it in a way easier to understand: there are degrees of motion experienced within the Earth plane that lie on a continuum that spans from physical manifesta-

*tions of the most dense matter to the higher exist-
ence of Spirit. Matter, energy, thought, and Spirit
form the continuum of this range of vibration experienced by all. Yet, regardless of the variations
of the vibrations, all is absorbed and contained
within the Universal Mind of Oneness.*

*Everything is connected through the Divine Mind
of Oneness. All is seen as the absolute, although
each item tends to carry its own identification and
appears to be separate. In the nature of higher realities, everything experienced is a part of the Oneness, and the individualistic vibrational pattern (or
frequency) of each item determines its position of
influence and strength.*

*The Law of Vibration reveals that higher powers,
and higher consciousness and understanding, reside on the end of the continuum that comprises the
highest vibrations of Spirit. Spirit is associated
with such terms as pure Light, the Merkabah, love,
and God consciousness. Physical dense matter is
defined as that which one experiences with the five
senses. Physical dense matter also represents the
human body (the vehicle that carries the soul). It
is also defined as the lower, heavier, and more subtle
vibrations, such as the energies experienced in the
heart and mind that cause mental pain and anger.*

*Since all is energy, it is easy to understand how all
objects and actions impact the total human being,
which is composed of nine subtle bodies. Body (the
physical body), mind (the mental body), and Spirit
are affected most by the Law of Vibration; yet the
influence of the All is present in everything that we
are.*

In understanding and using the Law of Vibration,

the aspirant learns to integrate the higher Light frequencies of Spirit into consciousness and the lower eight bodies, thus effecting transformation. Assimilating the higher frequencies into lower dense matter, through the direction and will of the mind and heart, allows the individual to raise his or her own vibratory patterns. This increased Light reveals itself in the aura around.

The wise, old ancients knew that the greatest power resides in the Light. They understood the Law of Vibration. They understood the ultimate strength of the lightning bolt and how Light energy stands at the point of creation. They also perceived the deeper construct of the etheric field that comprises the God Force and saw how this energy field resides within each individual, although it is unrealized in most.

Simply put, the ancients knew that HIGHER VIBRATIONS CONSUME AND TRANSFORM LOWER VIBRATIONS. Thus, the concept "love conquers all" reveals one of the greatest mysteries of creation. The more Light one assimilates into the body, mind, and Spirit, the faster the acceleration, enabling one to control life and manifest the perfect reality all around.

OUT OF LIGHT, ALL IS CREATED. All individuals who are experiencing an accelerated path to become One with the Higher Self shall instantly grasp the notion that when the Law of Vibration is understood fully, they will be able to apply this law and manifest a Heaven on Earth. When this moment is realized, the prophecy shall be fulfilled.

Since everything is on a continuum, the mission, then, is to move from the plane of dense matter and duality up to the plane of Oneness. This is accomplished by understanding those experiences and forms that have caused discomfort, pain, and sadness and replacing them with higher thoughts and experiences of love, joy, and peace. All that is experienced in life is nothing more than events designed within the Law of Vibration to provide Initiates opportunities to learn of the Law of Vibration and to choose to remain on that level, digress to a lower level, or aspire to a higher one. Once an individual moves to a higher level, that which was experienced on the lower level is never experienced again as a test of learning. The higher vibrational level assimilated within the nine bodies (by the choice the individual has made) serves to consume and transform the lower vibratory frequency. Consequently, since each thought, event, action, and emotion is assigned its own unique vibrational frequency, all that is of a lower nature is slowly "burned off." This phenomenon serves to continue to purify all of the lower nature within the subtle bodies and rests at the heart of purification.

All Initiates must learn the importance of purification, which only can be realized through the mind and heart connection. Purification also comes from the understanding that emotion is the cosmic glue, and that what is willed with strong emotion will be created. This is so.

Therefore, when one experiences the higher and lower natures at battle, it is important, on the road to mastery, to acknowledge BOTH sides of the duality and walk the middle of the road. In the Oneness, ALL must be addressed and understood— nothing can be omitted. The key to transformation, then, is not to attach any emotion to the lower vibratory patterns, but only to feel the strength of the love and higher energies. Once this is accomplished, the individual will move quickly through the experience, enabling manifestation of the higher kingdom of Light and love to be realized more quickly.

For now, this brief explanation shall suffice. Use it as a tool to carry the torch in the soul to the Higher Self.

I AM El Morya. Adonai.

Summary

Everything in the universe is in motion. Energy is never at rest. It is constantly in action, creating various effects. The differences between matter and energy are explained by the differences in their vibratory motions. Light, heat, magnetism, electricity, and sound are forms of vibratory motion, as are trees, desks, flowers, and animals.

* Everything in the universe is in motion, and objects and entities vibrate on a continuum.
* Our thoughts, emotions, desires, and wills give off vibrations which affect us and those around us.
* Higher powers, consciousness, and understanding reside in the higher vibrations. When humans embrace a higher consciousness, their auras increase to a frequency closer to the speed of Light.
* We learn to integrate higher frequencies of Spirit into consciousness and the lower eight bodies; thus, transformation occurs.
* Higher vibrations consume and change lower vibrations.
* What is willed with strong emotion will be created and become reality.
* Once an individual moves to a higher level of vibration, that which was experienced on a lower level is never experienced again.

Chapter 11

LAW OF ACTION

Action should culminate in wisdom.
The Bhagavad Gita

Many of us work with personal issues or with larger social causes to try to make our world a better place in which to live. Involvement with groups in an attempt to achieve a goal is often frustrating. We often can attract others who seem sincerely committed to the concern at hand. We can make plans. But unless there is a visible crisis, it is often difficult to get people to carry through at the level of action needed to solve problems. It seems that we move from problem to problem without demonstrating the actions required to make significant steps toward solving the problems.

Action inevitably involves some change in our behaviors. It requires discipline, and an effort to make changes in our lives. We develop clever ways to avoid taking action. We deal with the trivia, the things we know how to do, and avoid the level of effort required to deal with more difficult problems where the steps are not clear and the risk of failure is high. We are willing to settle for less than what we or our institutions are capable of achieving.

What we seem to have missed is the need to be able to determine our goals, to develop plans, and to strive to achieve these goals. When these actions are accompanied with positive thoughts and expressions of love, we are able to manifest and achieve our desires.

Our problems seem to lie in several areas. Strange as it may seem, many of us do not know what we desire. We want to be comfortable, to get along, and not to have serious problems, but we may not have goals that are accompanied by the passion to achieve them. Goals and desires are the fuel for success. Our increased awareness of the importance of goals now is incorporated in management circles as developing a vision of where we want to be in the future. It is this ideal state that many of us cannot visualize or allow ourselves to dream about.

A second problem is that we may not understand the actions or steps that are required to get to where we want to be. Knowing how to develop a program, or how to take the many smaller actions that lead to our desired goals, is an essential part of striving to achieve.

We may not have the will to persist in our beliefs and actions when we encounter conflict or difficulty. Persistence and the ability to stay with a dream constitute a critical part of success.

Finally, we may not understand the relationship between the physical and the spiritual. While action is essential in the Third Dimension, it also must be accompanied by positive thoughts and expressions of caring and love. We may not realize that a variety of forms of help are available to us from the Celestial World. We need only take the time to ask for this help. "Ask and it shall be given" must become a reality of our lives.

El Morya speaks of the importance of the Law of Action in the following message.

I greet you with the love of the Christos and the wisdom of the Buddha. I, El Morya, am pleased to bring to you the knowledge and understanding of how to apply the Universal Laws in the Third, Fourth, and Fifth Dimensions. Application of these laws is possible through the Law of Action.

In higher dimensions of time / space, such as the realms in the Fifth Dimension and higher, manifestation comes from thought and the expression of love emanating from within. In dimensions below the Fifth Dimension, such as the Third Dimension, in order for manifestation to occur, thoughts must be accompanied by action. That is because the Third Dimension is a three-dimensional existence and accompanies the physical world.

Things that reside in the Third Dimension on Earth are all solid, liquid, or gas, even though the foundation for all has its origin in the etheric. Density comprises existence on Earth. It is important to remember this concept when living in a third-dimensional reality. The reason this is so is because third-dimensional forms need a greater force to assist them to reposition the electron into other existences. It is because of density that the Law of Action must be applied for manifestation to be realized more easily on the Earth plane.

An understanding of the Law of Vibration and the principles that underlie this law provide the way for humans to raise themselves out of a third-dimensional reality into higher ones. Thoughts and changed consciousness are the keys to a successful transformation. As consciousness is raised, an in-

dividual slowly begins to change his or her vibrational rate, transforming from the Third Dimension and moving eventually into the Fifth.

As one's vibrational rate increases, the auric fields begin to align with the white Light. The greater the Light held within consciousness, the greater the power the person has to manifest things solely with the power of mind, accompanied by love. Before the vibrational frequency is raised to a high enough level, however, one must apply the Law of Action in order to manifest all that one wishes to create.

The reality today is that many souls remember the time when they could just "think things into action." They remember when life was not difficult and when their days were filled with pleasure, discipline, and dedication—to self and group advancement. The world is different now, and many get confused because they are not living the lives of harmony, peace, contentment, and abundance that they know are possible. They have not realized this higher existence yet because their thoughts are not strong enough and the Light within them is not great enough to sustain a higher existence. Many wonder why there is still perceived pain and suffering in their environments.

If I may be so bold, I will diagnose this situation. The reason individuals are not manifesting what they want, to the degree that they wish, is because they are not applying the Law of Action fully. Their souls remember an existence in Atlantis and other such realities when they did not need this law, but their minds have forgotten that they are now ingrained in a third-dimensional reality. If they apply more action to their dreams and focus their wills and emotions, all that they desire can come true.

Earth is now in the transition from the Third to the Fifth Dimension. Individuals presently residing on Earth carry vibrations ranging throughout all these dimensions—and even higher and lower ones. Those who have changed their consciousness successfully to match that of the higher dimensions display few to no problems in manifesting all that their hearts desire. Those whose vibrations match that of the Third Dimension (or lower) must understand that it takes action to move the electron to create what is in their dreams.

Before Earth is positioned firmly in the Fifth Dimension, many more years must pass. It will, therefore, take individuals an equal amount of time to change their vibrational frequencies because Earth and humanity are One. Because this is so, we advise that the Law of Action be taken seriously. By applying this law, more individuals will become co-creators with God and can bring Heaven to Earth. That is humanity's purpose for being.

The Law of Action means that an individual must engage in activities that support thoughts, dreams, emotions, and words. A commitment must be made first, however, for this step supports the basic principle of the Law of Action. The commitment then is turned into a plan, and the plan then is supported by passion. Lastly, tasks need to be completed, because the action on the physical plane forms the bonds that connect all aspects of the energies working toward manifestation.

Simply put: thoughts, emotions, words, and actions are the keys to God-realization. But God-realization also means:

OF YOU, YOU DO NOTHING. IT IS THE FATHER/MOTHER WITHIN YOU THAT DOES IT ALL.

Raising the Light within, living a life connected to the Higher Self, putting into action that which you want from within, and applying discipline and will power are the factors that set up the God Force to work through you. Become One with this Force and the will of God will become One with you.

Adonai, Dear Commanders of the Force. I AM El Morya.

Summary

Application of the Law of Action is a precondition for using the Universal Laws in effective ways. Actions may be understood in the following ways:

* Action requires a change in our behaviors, and it requires an ability to set goals and strive for their attainment or manifestation.
* Common difficulties in applying the Law of Action are inability to set meaningful goals, lack of skills or discipline to develop plans or a program for attaining desired goals, lack of persistence, and inability to link our physical and spiritual development.
* While manifestation can be achieved in the Fourth and Fifth Dimensions by thought and expressions of love, action is required for manifestation to occur in the Third Dimension.
* As we raise our vibrational rate, we are able to manifest things with the power of the mind, accompanied by love.
* When we apply the Law of Action we grow spiritually toward becoming co-creators with God.
* Individuals can apply the Law of Action by making a commitment and engaging in activities that support thoughts, dreams, emotions, words, and actions.

Chapter 12

LAW OF CORRESPONDENCE

Long before the emergence of the "new physics" many spiritually minded and artistic people understood the unity and wholeness of the universe. William Blake wrote:

> *To see a world in a grain of sand*
> *And a Heaven in a wild flower,*
> *Hold infinity in the palm of your hand,*
> *And eternity in an hour.*
> *Auguries of Innocence*

The term *metaphysics*, or the larger context of physics, symbolizes the truth of the Law of Correspondence. The principles or laws of physics that explain the physical world—energy, Light, vibration, and motion—have their corresponding principles in the etheric world or universe. The deep meaning of the Law of Correspondence is difficult for us to comprehend because our science and our world have been based on identifying the parts of systems or phenomena rather than looking at the whole and seeing interconnections and relationships.

Only recently have we realized the need to reverse our basic paradigms and views of metaphysics. Willis Harmon discusses the old, mechanistic view of the universe as M-1 physics, which is based on the belief that matter gives rise to mind. This view assumes that the basic material of the universe is matter and energy. Our consciousness emerges from matter such as the brain, and whatever we know must fit with our perceptions of the physical world.

Later, we moved to an M-2 view of the world based on the dualism articulated in Descartes' separation of science to deal with the physical world, leaving the church to deal with the mind-spirit view of the world. This view assumes that two types of energies make up the universe—matter-energy and mind-spirit.

Within recent times we have moved to M-3 metaphysics, which reverses the original premise, and says that mind gives rise to matter, since the basic energy of the universe is consciousness. First and foremost is universal consciousness, which also is called the Golden Liquid Light, the God Force, or the basic Oneness of the Universe.

The second consciousness to be considered is the degree to which individuals can move to the mainstream of the universal consciousness. Each individual is unique, with his or her own human beingness or essence. The essence of the individual determines his or her consciousness, and consciousness is the basis for the human mind. When we expand our minds, we acquire a higher spiritual consciousness. As we grow spiritually, we become one with the God Force.

This view of the world is supported further by our understanding that the world is holographic. A hologram is a photographic image that projects a three-dimensional image, which shows various views and images depending on the perspective. Contained in each small part of the whole is the whole itself. A holographic view of the world changes many of our views of reality. Some of these views (which also explain the Law of Correspondence) have been identified by Barbara Brennan (1987), author of the best selling book *Hands of Light*, as follows:

Consciousness is the basic reality

Each of us has unique characteristics which constitute the basis of our essence. Our consciousness is expressed through our intentions or our values. We develop perceptions of the world around us, which is our way of imposing an order or regularity on this world. We tend to perceive the world in ways which are consistent with our expectations, beliefs, and past experiences. Thus, we create our own experiences.

Everything is connected to everything else

Nothing in the universe exists separately or in isolation. Everything we do, say, or believe affects everything else immediately. When we behave in a positive, nurturing way it has an effect not only on the environment around us, but also on the many, complex planes of the universe, as discussed previously in the chapter on the Law of Divine Oneness.

Each piece contains the whole

Every cell within us contains intelligence and the whole pattern of our essence. We are beings with interacting systems which make up our wholeness. Similarly, we are part of others and of the world around us. There is a basic wisdom and knowledge within the universe which is beyond our physical reality.

While there are many other implications of the holographic universe, each of them impresses upon us the degree to which we create our reality and therefore must act responsibly. As more people gain this expanded consciousness and begin to live acknowledging responsibility for themselves and others, Earth moves closer to the Fifth Dimension.

All this documents that our views and perceptions of the world are indeed changing. No longer can we see ourselves as separate, disconnected entities. Instead, we are maturing into a species that must understand that we are part of a whole, finely tuned ecosystem, each part connected to and affecting the other parts.

The Law of Correspondence is THE KEY for understanding this connection, so let us read what El Morya has to say about this important principle.

It is with great pleasure that I begin to explain the Law of Correspondence—the law that eludes many Initiates interested in the path of Oneness. This law, often referred to as the principle of "As above, so below; as below so above," is the basis for understanding the interdimensional operations of the universe. The aspirant who strives to increase his or her understanding of the Universal Laws must integrate the knowledge that all planes of existence exist simultaneously, and that, in this synchronicity, all is in motion.

In examining the Law of Correspondence, it is important to understand three planes of existence. They are the physical, mental, and spiritual planes. These three planes comprise the basis for operations and govern the harmony and energy convergence of the soul wishing to bring Heaven on Earth. While there are many interdimensional levels existing within these three planes, all vibrating at different rates, for the purposes of this lesson, it is important to focus only on the three major divisions just described.

The term "correspondence" (corresponding) implies that all "things" existing within these planes of existence, whether seen or unseen, exist in harmony or agreement with the All. There is only Oneness, and this idea is critical to absorb. Just as individuals cannot step out of this Oneness, neither can any of the other elements found on these planes. Significant to this understanding is that all are truly in harmony, one to another.

Even though human beings perceive themselves to

be limited to what they see and experience, this does not mean that they are separated from the larger picture or the macrocosm. Key to understanding the Law of Correspondence is to know that agreements have been made in Universal Mind that all are in harmony with Divine Law. This Universal Mind is the force field or Golden Liquid Light called the God Force. Humans have been created and placed on Earth to learn this and to become co-creators with this force field, which is the basis for creation. If humans remain separate, never seeing this connection, they will pass out of embodiment in a separated state of existence. If they open their minds to this knowledge and see the universe in a different Light, by understanding that each individual IS A PART OF THIS WONDROUS FORCE FIELD, then they are destined to move forward in time and become demigods.

We smile at the term "gods in exile," for it depicts the situation and frustration that we perceive humanity to be in today. The physical, manifest world around is so strong that it keeps many in a state of unconsciousness. This state of mind is likened to that of the sleeping giant, who, when cloaked in the sleep state, is quiet and subdued. Awakened, the giant's potential can come forth to achieve great things. Magnificent deeds are destined to come forth from these sleeping giants in the Seventh Golden Age. Those who awaken will usher in the new millennium for the Children of the Golden Dawn.

The Law of Correspondence is the law that holds the Oneness together. As mentioned, its name is synonymous with the Golden Liquid Light. Contained within this pulsating, vibrating field of endless energy is all that is and ever will be. It is the etheric, or cosmic, glue that holds everything together and connects the physical planes with the mental and spiritual ones.

Knowing that all exists simultaneously in each moment of time / space means that the Initiate has the power to affect any and all things in any moment of time. The reasons why many have not accomplished this thus far on their journeys are because:

> *(1) they have not understood this law and consequently have not known that they could do so, and*
> *(2) humanity's will is weak.*

The mind, connected with the Universal Mind of the All, is the key to change and to creation. The strengthening of the mind comes from discipline and will power. The strength of will comes from the heart. Individuals have been distracted by the physical, manifest world, spending much of their time entertaining their five senses. Focusing attention on the outside has contributed to their forgetting the power within.

Going within allows the Initiate to connect the mind to other planes and dimensions of reality, for it is here that the soul connects with the All. When this connection is made, all power is returned. In the journey comes the awakening that all dimensional realities are connected. It is the wisest of souls who learns how to access these other realms.

The physical plane vibrates at the lowest vibrational rate, while the plane of Spirit vibrates at the highest. Within each plane are also subplanes of existence, but it is not necessary to describe that phenomenon here. It is only significant to know.

Let us use the thermometer as an example to explain these concepts and show how easy it is to visualize the Law of Correspondence at work.

The thermometer registers numerical readings ranging from low to high. Nowhere are there markings which indicate absolute divisions separating one from another, such as hot or cold. Yet we are aware that all measurements are contained within, and each division has its own unique vibration or measurement, different one from another.

The various, different vibrations contained within the All exist simultaneously like the variations within the thermometer. These range from the physical to the spiritual planes, for the purpose of this instruction. The difference between the thermometer and Universal Mind is that there are billions of unending variations within Universal Mind, whereas the thermometer registers a limited range. Yet every change of condition will affect the reading of the thermometer.

What is significant about the Law of Correspondence is that ALL LAWS EXIST WITHIN THIS CORRESPONDENCE; THEREFORE, ALL IS CONTAINED WITHIN IT. One plane of existence is affected by another and one plane affects another. All occur simultaneously. Consequently, all changes in one plane of existence affect the other planes as well. This includes thoughts, words, emotions, and actions. The Celestial Realms and angelic, devic, and elemental kingdoms all are interconnected with decisions humans make on Earth. There is no escaping this. All are one and all correspond to one another. This also applies to humanity's decisions and how they affect other people and the world.

When the aspirant begins to realize this truth, the world takes on a new meaning. With this knowledge, power within the mind and heart begins to grow. This is the beauty of this understanding. This knowledge is destined to transform the world when Initiates everywhere rise and begin to increase their individual Light frequencies through the power of the inner journeys and the mind.

Since Light is the highest vibrational frequency known to humanity, it is reasonable to conclude that Spirit is Light. Since Spirit is the Creator with the power of manifestation, learn to illumine the mind and the heart with the Light of the God Force, Dear Ones. Work with this state of mind to further your understanding of the Law of Correspondence. Become that which you already are. Become one with your destiny.

I, El Morya, will work with any Initiate who calls my name in the Light of the Most Radiant One. I shall direct the attention of the soul to finding the corresponding path that shall enlighten your world. Ask and Ye Shall Receive. THE TIME IS NOW. Come forward out of exile and build Heaven on Earth.

Adonai. In the Light of the Most High, I AM El Morya.

Summary

Much of our third-dimensional experience has focused on the analysis of discrete parts of the many systems around us. Only recently have we become aware of the many systems that exist, their interrelatedness, and the prevalence of patterns and order within seeming chaos or randomness. The Law of Correspondence helps us to see the unity and wholeness of the universe and how everything is connected to everything else. Some of the keys to understanding this law are as follows:

* Mind gives rise to matter.
* There are three planes of existence—physical, mental, and spiritual.
* When Oneness is present, all three planes are in harmony and agreement.
* The Universal Mind is the Golden Liquid Light called the God Force.
* Humans are part of this wondrous force field and are created to learn to become co-creators in this force field.
* The Law of Correspondence holds the Oneness together; it is the cosmic glue and connects the physical, mental, and spiritual planes.
* All laws exist within this interrelatedness or correspondence.
* All changes in one plane affect all the other planes.

Chapter 13

LAW OF CAUSE AND EFFECT

*Every Cause has its Effect; every Effect has its
Cause; everything happens according to Law;
Chance is a name for a Law not recognized;
There are many planes of causation, but noth-
ing escapes The Law.*

The Kybalion

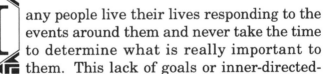

any people live their lives responding to the events around them and never take the time to determine what is really important to them. This lack of goals or inner-directedness places them in the position of being victims to the pressures of daily life. A major problem in their lives is lack of will and lack of clarity regarding goals or life directions. They are experiencing the results of the Law of Cause and Effect without realizing that they have the ability to influence the effects of the law in their lives.

The Law of Cause and Effect is the expression of Divine Order in the universe. The law states that nothing happens by chance or outside the Universal Laws. We may not always be able to identify the many, often complex, chains of events that produce specific effects, but this is the result of our incomplete knowledge. Events experienced may be the result of past life actions, the result of our present behaviors, or experiences provided from higher planes of existence to teach us how to master our intellectual and emotional behaviors.

Cause and effect does not deal with things so much as it deals with events. Every thought that we think, every act that we perform (individually or collectively), has its direct and indirect impact on the events which are part of the chain of cause and effect. Everything is like an ecosystem—connected and performing flawlessly according to the variables affecting the chain of events.

The Law of Cause and Effect may apply to long-term or short-term outcomes. Karma is an example of the manifestation of this law. Karma that used to take lifetimes to come around now can appear within minutes following a projected thought or spoken word.

While we cannot live outside the chain of cause and effect, we can exert our will and discipline to grow spiritually in ways which help us to use the law in positive ways. Each of us has free will, or the freedom to choose at least some of our behaviors. When we act, we have the choice of right action or wrong action directed toward ourselves or others. Right action advances the cause of God or Spirit. Wrong action is an act that goes against the cause of God or Spirit. When we assume control over our thoughts and actions, we have moved toward mastery and the ability to live within the laws in positive ways.

A common problem which leads to negative effects is that of living with unrealistic fears, anxieties, anger, melancholy, or worry. These are real emotions that we all experience, but if left unattended they can consume our minds. These mental and emotional states will generate consequences by drawing events to a person that continue to perpetuate these experiences.

As we move toward mastery, we are able to live by faith and remain in the Light. Learning to listen to our physical bodies, emotions, and thoughts gives us the ability to recognize and deal with these irrational states of mind, seeing them for what they really are, and learning to bless them and embrace them before letting them go.

Mastery of our emotional and intellectual behaviors must begin with forgiving ourselves and others. Harboring old grievances and resentments is a sure way of creating negative energies which will produce negative outcomes. Knowing how to heal old wounds in positive ways and moving into the Light is an important lesson in the mastery of our behaviors.

The Universal Laws are not barriers to our living happy and productive lives, but rather structures and guidelines for helping us evolve and become free. The Law of Cause and Effect provides us with the knowledge that all behaviors produce either positive or negative results. What do you choose for yourself and for those around you? What kind of life and future do you wish to create?

In the following transmission, El Morya discusses the Law of Cause and Effect.

Shalom to the Children of Light who are ready to become self-realized.

It is I, El Morya, tending to today's lesson that is destined to bring freedom to the masses. I come on the wings of the dove and hold the olive branch in my hand, offering it to all who are willing to accept it. The olive branch symbolizes peace, as it is through peace that humans will master the Law of Cause and Effect. If my humble gift is accepted, then the words in this passage will further your power because they shall describe the steps required to overcome the bondage of the human soul.

The Law of Cause and Effect is complicated on the

surface, yet simple within the order of the universe. The law briefly states that "Every cause creates an effect, and every effect has its origin in a cause." On the surface it appears complicated because there are so many forces that can produce effects. For example, there are the thoughts, feelings, words, or actions produced in any moment of time that affect an outcome later on; or there are forces set into motion from previous lifetimes or through genetics that must be realized. It is difficult to discern the cause when one is in the midst of solving a dilemma or learning from an experience. In the midst of confusion, what is important to remember is that all is created through perfect cycles of energy. This is truth because there is universal order in all things. That order says that everything moves in a circular fashion. This includes all experiences in every individual's life, as well as the forces of nature.

The Law of Cause and Effect contains certain interconnecting phenomena that must be understood when proceeding on the path to mastery. These phenomena are:

* ❋ *The strength of will;*
* ❋ *The clarity of the aspirant;*
* ❋ *The fear of the unknown and its effect on events;*
* ❋ *Forgiveness.*

Every person participates in creating his or her own reality through individual actions. The difference between an "average" individual and a master is that the average individual is tossed about like a boat on a high sea, following the stronger wills of others. Masters learn that by using higher laws against lower laws and applying higher prin-

ciples with strength of commitment, they create their own destinies and environment. Subconsciously, this is the state in which all wish to be. This, however, is a state few have achieved because the hearts and minds of most individuals are not strong enough to assume responsibility for creating their own realities.

Several planes of existence are operating simultaneously in the Law of Cause and Effect. Everything happens for a reason; there is no such thing as chance. All occurrences are continuous and unbroken, although the individual often does not understand the reason for the event. The higher planes are those that build mastery—the lower planes are those that complete unfinished business. The soul stays on the lower planes of existence for many lifetimes until it has released itself from karmic debts and responsibilities that have been harmful to growth.

When an Initiate begins to assume a higher state of consciousness, the Higher Self (which controls the higher planes of existence) brings experiences and lessons to the individual that build character. Karma is dissolved and replaced by Tests of Initiation to strengthen the soul. The Higher Self then defines personality characteristics that need refinement or strengthening and brings lessons with individuals (opponents) into a person's life to help that individual understand how to grow in the Light. Such examples might include lessons in:

* ❋ *Overcoming pride;*
* ❋ *Asserting with love;*
* ❋ *Learning unconditional love;*
* ❋ *Controlling fears;*
* ❋ *Surrendering ego to the will of God;*

✱ *Controlling the emotional and/or mental bodies;*

✱ *Desiring to be of world service.*

The lower planes of existence are those that keep individuals trapped in the wheel of rebirth, lifetime after lifetime, learning how to complete unfinished business with souls they have encountered. In these experiences, the individual often moves like a puppet at the direction of another individual's stronger will. Thoughts and emotions from stronger personalities often "cause" the individual to act and feel in ways that coincide with that stronger will. If the individual is not balanced within with the yin (female) and yang (male) energies and is not self-confident through self-love, then that individual will usually bow to the stronger will for approval or from lack of courage. Fear or the lack of confidence are the primary driving forces that keep individuals trapped in this wheel of rebirth. When there is something lacking within, humans try to fill the void through behaviors evident in the outer world.

The goal in mastery is to stay centered at all times and not to move to extreme positions of behavior. In this mode, the Initiates understand that they can experience maximum power and overcome all odds, unless fate dictates otherwise. Will is needed to stay centered, calm, and peaceful at all times. This is how will is used to master the Law of Cause and Effect.

A Master knows that any approach other than this one will never work. Moving to extreme positions of behavior only grounds the individual more firmly in the lower planes of existence. Taking extreme positions sets up situations through the wheel of cause and effect that continue to bring more of the same experiences to the soul. This occurs until the lesson to be learned is finally mastered, freeing the individual to move to a higher existence.

In the Law of Vibration, it was revealed that higher vibrations consume and transform lower vibrations. Lower vibrations never can change higher ones, for the higher energy is always too intense. Since all actions create other events, the Law of Cause and Effect teaches that the way to free oneself from events that appear negative and destructive is to begin the inward journey, monitoring all thoughts and feelings experienced.

Remember that the strength of the will drives the momentum in the Law of Cause and Effect. The will, when centered and in alignment with the heart and mind, has the power to perform miracles, and, in these moments, to control the electron spin. This is possible when the individual is both clear and free of judgment. It is also possible when he or she understands that it is Light that directs the currents of creation.

Another important concept of the Law of Cause and Effect is Karma, mentioned earlier. The popular descriptor for this phenomenon is "What you sow is what you reap." All that is experienced has had its roots grounded not only lifetimes ago, but also in this collective moment of time. This is truth.

When unpleasant events become a part of one's life, it is helpful to know that these events have come for one of two reasons:

1. Either there is unfinished business that must be resolved before the soul is allowed to move to a higher plane of existence, or

2. *There are lessons that must be learned to achieve a higher state of existence and enlightenment.*

There are no other reasons for karmic debts experienced within the Law of Cause and Effect. All is designed for humans to evolve to higher states of consciousness.

Since the Harmonic Convergence in 1987, all Children of Light have been freed of karmic debts, yet few have known this to be true. At that time, the dispensation was given that allowed all to begin their Tests of Initiation, thus freeing themselves to journey on their paths to mastery. This is not to say that Karma (both good and bad) has not been accrued, for all are still responsible for the individual daily actions that direct life. This is only stated to reveal that the events in one's life no longer are tied to the wheel of the past, but now are connected to higher planes of existence that free the soul to achieve higher states of enlightenment and power.

Nothing escapes the law. All is in Divine Order. There is no such thing as chance occurrence or coincidence. To say that coincidence exists is to say that the events so designated could exist outside of Universal Mind and order. This cannot be. All is Universal Mind and all is in order. All is law.

Therefore, what this means for the Initiate on the path is that one must begin to conquer the mind and the emotions. One must acquire self-love, enabling Light to flow continuously from the Source through consciousness and back to the Source. All must be continuous and experienced in a circular fashion. When this is accomplished, the individual assumes a position of using the higher planes of existence over the lower planes of existence, and creates the utopia that is longed for within. Thus, freedom is experienced and bondage is gone.

I trust that this adequately explains the Law of Cause and Effect. Go in peace, harmony, and balance. I AM El Morya.

Summary

The Law of Cause and Effect relates to our freedom of choice. While we have free will to choose our actions in life, we are held responsible by the Law of Cause and Effect. The difficulty most of us experience is learning that we have the ability to choose our outcomes and to develop the mastery over our behaviors needed to achieve positive results. In this sense, humans are provided the capability of moving beyond the Third Dimension and experiencing higher dimensions.

* Nothing occurs by chance or outside the Law of Cause and Effect.
* We are responsible for creating our own reality, for every action produces a reaction.
* We can learn to identify the events in our lives that are the result of current behaviors, the results of past Karma, or Tests of Initiation for our spiritual growth.
* Developing the strength of our will and the clarity of our goals provides us with the power to create our own reality.
* When we have not developed spiritual awareness, we remain trapped in separating behaviors which inhibit our growth; we are controlled by the wills of others, we lack self confidence, and it becomes a struggle to change our stereotypic behaviors.
* As we begin to achieve a higher level of consciousness in our lives, we are provided with lessons and experiences that enhance our spiritual growth and move us toward mastery.
* We gain control over our lives by avoiding extreme behaviors, developing a strong will and sense of purpose, and staying centered, calm, and peaceful at all times.

Chapter 14

LAW OF COMPENSATION

If you help others, you will be helped, perhaps tomorrow, perhaps in one thousand years, but you will be helped. Nature must pay off the debt. It is a mathematical law and all life is mathematics.

G. L. Gurdjieff

The Law of Compensation is the law which helps us to understand abundance and how we can deal with financial matters. The Law of Compensation is the Law of Cause and Effect as applied to blessings that are bestowed on us. While the Law of Cause and Effect deals primarily with events, the Law of Compensation deals with the material and spiritual gains we receive in life. It is in the manifestation of this law that we see the visible effects of our deeds as they are given to us in gifts, money, inheritances, friendships, and blessings.

Many of us do not receive these blessings as a result of the conscious and subconscious beliefs that direct the events of our lives. If we wish to master this law and receive abundance, we must break the poverty consciousness which comes from our conditioning in this lifetime and from the programming of past lives. We must leave the tapes of these experiences behind and see the world as a place of abundance, where there is plenty for everyone, instead of a world where there is not enough for all.

We need to overcome the programming of the past that was fed by statements such as:

> *Money is the root of all evil.*
> *The rich cannot be spiritual.*
> *To be spiritual means that we must renounce*
> *money and things in life that give us pleasure*
> *and comfort.*

If we are to break our poverty consciousness, we must reprogram our thinking so that our conscious and subconscious minds do not sabotage our due returns. Affirmations are a valuable way to do this.

People are successful in life because they do more for others and because they have an attitude that supports success. If you want to get more out of life, then you must give more with right thoughts, emotions, actions, and words every time you give a gift or perform a service for someone else.

The application of this law does not always mean that what you give is exactly what you will receive. Sometimes giving in one form (such as money) means that you will receive compensation in another form, such as a friend taking you out to lunch or someone giving you a beautiful gift. In addition, the law is extended by the Law of Tenfold Return. Whatever you give is returned in ways that are ten times the value of your gift.

Sometimes we have made an agreement to use this law in different ways. If you are a person who feels that you have given more than you have received, chances are that this is either because of karmic debt or because you have been using this law as a savings plan. Agreements could have been made where you gave freely with the understanding that the payments would come later in life—or even in a subsequent lifetime. You could be starting a savings plan of good Karma that will carry you into the future. Never despair of this law, regardless of how you feel you have been treated. Have faith always, and know that it is fair, just, and true.

Do not confuse the application of this law with the Tests of Initiation. Sometimes what has been delivered appears to be a punishment, whereas in reality it is not. It is a test to strengthen some weakness within. Discernment teaches us the difference between the two. Be mindful that what appears to be the opposite of a reward may actually turn out to be an incredible benefit and gift later on, once a test has been passed and a person has become the better for the experience. Patience is the key. Wait, and the gifts will be revealed.

Master El Morya describes the Law of Compensation in the following transmission.

Greetings, Oh Sisters and Brothers from the Stars.

I come forth to deliver this next piece of information which is pertinent for understanding the full context of the Universal Laws. It is with great pleasure that I deliver the following instruction to you, the recipients of the Divine knowledge of the universe. I come as your servant and elder brother, as I provide you the secrets for increasing your wealth.

Allow me to begin by asking you the question, "In what way may I serve you?" I begin in this way, for doing so provides an example of what comprises the basic foundation for the application of the Law of Compensation.

The Law of Compensation is an extension of the Law of Cause and Effect, in that it reflects the "just rewards" or "punishments" individuals receive for the seeds they have sown. It is an exact law, with its own deviations, that works to provide to the individual greater things than ever imagined. This occurs when the soul aligns with the Higher Self in service to others.

The Law of Compensation is about giving and receiving. It is the law that guarantees that each will be provided for by God. It is the manifestation of Divine Order in all things and that which grants freedom to the minds that work to dissolve the attitudes of poverty consciousness and insatiable needs.

The law is flawless in its design. Basically, it says that for everything given there shall be a return. But there is a twist to this law that not everyone realizes. This twist is called the Law of Tenfold Return. What this law reveals is that once a person learns to give freely from the heart, the universe returns the gift with a tenfold yield. This supports the premise that "It is better to give than to receive."

I give this knowledge freely from my heart, Dear Ones. Furthermore, I freely ask, "What more can I give in this moment of time?" In so doing, because my attitude, motive, and heart are all aligned with truth, I reveal to you now that I shall be rewarded tenfold for this offering.

For most, the Law of Tenfold Return goes into effect primarily when the individual learns to release fears that send the message that "there is not enough." Another condition that facilitates enactment of this law is when the auric fields of the Initiate are attuned to the higher vibrations of Light. Attaining a higher frequency in the Light automatically raises the body, mind, and Spirit into a higher

*dimension of mind, which releases the old pro-
gramming that keeps one in bondage.*

*One cannot separate the laws and their influence
on individuals in a universe of Oneness. Therefore,
it must be reinforced that compensation is also the
reflection of a person's multidimensional thinking.
The Most Radiant One stated this when He de-
clared, "As a man thinketh, so shall he become."*

*This command assures that what is reaped is the
just consequence of all that is sown. The Law of
Compensation assures that everything is fair and
all is in alignment with the Divine, for the laws are
not biased. Each soul is treated impartially and
indifferently by the laws. Each soul is its own
judge while on the Earth plane, for free will dictates the gifts that will be given to each.*

*Another factor that enters into just compensation is
the fulfillment of promises and contracts made between lifetimes. Each soul who comes to Earth is
on a mission from God, whether it realizes it or not.
Contracts are made in the etheric and reviewed
periodically in the dream states, assessing the standards and measures of performance for the individual in embodiment. When promises are kept, the
soul is rewarded tenfold. This is the mark of those
who possess the "Midas Touch."*

*When the word is not honored, a lower vibrational
frequency is initiated which sets the individual up
for what are termed "disappointments" and "frustrations," which are not readily understood on the
Earth plane. When one assesses the complexity of
all the dimensional realities and vibrational frequencies that impact the soul, one quickly sees that
alignment with the Light of the Higher Self is the*

only way out of bondage. All must be in the highest vibration and truth to control one's destiny. Connection to the Higher Self and to God's will grants peace, harmony, and a fulfilled life.

Free will is God's gift to humanity. This allows all individuals to choose their own rewards in life, based upon the application of integrity. Integrity is the key which grants the soul on the spiritual path greater gifts and rewards, including both spiritual and material offerings.

When a soul feels helpless to change life events, invoking the Law of the Perpetual Transmutation of Radiant Energy (in cooperation with the Higher Self) is the way to remedy the situation. Apply this law and wait for the returns. Applying this law creates Divine Order, and the compensation that comes surpasses all understanding.

Speaking of compensation, there is another important aspect of this law which includes payment to oneself. Too often individuals give to others and do not give to themselves. This depicts a lack of self-love and creates an imbalance in the energy fields that support the natural flow of energy. All must learn to love themselves FIRST, and from this state of mind, all else flows. The more you love yourselves, the more love you have to give to others. It is like a cup that is always full. The cup that overflows is the cup of Divine love that spills out into the universe, touching the robes of all others.

By not treating oneself with the same kindness bestowed upon others, a cycle for deprivation is established. Positive thoughts, attitudes, words, and actions are needed at all times to keep the energy flowing. Blockages create inequities, although from the universal perspective, inequities are only perceived and are not reality. Nevertheless, all must be kept in alignment with harmony and love, and this includes the love of self, which is contained within.

Overcompensation to others is another stumbling block to the smooth operations of this law. The human psyche is clever and can deceive one to believe that if one gives more to another, then that soul is deemed more worthy and loving. Therefore, giving must be a good and honorable thing in that it justifies one's own self-worth.

As was stated earlier, giving, and giving freely, IS an honorable thing and THE action which grants freedom. But if giving is done with the wrong motive, such as giving to make up for the lack of love within, then the energies once again are blocked. All must give equally to themselves and to others to keep the energy balanced.

Balance! Balance! Balance! This is the only path to follow when achieving mastery. If balance is maintained at all times and truth and integrity are adhered to, then the Law of Compensation shall be realized.

In honor of the God within, I, El Morya, do complete this transmission for the Divine. Go in Peace.

Summary

The Law of Compensation is the Law of Cause and Effect as it applies to material and spiritual gains in life. Some of the characteristics of its operation are as follows:

* ✳ We may not be able to receive abundance because of our beliefs and programming that we cannot be spiritual and also enjoy abundance. This is changed when we move into higher dimensions of the mind.
* ✳ We receive gifts and blessings according to the degree to which we have given to others.
* ✳ Our gifts to others are rewarded with a tenfold return for those gifts that we have given freely from our hearts.
* ✳ We must be able to love and give to ourselves first, as well as to be able to give to others.

Chapter 15

LAW OF ATTRACTION

What is hidden within will dictate what will appear on the outside.

El Morya

ost of us have had chance experiences in which our needs were met at exactly the right time—the page you turned to in a book which gave the information for which you were searching; the stranger you sat next to who answered a question you'd been thinking about; or the money that arrived just when you needed it. These are examples of the Law of Attraction.

The Law of Attraction extends the Law of Vibration in that we create or attract the things, events, and people that come into our lives. Our thoughts, feelings, words, and actions produce energies, and these energies attract like energies. Negative energies attract negative energies and positive energies produce positive energies.

Our task is to monitor and to see that our thoughts,

feelings, words, and actions are positive. This is often difficult for us to accomplish in a material world of thought-forms of violence, sex, and greed. While we cannot be protected from seemingly negative events, we can learn not to dwell on them and thus attract similar events into our lives.

An example of the power of this law may be seen in the copycat crimes or evil events which many, including children, see on television and in other media. When people observe certain phenomena some have a tendency to duplicate them. Just by thinking about things, they create similar events around them. There is strong evidence that the increase in violence among both adults and children is the result of negative images which are not balanced or placed in perspective.

A positive example of the Law of Attraction is that optimistic teachers who have higher expectations of children provide a climate in which children's learning and achievement are increased. Studies have identified similar outcomes among supervisors, or mentors, and adult workers.

When we think positive, loving thoughts we draw positive, loving people into our lives. We also influence the Tests of Initiation that we experience, for these tests are designed to increase our learning.

In the following message, El Morya reveals the secrets of the Law of Attraction.

It is with pleasure that I return to deliver another message regarding the Universal Laws. For this communication I shall focus on the Law of Attraction. This is the law that serves to frustrate many souls on the spiritual path, for it mirrors to them that what is hidden within.

The Law of Attraction demonstrates the power of the mind, heart, and will to project what is within, and the universe's ability to respond to this energy. It is likened to a cosmic magnet that draws to the person everything he or she focuses on or projects into the etheric.

In an earlier transmission it was established that manifestations are a result of multi-dimensional forces impacting the conscious and subconscious mind. Because this is so, it is essential that all persons watch carefully their thoughts, words, emotions, and actions, to assure that hidden, negative images, surrounded with emotions, are not stored within. This is emphasized because this is key to understanding the Law of Attraction.

Inner thoughts and emotions determine the level at which one vibrates. This is truth. One's vibrational rate is a frequency. This inner frequency creates a signal that is emitted outward. Once emitted, this signal begins to draw to it other things that reside on that same frequency. What is hidden within will dictate what will appear on the outside.

What the Law of Attraction also draws to the soul are one's Tests of Initiation, for the Higher Self understands every weakness within that creates a "void" or character flaw that must be "polished." The Higher Self is programmed to fill each void (frequency) that has not been learned or mastered with experiences needed to assure personal growth. The beauty of this law is that once lessons are learned, and the individual's vibrational rate rises higher, the tests never come again. They do not, because the soul rises above the vibrational level of those tests. The soul, now residing on a higher level, will receive only experiences that vibrate on this new level. The miracle is that the higher one goes, the better and better life becomes.

The Law of Attraction controls the rate and se-
quence of events that impact a person's life. Quick-
ness of mind and control over the emotional body
are the key elements that dictate the rate at which
events occur. Once individuals master control over
their mental and emotional bodies, they then expe-
rience only that which has been carefully pro-
grammed into their conscious and subconscious
minds. It is at this point that they demonstrate
more control over what happens in their lives.

If a person has not mastered the mental and emo-
tional bodies, and often performs erratically and
negatively, then the law returns to that person
events and people that reside on the same level of
discordance. These individuals feel as if they are
constantly swatting at flies, often wondering if they
ever will get rid of them. This is the state that
makes many people feel helpless and victimized.
Often individuals believe they are like ships being
tossed about on stormy waters.

I began this transmission by stating that this law
is frustrating to many. This is so because individu-
als do not understand that what is delivered to the
sender is what is built from within. It is inescap-
able. In a world bombarded with negative thought-
forms emanating from sources such as television,
discordant societal groups, troublesome group ini-
tiatives, war zones, ghettoes, painful and distress-
ing situations, and radios, it becomes difficult to
separate personal thoughts and images from that
which is not of one's own essence.

People must watch what is being fed into their
minds! To master this law, great discernment and
discipline are needed. Parents need to guide their
children better, and individuals must begin to se-

lect more carefully that which is allowed into their auric fields.

In the days of the ancients not many influences bombarded the mind. Today it is different. As Earth approaches the Fifth Dimension, there is an exponential increase in stimuli, and one must use great discernment in protecting the most precious "commodity" humans have—the mind. This must be done before mastery can be attained. Practice and a desire to control one's own thoughts and emotions are what dictate one's vibrational frequency.

Controlling vibrations is the key to mastering the Law of Attraction! If individuals could learn to control their vibrations at all times, and learn to reside on a higher frequency closer to Light, then all could control the events and souls that come into their lives.

There is, however, one exception to this law that must be explained.

Contracts souls make between lifetimes can appear to negate the effects of this law. An example would be when the Most Radiant One came to Earth 2,000 years ago and fulfilled his contract for the celestial plan. The amount of anger and hatred projected on him in the final hours was not an extension of the anger and hatred radiating from within his essence. Instead, it was delivered unto his soul because lying within his auric field was the program that was destined to transmute the world. His Higher Self came into this world with the plan that when the time was right, this program would activate, and, in so doing, would transmit the "void" that needed to be filled. This drew the events to him to fulfill his destiny, yet, at the same time, *raised his vibrational frequency to the point of ascension.*

Great Ones who come to Earth to fulfill missions for God enter the Earth atmosphere with the blueprint for transmuting designated energies for the world. These blueprints contain information and instructions on how to transmute knowledge, thoughts, emotions, and events. When the blueprints are activated, the universe responds to the frequencies programmed within and calls the images, people, and events to the scene for the dramas to be played out.

The Most Radiant One had only the vibrations of compassion and forgiveness within his essence. That is why he was selected to fulfill that role. His vibrational frequency was measured to be the highest on Earth. For the painful event that had to be fulfilled (that of transmuting the sins of the world), an extremely high vibration was needed, because humanity's consciousness was so dark and low. Therefore, a Being had to come forth that equalled the vibrational frequency at the opposite end of the spectrum. The strength of his Light was necessary to consume and transform the negativity of humanity.

If he had not been vibrating so highly, then an event of lesser consequences and impact would have occurred. It was because of his intense, radiant Light that the law could be fulfilled, but it took extreme circumstances to fulfill prophecy. This explanation also reflects the application of the Law of Rhythm, a law that shall be explained later. Because it will, I shall say nothing more about it at this time.

To the reader of these words, can you not see how

the applications of each law build one upon another? It is necessary to understand the ALL before you can fulfill that which you have come to Earth to do.

Learn the meaning and significance of all the laws, apply them to your life, and see how you truly are the co-creator with the Divine. Heaven is waiting to be brought to Earth once again. The Heavenly force awaits to assist you in this endeavor.

Hold your thoughts on God and on the Light, and Ye shall see the wonderment of your inner life as it begins to spring forth the fruits of your essence.

Beloved Ones, hear the inner voice within that speaks of your divinity. Do not be afraid to connect with this higher frequency. Visualize the Light in your daily meditations and prayers, and Ye eventually shall draw to you all that is of the highest.

God speed you on your journeys. I AM El Morya. Adonai.

Summary

The Law of Attraction helps us understand how we consciously and unconsciously choose the events in our lives.

✳ Our inner thoughts and emotions determine the level at which we vibrate. The level of our vibration attracts things and people operating at the same level of vibration.

✳ The level of vibration also determines our Tests of Initiation, for the Higher Self is expected to ensure mastery in the various areas of our own lives.

✳ When we have not mastered our mental and emotional bodies, we experience the discord of others in our own lives.

✳ As we gain mastery, we move toward creating the Fifth Dimension on Earth.

Chapter 16

LAW OF PERPETUAL TRANSMUTATION OF ENERGY

Good thoughts will produce good actions and bad thoughts will produce bad actions. Hatred does not cease by hatred at any time; hatred ceases by love.

Buddha

There are times when we may feel trapped and helpless, unable to deal with the problems of our daily lives. What we do not realize is that we can change the conditions of our lives. It is our ability to use the Law of Perpetual Transmutation of Energy that gives meaning to the concept of free WILL. We have the power to choose the directions of our lives.

It all begins with the principles of energy. The material universe is made up of various forms of energy. Motion is the only manifestation of energy. It may be the active or kinetic energy of the rays of the sun, ocean currents and tides, winds, waterfalls, or other forms of active energy, or it may be potential energy such as that contained in fossil fuels or other forms of inert energy. When energy is converted from passive to active energy, it is transmuted to other materials or changed to other forms. Transmission or transmutation of the forms of energy is a continuing process of the material universe.

Just as energy is changed in the material world, it also is being changed continually in our lives. The manifestations of our energy are found in our thoughts, our belief systems, our speech, and our actions. Each of us has some control over the ways we use these behaviors to send positive or negative energies to others or to maintain positive or negative thought-forms in our own lives. The process of sending out thoughts to others is known as transmutation of thought.

How does this operate? Every thought that we have produces two actions. The first action constitutes a vibratory energy, like sending out a wave from ourselves. The distance the wave travels and the intensity of the wave depend on our ability to focus and maintain our thoughts. When spiritual or positive people enter a room, their thoughts seek persons with thoughts similar to their own. All persons in the room will experience a raising of their vibrations, but the meanings are likely to be different for everyone in the room. Persons with higher thoughts and vibrations stimulate others to higher thoughts without conscious effort being exerted.

A second effect of thoughts is the creation of thought-forms. Every thought creates a materialized entity which operates on emotional and intellectual levels. Negative thought-forms may stay with an individual and increase in size over time. Persons with psychic vision often can see negative thoughts in the auras of other persons. Thought-forms can take on the form of entities that exist without our awareness.

Thoughts are forms of energy which may shape the conditions of our lives. For example, if a person wants to enjoy abundance but does not feel worthy or is unable to visualize gifts or wealth, this goal is unlikely to be achieved.

Thoughts are sent or transmitted to others. When we have positive thoughts, we send them to others and they respond quickly or over a period of time. Positive thoughts that are sent are replaced with positive thoughts; thus, we feed our own optimism and sense of well-being. We also feed the positive thoughts of others.

Similarly, if we think negative thoughts, we send negative impulses to others. This lowers their vibrations and sends low grade thought-forms into the environment. As negative thoughts are sent, they are replaced by the same.

It has been said that a large number of our sins or separations from God are committed with our mouths. We do not think about our thoughts and our speech, even though they impact our own present and future as well as the present and future of others.

If we are to grow spiritually, we must begin to examine our thoughts and understand that our beliefs and our thoughts do not represent reality. They are our perceptions of reality that are incomplete. When we realize this, we open ourselves to moving out to understand in new ways and to appreciate the diversity of people's perceptions. We can control our thoughts, our beliefs, our speech, and our actions, but to do so requires that we will ourselves to behave in different ways.

A beginning step is to clear our minds of past negative thoughts and feelings. We do this by forgiving past oversights, insults, or transgressions. It is the forgiveness that helps us clear our minds and fill them with positive thoughts and energies which enrich our lives. Where our thoughts are focused, our energies are focused. When we move to positive thinking, we free our energies for the positive activities of life and for our spiritual development.

Master El Morya explains this law and how it applies to our lives in the following way.

Greetings, Oh Children of the Divine. Once again it is I, El Morya, responding to the request to explain the next law. I transmit this next message with total love in my heart, and know that because

I do so, the words will be received within the heart centers of all who reside on that same frequency.

Today I will address the Law of Perpetual Transmutation of Energy. This is one of my favorite laws, for its application expresses the magic to be found in the Christos. Once understood, this law provides the answers many have yearned to know regarding how to change conditions in one's life from the point of stillness within.

So what does this mean in common terms? It means that all persons have within them the power to change all conditions in their lives, just by understanding how to use one Universal Law against another to facilitate the change. Simply put, since higher vibrations consume and transform lower ones, each person can become an alchemist of the heart, if he or she chooses to do so.

Since all is energy and everything is contained in Oneness, it is reasonable to conclude that everything is interrelated and affects everything else. But if this is truly the case, then one might suppose that all would continually be absorbed in the Light, and love and Light would reign on Earth. Looking around, the casual observer can see that this does not happen. So how, then, does this law work?

It works with the WILL, Dear Children of the Divine. It works when one chooses to transform the darkness into Light and when one has a desire to change surrounding conditions into a higher form of existence. This law is also a one-directional law; therefore, it is the key to one's harmony, peace, and love. Since higher vibrations only consume and change the lower vibrations, it is not possible to reverse the effects of this law. Lower forces, consumed

*by negativity, cannot apply this law to lower the fre-
quencies of higher vibrations, for its effects cannot
be reversed. It is the law.*

*It is with great pleasure, then, that I offer this law
to the Children of Light of the world to use as their
weapon to embrace the darkness and bring it into
the Light. There is no other law like this one, for
its application has the power to raise Earth's vibrations into the Christos energy, carrying it speedily
into the Fifth Dimension.*

*One uses this law by forgiving others, loving others,
seeing in others the differences as well as the similarities, and applying higher frequencies to situations in life that are considered to be discordant.*

*The highest frequency one can see is the color vio-
let. St. Germain is the ruler of the violet ray because he is the master alchemist. In his role as
Merlin, he came to Earth and brought the
alchemist's magic to assist in transforming the energies of separateness into those of balance. He was
the metaphysical king, while I, Arthur, was the
physical king. Together we reigned with the vision,
balance, insight, will, and courage that it took to re-
energize England and prepare her to assume the
vibrational frequencies that are destined to balance
the world. We did so through the application of the
Law of Perpetual Transmutation of Energy.*

*Violet is the favorite color of alchemists, and Mer-
lin knew of its power. Since this color holds the
highest vibrational frequency seen with the naked
eye, it has the power to change all the frequencies
that reside below it. Violet is the last color of the
rainbow, before it turns to ultraviolet and then is
reflected in the Light. It therefore holds the high-*

est coding of symbols, and can be used to change surrounding conditions.

Visualize this frequency daily and surround any condition in your life that is discordant with this color. See the condition change from a disharmonious one to one of peace and delight. Hold this vision with the strength of the will, always from the perspective from the Higher Self, and great miracles will begin to occur.

The key to its effective use is the Higher Self. Recognize this and all power shall be granted to you. The lower bodies have no power on their own; it is only the Light from the Higher Self that understands how to use this precious energy.

If one visualizes this frequency, consuming and transforming all lower, negative energies, the vibrations will change, first within the mind and then in the emotional body. The reason this is so is that negative entities cannot stay within this higher frequency for long. The strength of the will and the length of time this frequency is used will dictate how long it will take to clear a situation. When using this law, always remember the importance of the breath, for it is the breath that helps one command the emotional body.

Light is a higher frequency than violet. The white Light is the shield of protection. Visualize the Light within and around at all times, and it shall strengthen your will. With a stronger will, the soul's ability to manifest and transform events becomes more precise.

The Light also aligns the chakras with the Higher Self, thus providing the connection to the Great

Central Sun, and the Source of all there is. The Light strengthens one's faith, hope, and charitable nature, as well.

The third vibration that is important to know when using this law is pink. Pink is the color of self-love and resonates on the level of the soul. Surround others with this frequency and their attitudes will soften. Hold them in the soft glow of this field and watch their frowns slowly turn to smiles. The power of this frequency cannot be underestimated, for it generates much love throughout the universe.

The effects of this law are seen primarily when one meditates in silence and applies the principles to situations and events in life. Therefore, I invite all who wish to change the conditions around them to join with St. Germain in the stillness of the hearts and ask for guidance on its use. He shall assist all to become the magicians of the new millennium, but demands that the wills be strong.

Journey with Merlin once again, Dear Children of the Heart, and learn of the magic of the ancients.

I close this transmission with a song in my heart and look forward to your accomplishments as you create a beautiful world for your children.

I AM El Morya. So Be It! So It Is!

Summary

The Law of Perpetual Transmutation of Energy explains how our thoughts manifest positive or negative energy in our own lives and in the lives of others and how we may transcend negativity by applying higher frequencies to situations perceived as negative.

* The Law of Perpetual Transmutation of Energy is basic to our understanding that we are responsible for many of the conditions of our lives and that we have free will to change the nature of our lives and environments.

* Just as energy is changing continually in the material world, so energy is being sent with a predictable impact in the emotional and spiritual worlds.

* We use energy in our thoughts, our beliefs, our speech, and our actions; it is these behaviors which transmit and transmute energy to others, whether positive or negative.

* Positive energies attract positive energies and overcome negative energies through their higher vibrations.

* We control our transmission of energies through intent and will.

* We apply the Law by forgiving others, loving others, appreciating the uniqueness of others, and using higher frequencies in our lives.

* Violet color may be used to change conditions; white Light may be used as a protection; and pink may be used to increase self-love and the love of others.

Chapter 17

LAW OF RELATIVITY

God allows us to experience the low points of life in order to teach us lessons we could not learn in any other way.

C. S. Lewis

he Law of Relativity begins with our understanding that each of us is provided with problems or Tests of Initiation. These tests are designed to assess where we are on our spiritual paths and what experiences we need to learn.

Our response to these tests is important to our spiritual growth. On the one hand, we can compare ourselves to others and ask, "Why me? Why am I experiencing these problems when others do not experience the same problems?" We choose our response to these tests, and that response can advance or retard our spiritual progress.

When the heart and mind are connected, we realize the meaning of the tests and know that failure simply means that the next test will be more difficult. In this positive frame of mind, we say, "Thank you, Masters, for this Test of Initiation." When we look at our problem we consider that it might have been worse or more difficult.

The ways in which we view the world begin and end with our own minds and the meanings we choose. As we move on our spiritual paths we are able to see the positive aspects of our experiences, even the difficult ones.

El Morya speaks to us on the Law of Relativity.

This message on the Law of Relativity is protected in the Light of the Most Radiant One and transmitted with the vibration of the Highest. It speaks of observation and choice, and teaches the importance of applying the Law of Vibration to the choices each makes.

Inherent in understanding the Law of Relativity is an awareness of the Tests of Initiation, which are lessons that all must learn to become enlightened. These tests determine how quickly the soul advances on the spiritual path, and how many times it must be reborn on the Earth plane for the purpose of making choices again.

I, El Morya, speak with the wisdom my soul commanded when I was Solomon centuries ago. It is with great pleasure that I come forth today and transmit my understanding of this most important law.

Although the Law of Relativity has been in existence as long as the universe, it received its current name from the Pharisees of old. The Pharisees I speak of were the ones who lived when the Age of Pisces was new. These learned ones understood the importance of maintaining a higher standard of living while practicing spiritual laws. Many who resided in Israel enjoyed the status of their positions and protected their ranks by citing the laws as the defense for their actions. They spoke with precision, for they had memorized the laws, and their minds understood the impeccable application of these statutes in the world.

They were, however, remiss on one count. Their hearts were not connected to the spirit of the laws. An intellectual interpretation of the law often differs from the spiritual intent, which was usually the reason the law was created in the first place. Unless a soul is sufficiently advanced to accept the spirit of the law, its meaning and intent often are lost in the winds of time. The Law of Relativity is one of the laws that has been lost in the winds.

Basically, the Law of Relativity assures that each soul will receive a series of tests (problems, if you will), designed for the purpose of strengthening the Light within. As each soul is tested and provided with opportunities for advancement, options are given that guide the possible choices to be made. These options allow the soul to use the understanding of the Law of Vibration for either advancement or regression.

Everything in life is relative, Oh Sisters and Brothers on the path. All is the All. There are no judgments regarding good or bad, better or worse. Everything is relative, balanced within the mental and emotional state of the person in any given moment of time. The reason one believes that things are better or worse is because the mind makes comparisons with people, things, and events that are not relevant, and applies these comparisons to the present situation.

Each event in one's life stands alone and should not be compared with other things. That is because each event has its own vibrational frequency, with unique lessons to learn, and should be analyzed from the perspective of "What is it I am to learn from this situation?" Instead of approaching life from this perspective, individuals frequently choose to compare their lives and situations with those of others, and it is through these comparisons that they often become depressed, believing that others are more blessed than they are.

The Law of Relativity speaks to the fact that all things are known only through their relationship to the mind. The mind controls how one feels, what one believes, and how one behaves. It is a powerful tool—and God's gift to humanity. But the mind can be too clever sometimes, especially if it becomes disconnected from the heart. Too much analysis or reason sway one from seeing the higher truths. When this occurs, the individual becomes attached to the letter of the law and not to the spirit of it. This is what happened to many of the Pharisees of old.

The Law of Relativity brings clarity to the mind, for it cautions individuals not to compare current problems to former ones. Instead, the law guides each soul to look at challenges as opportunities for advancement and learning. Since each will be presented with Tests of Initiation, and everybody's tests will be different, it becomes obvious that the journey in life is not about comparisons, but about mastering the lessons each has come to learn.

The Law of Relativity is considered to be one of the more advanced laws. The key to using this law effectively comes through the control of one's mind.

When one learns to use the mind to focus only on the present situation, the soul is freed to pursue new and higher solutions for problem solving.

Learning to analyze each moment of time, staying connected with the heart, is the key to freedom. The law essentially reveals that in every moment of one's existence, the soul is provided with choices. The ultimate goal is to choose that which is beneficial and good for advancement, thus creating a higher frequency within.

When one does not understand this law, great repercussions may develop because choices made, not connected to the heart, can bring heavy returns of Karma. When people are pious and feel they are in a state of grace, they sometimes act righteously. This is especially true of those who also have memorized the laws. In this frame of mind, they can be compared to the Pharisees.

Keep in mind, Oh Children of Earth, that the souls of the Pharisees are still caught in the wheel of rebirth. The choices they made did not take into consideration the importance of the connection to the heart. Make all choices from the heart center, and the wheel of rebirth will no longer chain you to the Third Dimension. Let the Law of Relativity guide your understanding and set you free to pursue other forms of existence.

Come join us in the Fifth Dimension and higher. We shall teach you the higher truths that you are seeking to learn. All you need do is to assure that each choice you make is aligned with a higher frequency, and you shall quickly advance on the steps of the high Initiate.

May the Creator of All watch over your every foot-step. Go in peace. I AM El Morya.

Summary

The Law of Relativity deals with the ways in which we manage our thoughts as we face our problems and our Tests of Initiation. We may respond to these tests with self-pity, or we may look for the learning opportunities they bring.

※ Each of us is provided with Tests of Initiation to determine whether we have mastered lessons of spiritual growth.

※ Our responses to these tests may be judgmental in that we compare ourselves with others, or they may be positive in that we respond to the problems with mastery.

※ Our ability to respond positively requires that our hearts be connected to the spirit of the laws and that we use our tests to advance on our spiritual paths.

Chapter 18

LAW OF POLARITY

To destroy an undesirable rate of mental vibra-
tion, put into operation the Principle of Polar-
ity and concentrate upon the opposite pole to
that which you desire to suppress. Kill out the
undesirable by changing its polarity.

The Kybalion

he Law of Polarity states that everything is dual, that there are two poles or opposites to
everything found on the physical, mental, or
spiritual plane. Polarity is the difference in
dimension or direction, and it represents the two extremes of
one thing. In the physical world there is no summer without
winter. In the mental world there is no structure without
freedom, and in the spiritual world there is no good without
bad. In each instance, both of the poles have meaning.

The Law of Polarity considers an object or condition in
itself as unrelated to other objects or conditions. Thus, love
cannot be related to winter on a continuum because these
conditions are on different planes, or refer to different classes
of objects or relationships.

When we consider those conditions or objects found on

the same continuum, we soon realize that there are no absolutes. When does water move from hot to cold, or when does summer become winter? Opposites are two extremes of the same thing. The difference is simply the degree to which we perceive either pole as being on the same continuum.

If two poles are degrees of the same thing, then we have the power to move from one extreme to the other. We may dislike some individuals strongly and then, when we come to know these persons, feel compassion or love for them. We may dislike the discipline of exercise but, over time, learn to look forward to the high of working out. Or, we may think we cannot do without certain food items and then learn to dislike these same foods. These are examples of how we use the Law of Polarity on ourselves by moving from one extreme to another. Using this law is part of the discipline we need to change our lives.

What may be even more surprising, however, is that we can influence others in positive ways. When we dislike others, we can visualize them as being good and put violet light around them. We then may find that these persons have changed in some ways, and we may even learn to like or love them. Thus, we have the power to change our own feelings, and, often, the feelings and behaviors of others.

El Morya describes the Law of Polarity and the Celestial Hierarchy's views of what the law does for humanity.

Greetings, Oh Sisters and Brothers of the Stars. I, El Morya, come forth today to transmit the message on the Law of Polarity. I deliver these words as the Representative of the Council of Light from Lyra, and as the designated Ambassador for the Tribunal Council of the Galactic Command. These Councils pay tribute to the Law of Polarity because it is through the operations of this law that their work is deemed successful.

The Law of Polarity designates that everything has opposites and opposites are the same; they only differ in degrees. What is considered truth for one is the half truth for another. In all things there exists duality, which comprises the nature of the universe.

If opposites are really the same, then it is reasonable to conclude that love and hate are but two extremes of the same emotion residing on the same continuum. The differences between these two reactions lie in the degree of emotion expressed. The same holds true for concepts such as hot and cold or good and evil. Where does love begin and hate stop? Where does hot begin and cold stop? The answer resides not in a point on the scale, but in the degree of the mental and emotional attitude of the individual in any moment of time.

For the average student on the spiritual path, this law provides the power and keys for understanding transformation. Since all things contain the principle of polarity within them, then all things can be changed. The way things are changed is by directing the "charge" of energy along the continuum that resides between the two polarities. It is that simple. The power of the mind, which controls the emotions, is the key to understanding that ALL THINGS CAN BE CHANGED. The first step in change is CHOOSING TO DO SO.

Humans possess eight etheric bodies and one physical body. Four of these bodies are better understood, and, therefore, "used" more than the others. These are the physical, mental, emotional, and spiritual bodies.

In the universe, there are three primary planes of existence:

1. *The physical, which is the lowest, densest plane of matter;*
2. *The mental, which comprises the mental and emotional bodies; and*
3. *The spiritual, which includes the etheric and spiritual essences of the higher planes.*

The physical plane includes the physical body, the mental plane includes the mental and emotional bodies, and the spiritual plane includes the higher etheric bodies and encompasses the soul and Higher Self. Polarities exist on each of these planes of existence; yet the polarities within everything that resides on each plane cannot be crossed between the planes. That is because the vibrational frequencies residing within each of these planes are distinct unto themselves. For example, one cannot turn love into cold, or heat into evil. Therefore, each thing must be analyzed for its own essence and being. Each reaction emitted then must be analyzed for the frequency that it contains, and a decision can be made to change the behavior to either a higher or a lower one. This is possible, because all things reside on a continuum.

The power of the Law of Polarity comes from this understanding, for this knowledge gives the individual the foundation for choosing other responses. The universe, through the Law of Cause and Effect, will return whatever behavior is emitted from the source. If a lower behavior is sent, then the individual can expect events in his or her life to come around that will deliver a similar package of events or experiences.

Knowing that all reactions and emotions reside on a continuum aids the individual to achieve higher states of consciousness and to evolve. Nature is set up for all to evolve. That is the secret to life and to understanding the laws. Humans are to continue to raise their vibrations through the power of thoughts, the mind, emotions, and actions. This is accomplished through choice.

The key to mastering the Law of Polarity lies in one's ability to stay balanced, focused, and detached from the world and things around. Extreme reactions most assuredly bring returns that match the emotions and behaviors emitted. Balance is the key to success. Never forget this, and this Law shall come to serve you and raise your vibrations unto the Divine's.

Thank you for this opportunity to deliver this message of power. On behalf of the Council of Light from Lyra and the Tribunal Council of the Galactic Command, I bid you farewell for a brief moment in time.

Adonai. I AM El Morya.

Summary

The Law of Polarity expresses that we can change ourselves and even change others. We may do this in unconscious ways as we learn and experience new things or the same things in new ways, or we may use the law consciously to bring about change in ourselves and others. Some of the key understandings of this law are as follows:

* There are two poles, or opposites, to things or conditions found on the physical, mental, and spiritual planes.
* Polarity is the difference between the two extremes of one thing.
* There are no absolutes of difference between the extremes or poles of any one thing; rather, there are degrees of difference.
* When we choose to change, we can change our attitudes or behaviors on the continuum of extremes when we choose to do so.
* We can change the behaviors of others by raising our vibrations.
* Mastery of the Law of Polarity requires learning how to maintain balance, focus, and detachment from the distractions of the material world.

Chapter 19

LAW OF RHYTHM

Everything flows out and in; everything has its
tides; all things rise and fall; the measure of the
swing to the right, is the measure of the swing
to the left; rhythm compensates.

The Kybalion

he Laws of Vibration and Polarity are expanded when we add the Law of Rhythm. While every thing vibrates and moves, and has two poles or opposites, everything vibrates at or responds to a certain rhythm. This rhythm establishes seasons, cycles, stages of development, and patterns—all of these reflect the regularity of God's universe. It may also be viewed over long periods of time as the continual creation of the universe, the rise and fall of nations, and our own birth, death, and rebirth.

The cycles or rhythms apply to all areas of human life—the physical, mental, and spiritual. Many of the cycles in our lives and in nature occur in multiples of seven—seven days to the week, seven notes to the scale, seven rays of influence, etc. It has been said that human beings were designed by the Creator to live for twenty and one-half periods of seven years each, or about 144 years. Our failure to do this is the result of our inability to live within the laws of nature. Today we find many who are extending the life span from 68 or 70 years to 80, 90, or even more than 100 years.

In the natural order of the Law of Rhythm, we experience the positive cycles and the positive emotions of faith, generosity, kindness, patience, love, courage, and duty. Everything goes well and we feel happy and confident. We may describe this period as "being on a roll" or experiencing unusual luck. We feel this way because our lives are in balance.

When we move into the negative cycle our feelings and mental states change. We now may feel more fear, greed, envy, criticism, or hatred. Our natural tendency is to blame this on other people or events. We can overcome these feelings by transmuting the feeling and overcoming the negative. Our will or mental state is superior to the manifestations of this law. The rhythm continues, but the negative takes place on the lower, unconscious level. It is overcome or transmuted to a higher level by the use of our will to remain positive. We rise above the natural rhythm and do not experience the negative.

Since the Law of Rhythm is inevitable, we can adapt in ways by using our knowledge. We can plan new ventures at the times when things are moving to a positive side and we can remain positive to lessen or eliminate the effects of the negative.

We do this by learning to control our emotions at all times. We must work at reducing episodes of fear, worry, selfishness, greed, hatred, or other negative emotions. Even though we may have some of these feelings, we should strive to keep ourselves from owning expressions of these feelings. In this way we will not be subject to these emotions when the pendulum shifts again. When we allow negative emotions to be expressed, they remain with us and they provide the poles for shifts of the pendulum. When we are expressing positive emotions, the positive stays with us and assists us in transmuting the negative swings of the pendulum.

The key to success in mastering this law is balance.

Never allow your emotions to swing too far to the right or left. If you can accomplish this, life gets better and better.

El Morya describes the Law of Rhythm in the following way.

On behalf of the Light within each person who reads this message, I greet you from the heart of Sananda. It is I, El Morya, here to transmit the next message on the Law of Rhythm.

The universe moves in a cyclical fashion, with energy flowing one way and then the other. This movement is defined as the rhythm of the universe, and this rhythm is found in all things. It is called the Law of Rhythm.

The principles underlying this law are defined as the movements of the in-breath and the out-breath of God. Life moves in cycles and is constantly renewing itself, first from the highs and then from the lows, next from within and then from without. These rhythms connect the two extremes revealed in the Law of Polarity. These rhythmic motions are what constitute the heartbeat and the pulse of life itself.

The Law of Rhythm basically states that all things move in a cyclical fashion, like the pendulum swinging first to the right and then to the left. The tides flow in and the tides flow out; the sun rises and the sun sets. These rhythms constitute an order of renewal in the universe that can be either disruptive or pleasant, depending upon how one wishes to perceive these rhythms.

Like the physical plane, the mental and spiritual planes also have rhythms. Thus, individuals witness mood shifts and states of mental imbalance. These periods constitute some of the most difficult times that people experience, for the extremes drain individuals of precious energy and serve to lessen the mastery they command over their own mental and emotional bodies.

For every high there shall be a low. This is the Law of Rhythm. This is the only law the individual cannot learn to control. The only way in which one can command mastery over it is through mastering one's own emotional and mental states at all times. Doing so allows one to rise above this law.

Those who thoroughly enjoy life and are filled with excitement must also experience the extreme lows, for as the pendulum swings from the right and back to the left, the opposite event or experience must be brought to them. Once the individual tires of the lows, the soul is open to learn new ways to govern specific behavior patterns. This begins the process which leads to the lessening of the extreme depressions that intrude on one's life. When the Initiate commands this state of mind and demonstrates that he or she is ready to receive instruction on another, "better," way to experience life, he or she then is introduced to the Law of Rhythm.

The way in which one escapes from the effects of this law is to rise above it. That means that the only escape is to control the mental and emotional bodies at all times and to govern the extreme mood shifts that interfere with one's path. The individual learns to walk the center of the road, never getting too excited or allowing negative things to penetrate his or her consciousness.

Masters know that all is energy and that this precious life force is given to each to manage and use wisely for manifesting God's plan on Earth. Since energy can neither be created nor be destroyed, it must be transmuted. The Law of Rhythm teaches a way in which to transmute energy and manage the extreme rhythms in life.

The key to transmuting the effects of the Law of Rhythm is through the strength of the will. By applying one's will to manage reactions towards events in life, the individual actually can learn to detach emotionally from all experiences. Will power can be used to prevent the individual from getting too excited when events occur that serve only to steal the energy, under the guise of enthusiasm. When the highs are controlled, the swing of the pendulum will not be so extreme. Therefore, the polarized event that will come to the individual will be of a lesser negative quality, and will be easier to accept.

To be successful at rising above the Law of Rhythm and detaching emotionally, the Initiate must learn to walk the middle of the path at all times. This is the road to mastery. Few have been able to accomplish this in the past, however, which is why there are so few who have ascended from the Earth plane.

The time is come for more to make this journey and move into their Light Bodies to sit at the right hand of the Father/Mother Creator. Those who master the Law of Rhythm will surely be among those who will have seats reserved for this gathering. This law separates the Masters from the Initiates, the leaders from the followers. It is the turning point toward Spirit and the step away from the material world of the Third Dimension. Learn it well, Dear Children of the Command, for to understand it grants you your ticket to the stars.

Adonai, Oh Sisters and Brothers of the path. In the name and radiance of the Most High, I AM El Morya.

Summary

There are many rhythms in our lives that we cannot escape. We can overcome the effect of rhythms by remaining positive and transmuting the effects of negative rhythms or cycles.

* The universe moves in cyclical fashion, with energy moving one way and then another. This rhythm is found in all things and is known as the Law of Rhythm.
* Individuals experience mood shifts and mental imbalance as the negative cycle or rhythm is experienced.
* One can overcome the Law by mastering his or her mental and emotional states at all times.
* The individual overcomes or transmutes negative cycles by walking the center of the road or remaining calm and centered.
* It is our will power which allows us to master our mental and emotional states and to remain centered.

Chapter 20

LAW OF GENDER

Gender is in everything; everything has its Masculine and Feminine Principles; Gender manifests on all planes.

The Kybalion

T he Law of Gender is often difficult for people to understand because they assume it refers to the physical differences between men and women. Physical differences or sex are one small manifestation of the Law of Gender on the physical or organic plane. The term is used in a much larger context to refer to creation or production.

Masculine and feminine energies are found on all planes—physical, mental, and spiritual. Gender refers to a division of labor or effort which is required for all creativity. Gender is found in organic as well as inorganic matter and within the operations of heat, light, electricity, magnetism, attraction, repulsion, etc. In each instance, both masculine and feminine energies are essential—the masculine energy directs itself to the feminine energy, thereby initiating the creative process. The feminine energy is the one doing the active creative work, and this is true on all planes.

On the mental plane we are the Law of Gender manifested. Although male and female bodies and brains differ in significant ways, both sexes have the need and abilities to use both masculine and feminine energies. Both must be present in the creation process, and both sexes need to develop these skills.

Current brain research supports the distinction outlined above. The male brain usually emphasizes left brain thinking, and it appears to be suited for analytic functions. When these are employed, they culminate in the skill of initiation of action. On the other hand, female brains appear to demonstrate more right-brain activity and to be suited for synthetic functions. Both men and women can perform both sets of functions, but in different ways. In most cases, each of us has access to both masculine and feminine energies. Part of development, maturity, and spiritual growth is the ability to use both sets of energies based on the requirements of a given situation.

Masculine energies may not be used because of our fears of success and failure and ignorance of our missions. When we learn about our missions, we gain the confidence to act and to initiate.

Feminine energies sometimes are viewed as weak. Even though we must live lives of positive thoughts and actions which exhibit gentleness, patience, humility, self-control, graciousness of speech, sympathy, and wisdom, these are not manifested in passive ways. We are expected to use these positive behaviors in bringing about the Fifth Dimension. It is the feminine energies that will bring about a balance that will enable us to become co-creators with Spirit. In full spiritual development, masculine and feminine energies are understood and expressed by both women and men. It is then that we manifest the fullness of the human and third-dimensional experiences.

El Morya's message on the Law of Gender expands the concept.

I come once again to deliver the final message. Today I will speak on the Law of Gender. In so doing, I shall impart the wisdom of the ages, for in the understanding of this law comes the union with the Divine. I am delighted to begin, for there is so much to say. Therefore, I, El Morya, shall commence with this discourse.

The universe is made up of two active principles, yin and yang. Some call these the positive and negative aspects of life, while others refer to these as the polarization of the subparts. Regardless of what term is used, these two principles are found in every subparticle in the universe, and comprise the foundation for creation itself.

The Law of Gender is the expression of yin and yang, otherwise termed the feminine and masculine. The law states that these two principles reside within all things, and it is through these principles that humanity is able to create.

The Law of Gender is the creative force that runs from the inner into the outer world. It is the force of the Gods and the power of the giants. It creates life, even that which is born into the physical manifest world of "things," for both of the principles (yin / yang) must be present to build and to manifest in the third-dimensional reality, as well.

The receptive side of humanity's nature is often called the negative side. This is further termed the feminine or the yin. This is the force that creates, spins ideas, and weaves the threads to make the tapestry into a work of art.

The positive or directive side of humanity's nature is called the masculine or yang. This force is directed toward the creative force of the feminine principle. It is the originator of ideas and actions. The masculine energy is attracted to the feminine principle, and when they unite, they form a union that assures that the creative process will be realized.

These two forces are present in everything that exists. These forces are the great mystery of the universe. The natural attraction of the positive and negative energies are everywhere, for there is consciousness even in the atom. Remember that it has been stated earlier that God is thought. Therefore, the chi or prana that exists everywhere has intelligence. This intelligence, which has the power to create, is demonstrated in the Law of Gender.

It is important to understand this law if one wishes to advance, because mastery requires the person to command everything in the physical world. This means that individuals will be guided and tested until they are expert at manifestation and creation.

Of the two, creation appears to be the easiest, but in reality it is not. To truly create in the physical world, individuals must balance the yin and yang within to a point of stability. This means that they must have mastered how to receive dreams and visions and also how to turn them into reality, by creating in the physical world. When individuals are able to create and implement ideas, they position themselves in the field of Oneness. Very few souls ever achieve this kind of command over nature or themselves. This truth reveals another reason why so few ever become Masters.

When the yin and yang are balanced perfectly within the soul, the individual intuitively knows how and when to act appropriately in all situations. The balance of the positive and negative or masculine and feminine principles within brings the person to a point of androgyny, the state of mental balance that aligns the individual with the Higher Self.

Universes have been created when the feminine principle was unleashed, but they have been created only when this was ignited and balanced with the masculine principle. For centuries on Earth, the feminine principle has been thwarted, making it difficult for either men or women to exert their full human potential. Cultures, societies, individuals, sexes, and institutions all have participated in suppressing the feminine principle. As a result, creation has been stifled and destruction looms at every turn. The aggression from the masculine principle has thrown all things out of balance, leaving the world to wander aimlessly until the power can be restored.

A Golden Age, the seventh, to be precise, has been predicted for the millennium, because the cosmic conditions are ripe for the feminine energy to be restored on the planet. The Age of Aquarius has promised this. Philosophers, astrologers, and astronomers have known this since the beginning of time, for the Creator's pen has so recorded this edict. The Earth will venture into this new era and the balance will come forth, but first the balance must be realized within each individual.

Therefore, we offer the Law of Gender to you for contemplation. Learn of this law, for it is the source of all your power. It will teach you to become co-

creators with God. Learn to balance all thoughts, emotions, words, and actions with the principles of positive and negative responses. When you accomplish this, self-realization will be given.

The Higher Self is androgynous and waits to unite with the lower eight bodies. It cannot form the union, however, until the lower bodies are balanced with the yin and yang energies. The balance actually accelerates the electron spin to a point of stillness necessary for the merger to take place. Ascension does not occur until the union is perfect.

Therefore, I say unto you, hold the perfect stillness within, and balance the masculine and feminine principles in the soul. Learn to listen to the higher guidance of your inner voice, and know that when you do so, all will be perfectly aligned.

This concludes my message of the Law of Gender and seals the messages of twelve. On behalf of the higher Councils of Light who sanction these words, I leave you with this volume of information to ponder.

Read each message with the masculine energy in the forefront of your minds and direct all initial impulses to the intuitive feminine nature. Then, put the meaning of these messages into action through the creative process of the feminine energy. When applying these laws, discipline the mind, heart, and emotional bodies to follow the guidance of the Higher Self. By living the laws, your souls will soar, for the Light these laws will bring will truly set you free.

In the months and years to come, I remain your humble servant. Should you need help in understanding or applying the spirit of these laws, call for my assistance. I shall not let you down. I only wait to serve you in your quest for mastery.

Remember, the Ascended Realms cannot interfere or override humanity's free will. That is your gift from God. Should you knock on the door of the Divine and invite our assistance, we will guide and support your journey. The angelic kingdom will also come, for that is their responsibility and duty to God. Know this to be true.

Finally, remember that the Order of Melchizedek, of which I am a member, is your strength in the years to come. We assist all who are sincere seekers of the Light and who wish to journey to higher dimensions of time / space while still embodied on the physical plane. Ask and Ye shall receive our assistance, and know that you are protected in the Light of the Most Radiant One.

I now close this transmission with love and respect for all who read these words with their hearts. Carry your intent to the higher dimensions and join your elder sisters and brothers who await to receive you in the chambers of the Most High.

Good Day in the Light of the Most Radiant One. I AM El Morya.

Summary

The Law of Gender deals with the two activities needed to create or produce—the yin and the yang. These functions are complimentary and are found on all planes—physical, mental, and spiritual.

* Masculine and feminine energies must be developed in both women and men to be used in appropriate situations.
* The masculine and feminine energies are the foundation for creation in every part of the universe.
* Creation requires that we have balanced the yin and the yang, or the ability to dream dreams and bring them into reality.
* When we balance our masculine and feminine energies we move to a state of androgyny that aligns us with the Higher Self.
* The Seventh Golden Age will be a time for the restoration of feminine energy on the planet.
* When we are able to master the balance of our thoughts, emotions, words, and actions we unite the Higher Self with the lower eight bodies. This is necessary in order for ascension to occur.

A joyous person abounds with energy and feels buoyant because he or she is running a higher-frequency current of energy through his or her system.

Gary Zukav

Artwork by Jacquelyne A. Lotz

Chapter 21

INTRODUCTION TO PERSONAL TRANSFORMATION

I am One with the Violet Flame.
St. Germain

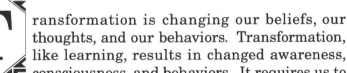ransformation is changing our beliefs, our thoughts, and our behaviors. Transformation, like learning, results in changed awareness, consciousness, and behaviors. It requires us to face our longings and our deeper-level knowledge, to gain the information and courage needed to determine their meanings for our lives, and to take the actions and steps necessary to gain the skills or clear the way for new levels of consciousness and understanding.

The process of transformation culminates in self-mastery. Self-mastery is achieved as we move to our reunion with our Higher Selves and the God Force. The merger of our physical selves with our Higher Selves is part of our becoming one with the Light and the God Force.

Transformation has been described as involving three

stages of mastery and development. Transformation begins with the opening of self to new ideas, new consciousness, and new information. Information gives us images and possibilities that we can test and determine the degree to which they seem right for us. This phase of transformation is an exploration, a seeking out of the unknown and a stretching of our beliefs. Previous sections of this book have provided examples of information that offers new possibilities. This information cannot be tested fully in the usual ways, but must be examined in our hearts and minds to determine its meaning for our lives.

The second phase of transformation occurs when we begin to integrate the information into our lives. We determine how the ideas and philosophies will be put into practice and how we will gain our own spiritual mastery. This is the phase of becoming Light beings and joining with our Higher Selves. It requires meditation, clearing of old beliefs, experiencing forgiveness of past and present transgressions or injustices, and learning to love and accept ourselves and others. There are many things that we can do to accelerate this process, which often is achieved as we are able to receive telepathic messages.

The last phase of transformation comprises mobilization of our self-mastery. We are able to live our Earth mission in powerful and fulfilling ways because we now are aligned in a real way with our Higher Selves and the God Force. We are living a fifth-dimensional life within a third-dimensional world. Ego is no longer the master of our lives, and we are preparing ourselves for our ascension. Our ascension, or the attainment of new levels of service and learning, frees us from the need to reincarnate to learn the lessons needed for self-mastery.

One of the primary lessons we learn as we move to self-mastery is the lesson of discipline, or the ability to control our physical, emotional, and intellectual functioning in ways that keep us in touch with positive views of our experiences and our abilities to view the third-dimensional experiences at higher levels. Being able to understand that the

Earth experience is an illusion that will be viewed in different ways as we become Spiritual Masters is part of our learning. It is easy to emphasize the discipline needed and forget the joy and the bliss that are experienced as we move through the process. We do experience peace, joy, and abundance as we are able to reunite with our Creator and move through the stages of transformation.

It is important to remember that we are never alone as we go through this process. Our guides, angels, the Ascended Masters, and many other sources of strength and growth are provided to us. The following section outlines some practical ideas and actions we can take to accelerate our progress on our journey to spiritual mastery.

Chapter 22

=======◇======

THE SUB-LAWS OF THE UNIVERSE

The Knowledge of man is as the waters, some descending from above, and some springing from beneath; the one informed by the Light of nature, the other inspired by Divine revelation.
Francis Bacon
(St. Germain)

he Universal Laws describe the fundamental principles governing the functioning of Earth and the Celestial Worlds. The Laws tell us that humans co-create with God by using their minds, that energy, vibration, Light, and motion make up the universe, that patterns of correspondence or consistency are part of our physical and spiritual worlds, and that there is a consequence or effect for everything that we do. These principles help us understand how and why things happen.

There are also human characteristics or traits related to the Universal Laws. These are referred to as the sub-laws, or the ways in which we put the Universal Laws into action in our lives. Each of the sub-laws is not simply a nice thing to do. Each has a spiritual purpose—a purpose designed to bring Heaven to Earth. In following the purposes of the sub-laws, we participate in the co-creation of the perfect world which has been envisioned for us by our Higher Selves.

We may agree with the purpose of the sub-laws and wish to live in accordance with them, but find that unresolved issues of past lifetimes or the limits of our current spiritual development place barriers in the paths of our realizing the purpose or benefits of the sub-laws. If we are to use the sub-laws well, it is essential that we learn how to overcome the barriers that prevent us from using them in effective ways. We can do this through our thought processes and through the words we speak, which reflect our thoughts in positive ways. These are the affirmations that bring our behaviors and our lives into alignment with Divine intent.

The following sub-laws detail the virtues that not only help us to grow spiritually, but also bring forth a higher existence on Earth. Each sub-law is described in terms of its alignment to the Higher Self and then examined from the perspective of the ego's influence on it. Finally, suggestions are given that will assist individuals to align their power with their Higher Selves, thus facilitating mastery in their lives.

SUB-LAWS OF THE UNIVERSE AND THE BEHAVIORS
AND ATTITUDES THAT DIMINISH AND SUSTAIN THEM

Sub-laws Governed by the Higher Self	Behaviors and Attitudes Governed by the Ego	Techniques for Aligning with the Higher Self
ASPIRATION TO A HIGHER POTENTIAL **Definition:** The higher force that instills within us the strong desire to achieve greater things. **Purpose:** The soul's ambition to evolve and journey back to the Source.	**Behaviors** Sabotaging your accomplishments Experiencing a lack of openness Failing to keep promises Lack of interest in life Criticizing others **Attitudes** Inability to set goals and objectives Fear of success and failure Fear of risks **Feelings of:** Vanity Diminishing energy Hopelessness Despair Death Playing it safe	Trust in the process and Divine Order of the universe. Make commitments and keep them. Follow your inspirations. See a part of yourself in everyone else, and emulate all that is good in others. Align with the Higher Self. Never stay around negative people for more than five minutes. Allow yourself to risk. **Remember:** God is in the details. **Affirmations** *I am getting better and better every day.* *The Light within me is expanding and producing miracles in my life.*

Sub-laws Governed by the Higher Self	Behaviors and Attitudes Governed by the Ego	Techniques for Aligning with the Higher Self
CHARITY	**Behaviors**	Give with no expectations of return.
Definition: Philanthropy or benevolent good will toward humanity. Lenient judgment of others.	General dislike for humanity Lack of trust	Give freely, knowing the law of tenfold return will serve.
	Attitudes	Feel the joy one receives when given a gift from the heart of another.
Purpose: A love for humanity demonstrated by giving, with no expectations of return.	Belief that you are being used or are unequal to another in power	See a part of yourself in everyone you observe.
	Poverty consciousness and belief that there is not enough abundance for all	Believe others will help you.
	Feelings of:	**Affirmations**
	Something lacking Insecurity Futility Malevolence Unworthiness Acquisition (Greed)	*There is plenty for everyone.* *Humanity's greatest strength is in its diversity.* *People everywhere are all children of one God.*

Sub-laws Governed by the Higher Self	Behaviors and Attitudes Governed by the Ego	Techniques for Aligning with the Higher Self
COMPASSION **Definition**: A sympathetic awareness of another's distress, often through unconditional love. **Purpose**: The quality that teaches that there is perfection in all things and that we are to have sympathy for others, even though they may not see things the way we do. Compassion replaces judgment.	**Behaviors** Behaving cruelly toward people and animals Persecuting others Tyrannizing others Judging others Inflicting injustices or injuries on others as punishment **Attitudes** Need to feel superior **Feelings of:** Being alone Hatred Severity Anger Nonforgiveness Revenge Disappointment Noninvolvement Apathy	Stay silent and "bite your tongue" before saying something cruel. Listen to others to understand their perspectives. Stop judging yourself and others. Practice thinking kind thoughts. Practice random acts of kindness. Distance yourself from others and lovingly observe them. Show tenderness, objectivity, and empathy towards others without smothering them. **Affirmations** *I no longer judge myself or others.* *I accept myself and others unconditionally.*

Sub-laws Governed by the Higher Self	Behaviors and Attitudes Governed by the Ego	Techniques for Aligning with the Higher Self
COURAGE **Definition**: Firmness of mind and action in the face of opposition. **Purpose**: The attribute that assists us to complete great things, no matter how large or small the contributions.	**Behaviors** Sense of imbalance and lack of ability to stand in your truth Allowing others to take your power Allowing yourself to be intimidated **Attitudes** Feeling that you have to conform to peer pressure Fear of failure Fear of confrontation **Feelings of:** Cowardice Timidity Weakness Faintheartedness Ambivalence	Stay calm and centered in the midst of chaos and opposition, and allow your Higher Self to guide you. Never fight emotion with emotion. Stick to the facts and data. Analyze worst case scenarios, make a plan, and follow through. Do it! Respect the timing and sequencing of all critical events. **Affirmations** *I am confident that I am fulfilling my Divine Plan.* *My inner guidance is clear, and I now have the courage to follow it.* *I now have the confidence to speak my truth.*

Sub-laws Governed by the Higher Self	Behaviors and Attitudes Governed by the Ego	Techniques for Aligning with the Higher Self
DEDICATION **Definition**: Devotion or commitment to a cause, person, or mission. **Purpose**: An act of commitment, based on great love and desire, to serve humanity. It is this action that separates the Masters from the Initiates.	**Behaviors** Uncaring mannerisms Sense of hopelessness or despair Inability or lack of desire to set goals and objectives Lack of ability to stay focused or committed Feeling that you are disconnected from God Listening to others before listening to your inner guidance Apathy toward self-improvement **Attitudes** Lack of discipline Lack of will or commitment **Feelings of**: Indifference Alienation Unconcern Passiveness Disorganization	Have the courage to operate on the Light level, which understands that we have a higher purpose in life. Request daily that the Light penetrate your essence and give you the energy and strength needed to pursue your life's plan. Set goals and objectives, and make a plan to reach them. Learn to trust and follow your inner guidance. **Affirmations** *I am now fulfilling my mission on Earth.* *I am now employed in the perfect job for me.* *I understand my higher purpose, and joyfully complete the tasks to fulfill it.*

Sub-laws Governed by the Higher Self	Behaviors and Attitudes Governed by the Ego	Techniques for Aligning with the Higher Self
FAITH **Definition**: Trust and conviction in a belief for which there is no proof. **Purpose**: Confidence in the Universal Laws and the Divine harmony of the universe.	**Behaviors** Need to control Need for material confirmation **Attitudes** Belief that ego is in charge and not Spirit Fear and dislike of what you receive Belief you are unworthy **Feelings of:** Skepticism Doubt Denial Distrust Suspicion Rejection Fear	Anchor the Light within on a daily basis. Recognize that there is purpose in all things. **Affirmations** *Let God's will be done through me.* *I trust in God to show me the way.*

Sub-laws Governed by the Higher Self	Behaviors and Attitudes Governed by the Ego	Techniques for Aligning with the Higher Self
FORGIVENESS **Definition:** Letting go of judgment, resentment, or a claim against another. An abundant act. **Purpose:** Unconditional love that absolves negative Karma and frees ourselves and others.	**Behaviors** Holding judgment or anger toward another Inability to forgive yourself Blaming others and holding grudges **Attitudes** Belief that if you forgive, you may lose control over others Desire to discredit, censure, accuse, or indict another Belief that if you forgive, you were wrong **Feelings of:** Fear Anger Resentment	Breathe deeply, relax, and let the feeling go. Allow the God Force energy to flow through you. Practice unconditional love. Do not take another person's words or actions personally. Remain calm and balanced at all times. **Affirmations** *I forgive myself for _____ .* *I forgive _____ for _____ .* *I release all negative and limiting beliefs.*

262

Sub-laws Governed by the Higher Self	Behaviors and Attitudes Governed by the Ego	Techniques for Aligning with the Higher Self
GENEROSITY **Definition**: An openhearted, liberal, unselfish act of kindness or gift bestowed upon another. **Purpose**: An act that grants liberty to us and frees us to evolve.	**Behavior** Lack of self-love which inhibits you from giving freely to yourself or others Overcompensation by giving too generously to others and not giving enough to yourself **Attitudes** Belief that you are separated from the Source Belief that you may not have enough **Feelings of**: Selfishness Greed Pettiness Stinginess Miserliness Meanness Insecurity	**Follow the Golden Rule**: "Do unto others as you would have them do unto you." Give yourself gifts, and enjoy receiving them. **Affirmations** *I am a radiant Being, and I love all of me.* *There is abundance for everyone, and I am ready to receive my share.*

Sub-laws Governed by the Higher Self	Behaviors and Attitudes Governed by the Ego	Techniques for Aligning with the Higher Self
GRACE **Definition**: Unmerited Divine assistance given for humanity's sanctification. **Purpose**: The quality that flows through a person giving a sense of beauty, balance, harmony, and charm of movement and form.	**Behaviors** Expression of rigidity Inaction or laziness Insensitivity toward others Disregard for details and excellence, and the skills needed for refinement in these areas Inability to differentiate another's problems from your own **Attitudes** Belief of personal importance or preoccupation with self **Feelings of:** Awkwardness Vulgarity Rudeness Carelessness Negligence Clumsiness Stress Indifference	Monitor your inner dialogue and beliefs, and bring discordant thoughts and actions into balance. Practice balance and harmony. Learn to breathe deeply, and calm yourself at all times. Identify weaknesses in your skill areas, and strive to improve upon them. Request that the essences of the Ascended Masters and all their grace and beauty merge with your consciousness. **Affirmations** *I am that I am.* *I am the Light of the world.* *My discernment improves every day.* *I complete all my work accurately, perfectly, easily, and effortlessly.*

Sub-laws Governed by the Higher Self	Behaviors and Attitudes Governed by the Ego	Techniques for Aligning with the Higher Self
HONESTY **Definition**: Honor and integrity of character and action. Truth in action. **Purpose**: The state of mind that changes our destiny by eliminating negative Karma and replacing it with positive Karma.	**Behavior** Need to cheat or trick another Living under false pretenses Engaging in deception Stealing or cheating another **Attitudes** Lowering your standards to accommodate peer pressures Feeling that you need to protect yourself or you may not get what you want or may be harmed Feeling unclear on issues or facts Lack of respect for others' abilities to deal with truth **Feelings of**: Inadequacy Deprivation Panic Malice Unfaithfulness Lack of self-respect	Monitor all your thoughts and actions on an ongoing basis. Listen to your conscience. Identify with role models who exemplify integrity and honesty. Be pure of heart. Do not give in to temptation and accrue the negative Karma for misdeeds. **Affirmations** *I am a person of integrity and can be trusted.* *I value equity and fairness and strive to live my life around these principles.* *I now live a life applying Universal Laws in Divine harmony.*

265

Sub-laws Governed by the Higher Self	Behaviors and Attitudes Governed by the Ego	Techniques for Aligning with the Higher Self
HOPE **Definition**: An unending confidence that an expectation will be fulfilled. **Purpose**: A trust in the soul's ability to evolve.	**Behaviors** Lowered expectations Not having dreams of a better way of life Inability to envision a better future **Attitudes** Belief that you are abandoned Feelings of: Discouragement Disappointment Despair Pessimism Fear Rejection Worry Passivity	Trust your inner guidance. Hold onto your dreams. Believe in Oneness, not separateness. Know that life is not static, but a process. Step back. Look at the whole picture. Believe that from every negative situation comes a positive one. **Affirmations** *Divine love flows through me and will guide me on my perfect path.* *The Light within my soul creates miracles in my life.* *My life is perfect and in Divine harmony.*

Sub-laws Governed by the Higher Self	Behaviors and Attitudes Governed by the Ego	Techniques for Aligning with the Higher Self
JOY **Definition**: The expression of feeling much delight, glad feelings, and happiness. **Purpose**: The state of mind that assists us to see the perfection and beauty of God's plan in every waking moment.	**Behaviors** Creating hardships, misery, and heartaches Discounting others' happiness and delight **Attitudes** Worrying that life is not perfect Belief that hard times are necessary, and we need to be punished Belief that life is serious **Feelings of:** Gloom Despair Unhappiness Misfortune Sorrow Inadequacy	Remember that everything happens for a reason, and take all challenges as opportunities for growth. Meditate on lessons that need to be learned. Pray for strength and guidance to stay in touch with the happiness within. Release all fears and worries and ask God to handle all the problems that seem insurmountable. **Affirmations** *I surrender to the Higher Self.* *Show me the way to happiness and joy.* *I now see the perfection in all things.* *I now embrace happiness and delight in the world around me.*

Sub-laws Governed by the Higher Self	Behaviors and Attitudes Governed by the Ego	Techniques for Aligning with the Higher Self
KINDNESS **Definition**: The state or habit of treating others kindly and with respect. **Purpose**: The attribute that drives us to recognize Oneness and to be empathetic toward others.	**Behaviors** Acts of coldheartedness Unfriendly behavior Uncaring or even malevolence toward others Lack of generosity Lack of recognition or response **Attitudes** Uncontrolled desire to dominate for personal recognition Concern about status **Feelings of**: Superiority Bitterness Ruthlessness Harshness Cruelty Greediness Indifference	Say "thank you." Show sympathy and compassion toward others. Show affection for your friends and family. Stay centered and calm. Recognize the good in others. Reward others, especially when they're not expecting it. Praise and recognize those around you. **Affirmations** *I do things for others, and it makes me feel good.* *I enjoy making others happy.* *When I help others, I help myself.*

Sub-laws Governed by the Higher Self	Behaviors and Attitudes Governed by the Ego	Techniques for Aligning with the Higher Self
LEADERSHIP **Definition:** The position in which one guides or directs. **Purpose:** The divinely inspired quality that infuses energy into others who support your vision. Collectively, good leadership facilitates the fulfillment of God's plan on Earth.	**Behavior** Cowardice or sheepishness Acting like a dictator or bully Inability to delegate responsibility Inability to follow through with tasks Indecisiveness and lack of a clear plan Lack of commitment Lack of self-confidence **Attitudes** Forgetting with whom you are connected Fear of non-approval Fear of failure **Feelings of:** Unworthiness Procrastination Incompetency	Follow your vision and inner convictions, and articulate them clearly to others. Have the courage to speak the truth. Complete all tasks in the pursuit of excellence. Guide others with love. Stay positive. Visualize yourself and your team completing a project successfully. Praise and reward others. Acknowledge your strengths and talents, and feel good about them. **Affirmations** *I work well with others.* *I am now completing God's Divine plan on Earth.* *Every day is more fulfilling than the previous one.* *I am a co-creator with others, performing in Divine harmony.*

Sub-laws Governed by the Higher Self	Behaviors and Attitudes Governed by the Ego	Techniques for Aligning with the Higher Self
NONINTERFERENCE **Definition**: The state or fact of not intervening in another person's path by judging or interfering with their actions or decisions. **Purpose**: This quality allows all to grow at their own paces and eliminates unwanted negative Karma that can impede one's progress.	**Behaviors** Conflict with another Forcibly meddling in the affairs of others Showing little respect for people and the decisions they make Courting another or their possessions Prying into business not your own **Attitudes** Irrational need to feel needed and appreciated Need to control others **Feelings of:** Envy Vanity Strong will Self-righteousness Infallibility	Allow others to make choices and live by their decisions. Get out of the head, and move more to the heart. Value people and relationships more than "winning." Ask for Divine assistance to show you the way to stop interfering in another's life. Request that the angels help you see the bigger picture. Restrain from action, and support through prayer. **Affirmations** *I honor my own path and respect the paths of others.* *I honor all for their choices and the decisions they make.*

Sub-laws Governed by the Higher Self	Behaviors and Attitudes Governed by the Ego	Techniques for Aligning with the Higher Self
PATIENCE **Definition**: Forbearance, steadfastness in the face of trials or delays. Having the ability to bear misfortune or inaction calmly without complaint. **Purpose**: The quality of balance that keeps the male and female energies within balanced. The composure necessary for ascension.	**Behaviors** Restless nature Inability to control emotions—excitability Lack of will and control of the intellect needed to stay calm **Attitudes** Uneasy feelings about another's abilities Discouragement regarding life and others **Feelings of**: Anger Discouragement Passion Overexcitement Lack of focus	Hold your composure in all situations. Breathe deeply and rhythmically. Never respond until you have all the facts and data. Remember that we are living an illusion and that all events in life are merely tests for mastery. **Affirmations** *I am attached to nothing.* *Nothing has meaning. I am calm and centered at all times.* *I complete all my work with little effort and stress.* *I see the perfection in all things.*

271

Sub-laws Governed by the Higher Self	Behaviors and Attitudes Governed by the Ego	Techniques for Aligning with the Higher Self
PRAISE **Definition**: To commend, recognize, compliment, or glorify. **Purpose**: The expression of appreciation that allows us to see the beauty in others.	**Behaviors** Criticizing others Slandering another Diminishing the work and achievements of others **Attitudes** Taking others for granted Feeling that you are diminishing yourself by complementing others Not recognizing others' efforts **Feelings of:** Indifference Rejection Separation Sarcasm Condemnation Satire Disapproval Hate Envy Jealousy	See beauty in others. Get in touch with the Goddess energy within and empower others by making them feel good. Ask for the ability to see who needs praise. Remember your intention to stay connected to your Higher Self. Enjoy how good it feels to make another happy. **Affirmations** *Our world and its people are beautiful.* *I now release all negative judgments.* *I free myself to evolve.* *I now let go of all negative self-criticism.* *I love myself for who I am.*

Sub-laws Governed by the Higher Self	Behaviors and Attitudes Governed by the Ego	Techniques for Aligning with the Higher Self
RESPONSIBILITY **Definition**: The act of being accountable by having the ability to distinguish right from wrong and following through with conviction. **Purpose**: The attribute that assists in developing standards that help one follow Buddha's Eightfold Path: Right Seeing Right Thought Right Speech Right Action Right Living Right Endeavor Right Mindedness Right Concentration	**Behavior** Lack of commitment Hypocrisy—saying one thing and doing another **Attitudes** Sense of being overwhelmed and feeling that your job description is too much to handle Feelings of imbalance between the male and female energies within Believing that you do not make a difference **Feelings of:** Laziness Negativity Hopelessness Uncaring Irresponsibility Unaccountability Helplessness	Remember that you chose your own path. Remember the commitments and contracts you "signed" before coming into embodiment. Break down all duties into tasks that have a beginning and an end. Hold on to your faith. Discipline yourself. Work to achieve mental and emotional clarity. Surround yourself with like-minded people. **Affirmation** *I now complete all my tasks easily and effortlessly.*

273

Sub-laws Governed by the Higher Self	Behaviors and Attitudes Governed by the Ego	Techniques for Aligning with the Higher Self
SELF-LOVE **Definition:** To value, honor, and respect one's being (body, mind, and Spirit) with full awareness of one's own inherent worth. **Purpose:** The state of being that teaches us to love others unconditionally while accepting ourselves for our perfections in the moment.	**Behaviors** Engaging in self-condemning statements Setting yourself up for failure **Attitudes** Expressing feelings of self-deprecation Expressing feelings of dissatisfaction, bitterness, or revulsion **Feelings of:** Self-hate Self-loathing Self-scorn Abhorrence	Trust yourself to do random acts of kindness. "Breathe Pink," and allow the color to change your feelings. Be charitable to others. Smile! Allow yourself to feel all your emotions, and let the negative thoughts pass through you. **Affirmations** *I love all of me—my body, mind, and emotions.* *I am a radiant Being of Light and love.* *I am perfect and I embrace the totality of my Being.*

Sub-laws Governed by the Higher Self	Behaviors and Attitudes Governed by the Ego	Techniques for Aligning with the Higher Self
THANKFULNESS **Definition**: The act of expressing gratitude for a benefit received. **Purpose**: An act of kindness that frees the heart to focus on the quality of the moment.	**Behaviors** Not acknowledging your needs Taking others' kindnesses for granted Ignoring the gifts of others **Attitudes** Feeling that you are blocked from Spirit Perception of scarcity State of consciousness where you impose expectations on others **Feelings of:** Unfaithfulness Carelessness Insensitivity Forgetfulness Moodiness Discontent Criticism Arrogance	Get in the habit of thanking God every day for all that you receive. Ask for the wisdom to understand all that is received as blessings. Make a list of all your blessings. Say "thank you" to obstacles and challenges for the lessons they bring. **Affirmations** *The universe is good to me and I am grateful.* *I thank God for showing me the way.* *I thank God for all my lessons, for they continue to make me a better person.*

Sub-laws Governed by the Higher Self	Behaviors and Attitudes Governed by the Ego	Techniques for Aligning with the Higher Self
UNCONDITIONAL LOVE **Definition**: Absolute acceptance of another without any sign of judgment. **Purpose**: The expression of God through the soul that grants us freedom in the Light.	**Behavior** Criticizing and judging others to make yourself look better Self-criticism **Attitudes** Experiencing any feeling or vibration that is not calm, peaceful, and loving Lack of ability to forgive or sacrifice **Feelings of:** Fear Anger Hostility Low self-esteem Piousness	Get in touch with your inner child to determine if or where it is wounded. Call forth the experiences, bless them, and forgive yourself and others. Observe others from a detached standpoint. Visualize the Light within permeating every cell of your body. Meditate daily to quiet the mind. See God in all things. Know that you are a point of Light and that God is within. **Affirmations** *I love to give and to receive.* *I give thanks to God for all that I am.* *Life is beautiful and I see perfection in all things.*

Summary

The ability to live in harmony with the sub-laws of the universe is one of the primary goals of our many incarnations on Earth. When we live within the values and purposes outlined by the sub-laws, we demonstrate that we have chosen to live in agreement with our Creator. We not only are created in the image of our Creator, but we also are moving toward agreement with the world and ways of life that the Creator has provided for us.

Talking about the sub-laws or characteristics of our lives is easy. Living them in consistent ways by demonstrating positive thoughts, words, and actions is much more difficult. The sub-laws listed in this chapter provide an index for helping us to live better lives. Using this listing of the sub-laws requires the following steps:

* ✳ Carefully read the definition and purpose of each of the sub-laws and make a list of those that seem most unfilled in your life.
* ✳ Study the ways in which you can achieve the purpose of the laws by aligning with them and with your Higher Self.
* ✳ Study how our attainment of the sub-laws is blocked by the will of the ego.
* ✳ Develop a plan for practicing right thoughts, demonstrating the intent of your thoughts in your behaviors, and affirming your intent to think right thoughts on a daily basis.

Many chapters in this book provide explanations of God's intent. This chapter helps us understand:

* ✳ The purposes and skills needed for living in the Light.
* ✳ The ways in which we can master the curriculum of the Third Dimension, which ultimately prepares us for entry into the Fifth.

Chapter 23

MEDITATION AND PRAYER

He who lives in harmony with himself lives in harmony with the universe.

Marcus Aurelius

rom birth, we identify ourselves with our five senses. We are told that we look like our father or mother and grow up hearing stories about our freckles, blond hair, and capabilities. In short, it is reinforced constantly that we are our bodies. Our identity is connected to this physical imprint. We gaze into the mirror and think that the reflection is who we are.

The reality is that we are not the body. We are something else much more expansive than the body. We are actually the expression of Universal Mind energy and Light, and it is this energy that creates our thoughts, words, emotions, and actions. Since we can think about our thoughts, we are not our thoughts. Since we can analyze our emotions, we are not our emotions. Since we can observe and analyze our bodies, we cannot be our bodies.

The body is not capable of doing anything on its own. During the course of our lives, the body will age and eventually die. We will not, because we are not the body. The body is only the vehicle that transports us as we journey in this third-dimensional reality.

Everything in the physical world is created first out of mental energy. When we think we are unhappy, we are. When we believe we are excited, we behave that way. Whatever we think, we have the power to become. Some people believe that we are the negative thoughts that frustrate and control us, but we are not. And aren't you glad? We live in a sea of thought-forms encasing the planet, many of which are not of the highest. These thought-forms have a tendency to gravitate to us, depending upon our mood and what we attract to us. The thoughts we choose to own exist as the original, creative forces that guide our paths.

Once we realize that we are not our thoughts and emotions, we can begin to control them. We do this by choosing to think or feel otherwise. Whenever we do not like how we are feeling, we should choose to experience something else.

It is difficult for most of us to break from the illusion of who we think we are, especially when our five senses are alive and functioning so well. There is a way to do so, however, and that way is through meditation. By meditating, we can become aware of all that is not the body and all that is pure consciousness. Meditation leads us to discover who we really are.

Meditation

Meditation is deep and continuous thought that allows us to travel inward to reflect on sacred matters. The act of meditation can cause our brain waves to slow down to such a degree that we are able to use more of our mind. This action, once achieved, allows us to reflect on the inner aspects of the mind. Deeper meditations connect us to the spark of the Divine and the Light within. Once this has been accomplished and the connection to the Higher Self has been made, we are assured of living harmonious, abundant, loving lives if we follow the guidance emanating from within ourselves.

Why should we meditate?

Meditation assists us to find bliss, inner harmony, and centeredness. It is the only way to find the peace within and to connect to it so that we can live it. Peace can never be found or experienced outside of oneself. It is found when we learn to control our mental and emotional bodies and stay centered within. Meditation teaches us how to master this state of mind, and once we do, we discover who we really are.

Meditation is the path of all the wise sages who have journeyed before us, and it will continue to be the road to freedom for many more in the years to come. In one of Ascended Master Kuthumi's earlier incarnations he played the role of Pythagoras. During that lifetime he was quoted as saying:

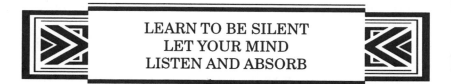

LEARN TO BE SILENT
LET YOUR MIND
LISTEN AND ABSORB

Pythagoras lived in approximately 600 B.C. and knew then what many still have not learned today. How many years must these Ascended Masters patiently continue to guide us before we learn?

Why is proper breathing important?

Very few individuals on Earth understand the importance of the breath. Breathing is life itself. It is the connection to health. Evidence of this statement is shown in the number of individuals with poor posture and caved-in chests, and those who are contracting diseases in the respiratory areas. If we could develop only one generation of children who breathe correctly, diseases could almost be eliminated.

Kuthumi states in many transmissions:

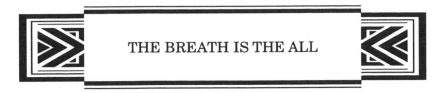

THE BREATH IS THE ALL

He emphasizes this, for it is through the breath that we connect with *prana*. Kuthumi defines prana as "the life force energy that feeds the soul." He goes on to explain further that "it is the nutrition line emanating from the Higher Self that provides the essential ingredients for all nine bodies to function in unison." In the Sanskrit language, the term means absolute energy, or the Source of All there is. It is used by the soul for all manifestation. Those individuals who have stored prana successfully, either deliberately or subconsciously, radiate a vitality and power that are experienced by all who are in their presence. It is prana that heals through the hands and auric fields of the Masters. It is this force field of energy that will continue to build in the individuals who consciously journey to the Light and who eventually will create Heaven on Earth, as prophesied.

Peoples in the Far East (such as the Orient and India) have known about prana for centuries. Some individuals in the west are beginning to understand it. A few prophets have predicted, however, that because of the western ego, prana will not be accepted in western culture until a scientist "discovers" it, quantifies it, and renames it, thus making it a commodity. We wonder if this will constitute the basis for a Nobel Prize.

How should we meditate?

We are what we eat! What we eat will determine what we think. Therefore, do not meditate within two hours of eating. Fasting is a well-known way to enhance the meditative state.

The process of meditation is enhanced if you sit with your spine straight. Do not sit on the ground, because the energies will be pulled into the Earth. Instead, sit on a pillow or rug, with your legs crossed.

Breathe deeply and rhythmically, inhaling through your nose, while your chest and solar plexus both expand. Breathe in fresh air, if possible. Slowly let the air out of your mouth, keeping your chest firmly in place and pushing up gently from your solar plexus. Try to exhale all the old, stale air.

Never inhale through your mouth. Humans are the only animals who sometimes breathe through their mouths, which is one of the causes of diseases. This is because the mouth provides no protection for the organs within.

Hold the air within for a few seconds before exhaling. This might make you feel a little light-headed. Focus your attention on any part of your body that is holding tension—the neck, shoulders, face, legs, etc.—and release the tension into the universe.

With eyes closed, visualize a golden Light within your head. See it slowly expand and fill your entire body with Light. Try to hold your full concentration on the Light, until you can see every cell in your body filled with this frequency. Continue to breathe deeply.

> *Controlling the breath, and thus calming the nerves, is a prerequisite to controlling the mind and the body.*
>
> Swami Rama

While visualizing the Light within, allow all thoughts to pass through your mind. Hold your vision on the Light.

What happens if thoughts bombard your mind and you cannot clear your head?

It is common for most people to experience thoughts that agitate the mind. If this happens, let the thoughts pass through like clouds passing across the sky, and bring your focus back to the Light. Do not hold onto any thoughts or feelings. Instead, just bless them, thank them for being there, and allow them to drift slowly away. Never attach judgment or self-criticism if you cannot hold the focus for long. Just experience the process and strive to do better each day. Be earnest in your desire to accomplish this, however. Discipline is necessary to achieve a higher state of consciousness.

The challenge is to conquer the desires of the ego. This usually takes a long time to accomplish. Do not expect victory immediately, but keep trying to conquer the thoughts and focus on the Light. Once you can do this, you stand on the threshold of becoming more than the sum of the parts of your existence.

How long should we meditate?

Each person must determine individually how long to meditate each day. Even as few as sixteen minutes a day will begin to produce miracles in one's life.

Discipline is also important. If a meditation can be completed at the same time each day, greater effects often are experienced. Some people prefer evenings, while others start the day with a moment or two of silence. The ultimate goal is to become a walking meditation every moment of the day.

What are the stages of meditation?

Sai Baba, a great Avatar living in India, presently holding the Christ consciousness for the world, teaches that there are three stages of meditation: concentration, contemplation, and true meditation.

Stage I — Concentration. The stage of concentration requires discipline over our thoughts and actions. Staring at a mandala (a circular pattern with concentric, geometric symbols and forms that represent the universe) for several seconds without blinking will enhance deep concentration, as will holding our thoughts still while focusing on the Light. To learn to meditate we must desire to learn the art of concentration, and then use this power to conquer our mental and emotional bodies. At this stage, we must command our breathing, taking deep rhythmic breaths and inhaling the life force energy of the universe.

Stage II — Contemplation. The contemplative stage requires the ability to focus internally—for example, visualizing the Light within. One of the greatest meditations that should be mastered is to see the Light within emanating from every part of our body. When this can be accomplished successfully and the mind can hold this thought for an extended period of time, consciousness will expand. Light is the great purifier of the universe. It dissolves all that is not of the highest, and is a transforming power. By focusing on the Light, all eventually is renewed, for it has an "IQ" greater than ours and understands all that we need. Therefore, by focusing our attention on the Light, we draw to us all that we need, whether we understand it in the moment or not. An excellent mantra to say daily that will facilitate this is:

I AM THE LIGHT OF THE WORLD

Stage III — Meditation. The stage of true meditation is mastered when the one who is meditating no longer feels that he or she is doing it. In other words, when the person and the Light merge and become One, then higher consciousness is experienced and understood.

Prayer

Daily prayer is another extremely powerful way in which we can achieve harmony in life. Prayer is a plea or entreaty addressed to God, asking for a special favor or request.

It is also a form of giving thanks. Did you know that prayers, when aligned with Divine harmony, are always answered in some form? That is the rule. Since this is law, we should have confidence that what we ask for will be realized.

The Ascended Masters constantly remind us of the sayings:

> *Ask, and it shall be given you;*
> *Seek, and Ye shall find;*
> *Knock and it shall be opened unto you.*

Matthew 7:7, King James Version of the Bible

When one asks, the request is granted; when one knocks, the door opens; and when one seeks, the answers are found. This is law.

Prayer is speaking to God, while meditation is listening to God. Since we spend so much of our time talking, it is a good practice to learn to focus our thoughts and words into constant prayers. Focusing our energy will always assist us to bring Divine harmony into our lives.

Some people do not know how to pray. They think that a formal verse has to be spoken or a structured thought emitted. Not true! A smile with a song of gratitude in the heart is the best prayer of all. Learn to be in this state at all times, and you will become a living prayer.

> *There is only one God and He is omnipresent.*
> *There is only one religion, the religion of love.*
> *There is only one caste, the caste of humanity.*
> *There is only one language, the language of*
> *the heart.*

Sai Baba

Living a life of truth, right speech, peace, harmony, love, and nonviolence fulfills the language of the heart. This is what we have come to learn.

Summary

Many of us live with the illusion that our identity is our body, our physical senses, and our experiences in the physical world. In truth, we are much more. We are expressions of Universal Mind energy and Light and our bodies are vehicles which facilitate our experiences in a third-dimensional world. Everything in the physical world is first created out of mental energy. Just as we were created from universal mind energy, we also create our reality from our mind energy.

There are two basic ways to get in touch with our real identities and learn about our missions and purposes—meditation and prayer. Meditation is listening to God, and prayer is speaking to God. Both allow us to contact our Higher Selves and make the connections beyond the physical world.

Meditation is deep and continuous thought and concentration that allows us to travel inward to reflect on our realities beyond the third-dimensional world. Deep meditation connects us to the spark of the Divine and Light within. It is the way we learn to control our mental and emotional bodies and discover who we really are.

Meditation begins with an understanding of the importance of deep breathing. Breath is "the nutrition line emanating from the Higher Self that provides the essential ingredients for all nine bodies to function in unison." It is our forcefield of energy that enables us to journey and remain in the Light.

Guidelines for our meditation include the following:

* Do not meditate within two hours of eating.
* Sit with your spine straight.
* Breathe deeply and rhythmically.
* Hold the air within you for a few seconds before exhaling.
* With eyes closed, visualize Golden Light within your head. See it expand and fill the body.

Prayer is another way of going within and making contact beyond the physical world. Prayer is a plea to God for a special favor or request or a means of giving thanks. It may be a formal prayer or request or our ongoing dialogue with our Creator. Prayer is an active vital force in our lives when we use it, because our prayers are always answered.

Chapter 24

AFFIRMATIONS AND MANIFESTATION

What things soever Ye desire, when Ye pray, believe that Ye receive them, and Ye shall have them.

Mark 11:24

aster Athena discussed the Divine Concept of Oneness in Chapter 9. She said that the universe and everything in it is mind or thought within the field of pure energy and Light.

Since we are One with this energy, our boundaries are limitless, and we have the power to affect everything around us. We can even affect conditions and events at a distance, although few of us have realized this potential. We only have to move our consciousness to our point of power through our Higher Selves, and then let the universe do its work of supporting our dreams, visions, decrees, and actions. As long as we are working through the Higher Self, we can be assured that we are bringing God's perfect plan through for our highest good and not the will of our egos.

The use of affirmations is an important tool in discovering personal power. This is primarily because when we affirm something by saying it aloud, we add the energy of sound to the thought. Sound is the second most important form of energy with which we can work. Light and sound are the basis for all manifestation and the ingredients with which the Universal Mind and the Golden Liquid Light work.

In studying the Law of Vibration, we learned that everything has its own unique vibratory frequency (sound), and that higher vibrations consume and transform lower vibrations. Applying this concept further, we begin to realize that the higher the vibration we personally maintain (that which is closer to Light), the more power we have to create and manifest that which is our perfect plan. This is another reason why it is so important for us to become Beings of Light. Remember the saying, *I AM the Light of the world*? It was stated with purpose.

We all have experienced the "talking" that goes on inside our minds. To most of us, it seems as if this happens continuously, and we keep a running commentary on almost everything that happens to us or around us. Unfortunately, much of this talking comes from what have been called "old tapes"—thoughts and ideas that we have carried around inside us for years.

Saying affirmations helps free us from these tapes and the negativity that often accompanies them by replacing them with positive, reinforcing thoughts. This is not difficult to learn or to do, and, in fact, can be done at almost any time and in almost any place. Affirmations can be used once a day or as often as desired. They can be spoken, changed, written, or thought.

Affirmations are, simply put, positive statements. They can be either specific or general, depending on one's need. Their number is infinite, because they can take the form of any positive statement that one wishes to make. By using them, an individual *makes firm* what he or she is trying to bring about in life, whether it be a change in jobs, a better relationship, a promotion, a healing, or something else.

The most powerful affirmations usually include a spiritual reference to God, Jesus, Buddha, Divine Love, the Ascended Masters, or whomever one feels comfortable with or is most inspired by.

The process of manifesting with affirmations requires five basic steps.

Step One. The first step requires that you visualize what you need. (Notice that the word *need* and not *want* is used. If we deliberately begin to visualize everything we want, chaos can result around us.) In the business and educational worlds, this step is considered to be goal setting, or forming the vision. Know where you are going and what you wish to accomplish.

On some level, each of us knows the inner plan that will bring the greatest harmony and joy to our lives. If you cannot identify your goals, meditate and ask that the vision be revealed to you. In time, all will come forth. The amount of Light you have been able to assimilate into your consciousness will correlate directly to the amount of time it will take to retrieve the answers—the more Light, the less time.

It is important to remember that you do not have to have a perfectly clear vision outlining every detail of what it is that you need. In fact, in the beginning it is desirable that you do not. Once you put your affirmation out into the universe, you might actually limit the gift that will come to you if you are too restricting.

Step Two. The second step requires that you focus your energies. One of the greatest problems people have today involves the number of choices available to them. There are so many choices that individuals often become confused. This confusion can lead to apathy, inactivity, or frustration.

What causes this state of mind and behavior? Believe it or not, it is the EGO. The ego pulls our attention to the wants rather than the needs. When a person seriously embarks on the spiritual path, one of the first contests he or she experiences is the battle between the ego and the Higher Self, or the will of God.

The ego pulls us in several directions, making it difficult to focus. The Higher Self has no difficulty whatsoever. Can you imagine Ascended Masters Kuthumi or El Morya running around perplexed and confused because of the multitude of choices they have to deal with? Never!

They, as Ascended Beings of Light, overcame those tests long ago and work only within the Universal Laws. In alignment with God's will, they select the choices that are presented through the Light stream of consciousness and move with grace and harmony every step of the way. This mode of operation produces perfection, harmony, and abundance because God's plan offers this to all. It is the ego and the lessons that ego must learn that make the path difficult to travel.

We, in embodiment, can travel the same path as the Ascended Masters if we wish. We only need to become aware of the tools that are available to assist us. The first of these tools is the understanding that we must simplify our lives! It really is that simple, although not so easy to accomplish. Our life-styles are complex, and the forces around us often bombard us, making it difficult to focus and think clearly. Here are some suggestions to help you:

* Make all decisions while in a relaxed state of mind.
* Realize that everything in the physical world is an illusion, and select one thing that appeals to you. Instantly, let everything else go. Just pick one thing. Focus your energy on this new point, and watch how quickly the mind begins to strengthen once a decision is made.
* Relax and meditate on your idea of a perfect situation for you. See yourself at work or play doing what you enjoy the most. Keep the vision, focus, and define it in detail.
* Write down your vision. Describe it completely, if this helps you form the thought.

Step Three. The third step requires that you write out your thoughts in the form of affirmations describing the vision as though they had already manifested and you were participating in them. Be sure to write all affirmations in the present tense.

Place the affirmations on a mirror or the refrigerator so that you are reminded constantly to focus on this ideal situation. Remember, the more mental energy you put into your affirmations, the sooner they will manifest.

Step Four. The fourth step requires that you say your affirmations aloud. Say them in the car, walking around the house, or in any other place where you can concentrate and not disturb others. Looking at oneself in a mirror while saying them appears to bring more energy to the decrees. Try this if you feel comfortable with it.

NOTE: An important key to success lies at this stage of the process. Therefore, read this next section carefully.

It is important to remember that, of the four forms of energy (thoughts, words, emotions, and actions), emotion is the cosmic glue. Beliefs and emotions solidify thoughts faster than the other three forms of energy.

When you begin to develop some affirmations designed to improve your life and change the reality (illusion) around you, you might not believe them right away. An example of this might have to do with affirmations regarding abundance. If your past has shown you poverty, hard times, and little prosperity, it might be difficult to say and believe in an affirmation designed to place you in abundance. The affirmation "Financial abundance is mine, and I accept it freely" is easier to say than to believe if one has had several years of hard times.

If you are saying one thing, but deeply believing something else, it will take longer for you to push the energy in a circular pattern into the physical world and realize your manifestation. Or, the manifestation might take other forms. A little abundance might begin to flow, only to be sabotaged because you do not feel deserving. The ego's confirmation of "I told you so, and I do not deserve it" will certainly come into play to justify the deep emotions behind this belief system. So while the Higher Self (through the Light stream of consciousness) is working to bring you what you deserve, your ego and your ingrained habits and beliefs (emotions) will be working to deny you what you want.

Here's how to conquer this situation. Do not give up. Keep saying your affirmations. When you see something develop, immediately claim your power and accept that you have participated in co-creating this event. Watch for all signs of the desired manifestation, because it might not come only in the form of monetary support. For example, it could come through someone offering to buy you lunch or someone else giving you something you have needed for your home. Just know that the universe (God) works in mysterious ways. Accept everything as a sign of your power to manifest, and immediately give silent thanks for your gifts. Say thanks to whomever you identify with: God, Jesus (Sananda), Mother Mary, the Ascended Masters, the Angels, Vishnu, Viracocha, Buddha, etc. It is vital to remember to do this, for it keeps the wheel of gratitude and energy turning.

A balanced attitude and astute awareness of the signs around you will assist you to develop self confidence in yourself and in this system. When you begin to develop a sense of confidence in what you are able to do, your belief system will start to strengthen. The new beliefs will then become the "cosmic glue" and will enhance the manifestation process so that you can realize things more quickly.

When you first begin to say affirmations that are not a part of your reality, it is critical that you block that so-called "reality" and say affirmations with strength and commitment. If weeks go by and nothing is realized, do not stop saying them. It may be that you have put so many thoughts and beliefs regarding not having something into your wheel of energy that it will take months before the cycle can play itself out. If this happens to you, your faith surely will be tested. How strong are you? How strong is your faith? How much do you believe in the power of the Light?

Step Five. The fifth step requires you to develop and

strengthen your will and begin to "will" your affirmations. Decree with power and strength. Then detach from your need, and let it go into the universe. Do not try to outguess the result. Just decree it, and wait for it to return to you in some form. Trust that the Light and the God Force have more intelligence than you do and that the perfect situation will begin to take form around you.

We can use affirmations not only for ourselves, but also for others. Only use them for decreeing positive things. You also must ask permission of the other person's Higher Self to do this. This assures that you are not interfering with his or her path. Interfering without permission brings the karmic debts back to the sender! Always remember that all energy travels in circles. What is willed on one level, regardless of who the recipient of the decree may be, MUST come back to the originator. There is no escaping the Law of Cause and Effect. What you sow is what you reap. If you think you can get around this Universal Law, you are mistaken.

If you think only positive, loving things, you will experience a life filled with love and Light. If you use the energy to will wrongful or harmful things on another, you will reap all that you sow. The difference between the past and the present time is that we are entering the Fifth Dimension, where all energies will continue to accelerate. It is the time of the quantum leap. Consequently, it no longer will take several lifetimes for energy to return to its sender, as it did in the past.

In the new millennium, energy will travel at closer to the speed of Light, and all thought-forms will return to the sender almost immediately. In other words, all Karma will be experienced instantly or in the same lifetime. This is one reason why it is safe to print this information now, for no one will escape the effects of what they sow. Individuals who choose to misuse their power eventually will get so tired and sick of reaping what they have sown that they will give up negativity out of sheer exhaustion.

Nevertheless, one must show great discretion in how this power is used. A safety net for using affirmations is to include a caveat that your decrees are for the most positive benefits for all concerned. Then let them drift off into the universe, allowing the celestials to work for you to bring blessings and joy to all.

The rationale for learning and using affirmations is that this method is one of many ways to create a Heaven on Earth. Picture what the world would be like if everyone began affirming and decreeing only positive, loving things. Or, imagine mass consciousness gaining momentum in the Light with more and more people turning their thoughts and actions toward the positive uses of energy. The world's present condition could change in a twinkling of an eye.

Jesus understood what it would take to bring the world into the Fifth Dimension. But, because it is up to us to change the vibrational frequency and raise it to a higher level, even he cannot predict when this moment will occur. Our mission is to hold the Light for the world, regardless of what goes on around us. As more and more people hold the positions and become the Light, this frequency will slowly affect everyone and everything on the planet through the Law of Vibration. *Be patient, Be silent, and Be the Light,* as Master Kuthumi has said. *Victory is assured.*

Affirmations manifest for individuals on different levels of development and commitment. The lower levels concern issues such as wanting or needing physical objects or specific events in one's life. Higher uses of affirmations involve concerns such as health, happiness, world service, mission fulfillment, and peace.

Some of the most powerful decrees are stated through the Higher Self, using the power of the violet frequency and celestial kingdoms for assistance. Since the violet frequency dissolves negativity, another level of power is added to the decree. Some examples of these higher decrees are:

> *Through the power of the Higher Self, I command and demand that the violet frequency blaze ahead of me and dissolve all negativity.*

I request that the angels of the Violet Flame Temple surround me with golden Light and release me from all struggles and limitations that are preventing me from fulfilling God's will on Earth.

Through my beloved I AM Presence, I move into the higher frequency of the Light and surround myself with the protection of Archangel Michael and the Sword of Blue Flame. I command that my life be purified of all negative thought-forms and that perfection come into my life.

Through my beloved I AM Presence, I AM Light and Love.

Through my beloved I AM Presence, I command that all mistakes of the past be replaced with perfection and that all things be purified before I approach.

Some examples of affirmations that can be used to improve the conditions in your immediate environment are:

I AM Radiant and a Being of Light and Love.
Miracles happen wherever I go.
All that I need comes to me easily.
Love comes to me easily and effortlessly, and I accept it now.
My health and body are perfect, and I am stronger every day.
I am now employed in the perfect job for me.
I complete all my work perfectly, quickly, easily, and effortlessly.
Abundance comes to me effortlessly, and I am grateful and I deserve it.

Finally, affirmations should be phrased so that they:

* Fit your own personal needs or provide assistance to others.
* Accentuate the positive without ever using negative phrases. The God Force is love and Light—only the positive. It does not recognize the negative. The emphasis should be on what you can do or want rather than what you cannot do or do not want.
* Are short and simple.
* Are always stated in the present tense, with the understanding that the request has already been fulfilled.
* Create new opportunities.

Summary

One of the ways that we can affect our lives and the conditions around us is through the use of affirmations. When we move our consciousness to the Higher Self, we have access to the universe to support our dreams, visions, decrees, and actions. When we state things aloud, we add the energy of sound to thought. Saying affirmations frees us from the tapes and negativity of the past and moves us to positive, reinforcing thoughts.

* ✳ We send energy into the world when we make positive statements or affirmations of our needs which can support the realization of these needs as well as changing previous negative thoughts about ourselves.
* ✳ Affirmations are positive statements which may be spoken, written, or thought.
* ✳ Manifestation is assisted when you:
  * ◆ Visualize what you need;
  * ◆ Focus your energies on specific needs;
  * ◆ Write down your thoughts; and
  * ◆ Strengthen and develop your will.

Chapter 25

ABUNDANCE

*No limits are set to the ascent of man, and to
each and everyone the highest stands open.
Here it is only your personal choice that decides.*
Hasidic saying

Have you ever wondered why there is so much poverty in a world overflowing with wisdom and wealth? Have you noticed how many individuals have difficulty manifesting abundance? Poverty is the opposite of abundance. Therefore, a discussion of poverty may help us understand how we can manifest abundance. In this chapter we will look at the process we have been using to create unprosperous beliefs so deep within us that we are not even aware they are there. Then, we will see how those beliefs actually have shaped the world around us.

One of the reasons poverty is so widespread is that poverty consciousness exists in the world. People see poverty on television, and in movies, magazines, and periodicals as well as in neighborhoods. If the pictures and stories are graphic enough, we believe them, discuss them, and think about them. These images are implanted in our conscious minds, and then transferred deep into our subconscious minds.

In addition, newspapers, magazines, and other media daily report these conditions as reality. The media's entire justification for continuing to focus on negative reports rests on the premise that this is real, so we must continue to see it and dwell on it.

Well, poverty is real, for the moment in which it exists. But poverty exists because people have created it with the power of their collective thoughts, beliefs, words, and actions. It is a vicious cycle that is self-perpetuating. If we see poverty, we believe it to be real. If we believe it to be real, our thoughts, feelings, words, and actions continue to create it. As we continue to create more apparent poverty in the world, many people begin to fear that perhaps it will touch their own lives. Fear (the cosmic glue) brings more poverty into reality. Therefore, we talk about it more.... Get the picture?

Because we have forgotten momentarily that we have the power to create our own reality, we have allowed the media and news to program us into creating a world that is less than perfect, harmonious, beautiful, and abundant. Carrying this process one step further, people begin to feel helpless to change these conditions, which only serves to perpetuate them.

We also have poverty consciousness because of our past life experiences. Many people today have had previous incarnations in convents, lamaseries, temples, or monasteries. In these past lives, vows of poverty were taken so many times that they left a permanent impression in our Akashic Records that poverty is holy. This belief is stamped so deep in some of us that it is nearly impossible to break this attitude. To believe otherwise takes a strength and discipline that most people are not accustomed to displaying. We were such good students in those former lifetimes that we all received an "A" for learning poverty consciousness. Some souls may even have earned an "A+" if they really struggled and were recognized for the burdens that they carried. This, of course, glorified the belief and made it all the more difficult to break.

The truth is that vows of poverty were appropriate for those former lifetimes and the conditions under which individuals chose to live. They are even appropriate today if a soul needs such an experience in order to evolve. As a matter of fact, vows of poverty must be taken at certain times in humanity's evolutionary development, because they help devotees to detach from the materialistic world and focus totally on the spiritual path. Such an existence eliminates distractions and sets up conditions whereby individuals devote their lives to learning religious and spiritual teachings.

Unfortunately, one does not have to spend a lifetime in a monastery or convent to learn other truths about poverty. Today, teachers and role models are everywhere suggesting that poverty is good because it makes us spiritual or holy. There is an underlying spiritual precept that if we struggle, we are noble because we earn more rewards on the path to God. Concepts such as these have been taught in nearly every major world religion for the past two thousand years (and perhaps even longer), stamping into the soul the notion that poverty makes us better people. Beliefs such as these even contribute to preventing people from aspiring to higher goals, because they believe that suffering is what God intends for them to do.

Nearly everyone carries Akashic Record memories from one of the two situations described above: past life experiences or present spiritual teachings. Because this is so, it makes it easier for the media to program individuals into accepting, believing, and fearing what they broadcast. Thus we participate in creating it.

Poverty consciousness runs deep in our cellular, Akashic Record, and past life remembrances. We believe the stories we hear to be true because they reflect "reality," and they also resonate within our emotional bodies at the soul level. Therefore, we do nothing to change this reality. Many of us live on emotions, failing to balance our emotions with logic. By accepting another person's beliefs as our own truths, we prevent ourselves from seeing what is needed today.

Ascended Master Kuthumi has reminded us repeatedly that our two weakest bodies are our mental and emotional bodies. He says that, on the road to mastery, Masters learn to control both their thoughts and their emotions. In other words, Masters CHOOSE what they think every moment of the day and CHOOSE how they feel, as well. Yet, how many of us can say that we are not influenced by the media? We believe all that we see, rather than see what we believe. That's the problem. We do not CHOOSE what we think every moment of the day, nor do we CHOOSE how we will feel. Instead, thought-forms and attitudes of others permeate our consciousness and we turn our lives over to them by buying into their beliefs, attitudes, emotions, and actions instead of creating our own.

Now that we understand that each one of us is the creator of our own reality and that our beliefs and emotions are the "cosmic glue" for manifestation, we can begin to understand how we have created such a mess in the world. The universe is truly a universe of abundance, yet we have thought it into one of poverty and pain.

God is Light, love, and abundance. The electron is the electron no matter how it manifests. Energy is energy! It is neutral and will move on the path of least resistance, depending upon how we direct it. It is, therefore, up to us to decide what we will create.

Choosing between poverty or abundance is a good way to start. Which do you choose? Remember that to choose one means that you must let the other one go. Are you ready to do this? Monitor your thoughts and beliefs, and then decide just how willing you are to let the negative ones go.

Einstein understood the concepts that are being discussed here and tried to tell us in a different way. Once a reporter asked him, "What is the most important question in the world?" He replied, "The most important question in the world is, do you want a peaceful, happy, abundant world in which to live, or do you want a foreboding, fearful, and scarce world?"

The reporter, slightly puzzled, asked, "Why is this the most important question in the world?"

Einstein replied, "Because whatever you choose, you will create."

NOW IS THE TIME to remember who we are. We must realize the power that lies within us and use this power to create Heaven on Earth. We must BE the Light, and integrate spirituality into everything on Earth. Never before have humans had to do this. This is a part of the Divine celestial plan to assist Earth to move into the Fifth Dimension.

The millennium holds the promise that Heaven will be created on Earth, and this will be accomplished by grounding spirituality into all walks of life. We are the Light and the co-creators with God, and it is our responsibility to use this Light to bring peace, love, happiness, and abundance to the planet.

It is time to practice being fifth-dimensional beings. Let's put on our thinking hats, and use the higher-level creative powers that have been given to us. At the heart of empowerment is the concept that a person can manifest all he or she needs to live in peace and harmony. Empowerment is never associated with the homeless, starving, or unfortunate. It is always connected with the strong and those who take charge of their lives and assist others to do the same. Let's challenge the old beliefs about abundance and use our logic to change our thinking. God's plan calls for abundance, happiness, peace, and love to be shared by all.

Upon examining some of the lives of the Ascended Masters, we notice that, in their final incarnations, they lived lives where they did not have to worry about poverty. Once they learned about the Universal Laws and their own power, they often chose lives of abundance and wealth. El Morya was King Solomon and later King Arthur; Kuthumi was Pythagoras and Shah Jahan, the Emperor of India who built the Taj Mahal; Monka was Viracocha, the head of the Inca civilization; Serapis Bey was the Pharaoh Akhnaton; St. Germain was Merlin and later incarnated as Shakespeare. A former incarnation of Jesus was Joseph, son of Isaac. Joseph later became the governor of Egypt and held power next to the Pharaoh. All these life styles had one thing in common—affluence. Do you think they lived in poverty and struggled? Of course not, and they are now Ascended Masters.

Just as we are doing, they balanced their lifetimes among less affluent and more affluent roles. Now that we have come to the end of these lessons, it is time to use our knowledge and experiences and live in abundance, too. Just like the Ascended Masters, we have learned the Universal Laws, and it is now time to balance this instruction in our everyday existences.

It is not poverty that makes one spiritual or noble. It is the quality of one's life and how one lives in each moment of each day that does it. There is nothing wrong with living a spiritual life in abundance and using higher principles and love to give to others and assist them on their paths.

You can and should begin to enjoy abundance. The first step is to analyze your thoughts and change those that are not in alignment with your new goals. Then you must begin consciously to give and receive. One of the best ways to start receiving is to start giving. If blockages are present, making it difficult for you to receive graciously, try a new approach to start the energy flowing. Command and demand the Law of Tenfold Return to work for you, so that you may use this energy to bring happiness and peace to others around you. The more you receive, the more you can give. When you give, do not be afraid to say the following affirmation:

> *This gift is given freely and with love to help bring abundance to Earth. I am a co-creator with God, and, in giving, I expect my tenfold return.*

If you follow this principle, the Law of Tenfold Return begins to operate in your life more quickly. Saying a decree like this serves to move blockages out of the way.

When we first begin to see the effects of this law, we have a tendency to deny that we could have participated in creating such a blessing. Then, after a few examples are provided to us, our emotional bodies will begin to believe. Once we believe, the cosmic glue begins to create at will. It is here that our faith usually becomes so strong that we no longer have to use decrees. We can move on to giving freely from the heart, enjoying giving just for the sake of it.

No matter what path you choose to begin to create abundance, begin today, and DO IT!

Summary

One of the most basic fears that people experience is the fear of poverty. Poverty consciousness comes from the media, our observations of suffering, and our past life experiences. There is a widespread belief that vows of poverty are necessary for spiritual development. While poverty experiences may be needed to learn important spiritual lessons, they are not required for spiritual growth.

God is Light, love, and abundance. We create our poverty and our abundance as a result of our thoughts, beliefs, words, and actions. We choose what we create. It is our responsibility to rise above our fears and take charge of creating abundance, happiness, peace, and love for all.

Our success in creating abundance is involved with its meaning in our lives and how we use our abundance. If we become greedy or do not use our abundance wisely, we may experience lessons which teach us how to use abundance. While we need to love and give to ourselves, we must also love and share with our brothers and sisters. In return, we receive more.

The Law of Tenfold Return states that when we give, we receive a tenfold return. Saying a decree may remove blockages and help us manifest abundance. Later, we may no longer need to say decrees as we learn to give freely from the heart.

Chapter 26

DISCERNMENT

To doubt yourself is to doubt the wisdom and
viability of the human design. To fully trust in
God you must also trust yourself. No one is cre-
ated without everything required to make
healthy, wholesome decisions.

Ken Carey
The Third Millennium

iscernment, or the process by which we evaluate situations and make decisions, is a critical aspect of our growth, our spiritual development, and our ability to create communities
that contribute to our collective well-being. There are many
indications that the world is experiencing rapid change and
profound transformation. This process, which has been ongoing for many years, has initiated a period of change not experienced at any previous time in our past history. This
period of change and transformation will last into the next
century, and will lead to a new level of civilization, a move to
a fifth-dimensional planet.

Moving to a new way of living cannot be achieved
without acquiring a new level of thinking and a higher consciousness. Developing a higher consciousness is accom-

plished by using both our rational thinking skills and our intuitions, or that which we feel and know without subjecting it to rational tests. We must rethink our beliefs, purposes, priorities, and patterns of behaving. We need to move to new levels of discernment.

Discernment is the ability to make discriminations, to make choices, and to make decisions. It is also the art of asking sensitive questions of ourselves and others in order to see deeper meanings and implications. The process of discernment involves four interrelated processes: perception, intuition, decision-making, and action. The core of each of these processes is comprised of trust in ourselves, faith in our Creator, and love, which is the energy that helps us expand our consciousness.

Discernment begins with perception, or the mind-set we use to view ourselves and the world we experience. Our experiences in the world shape our perceptions and beliefs. Our world view is a combination of our inner reality, or the ways in which we have internalized and used our experiences, and the realities of the external world. As we change and/or the world changes around us, we need to rethink our world view or mind-set.

Today, as we are faced with ongoing change in every aspect of our lives, being aware of these changes becomes an important task in our survival and continued well-being. We see companies and organizations collapse because they have not been able to change their ways of thinking and behaving. Individuals experience frustration when they have not spent time anticipating changes and responding to the need for change.

The most fundamental changes are likely to occur in our spiritual views, as we move from self-consciousness to group-consciousness to soul-consciousness to God-consciousness. Our perceptions and our values change as we progress on our spiritual path. As we move through these stages, our consistent concerns are to move toward more complete identity with the Creator, greater trust in the Creator, and greater trust in ourselves—that the decisions we make at any time are expressions of our free will and perfect for our level of development. It is also important that we learn to discern what is helpful for our advancement and what is not helpful, so that the decisions we make can accelerate us on our paths.

As individuals become more spiritual, their perceptions change. They drop their duality consciousness and begin to see the world in terms of lessons to be learned and tests designed to facilitate empowerment. This change in perception requires a strong sense of discernment, for we may be brought down many wrong alleys just because we have not learned the art of discernment. While no harm may come from making poor choices, poor decisions may make the journey more difficult. If our goal is to achieve a life of peace, harmony, abundance, and love as quickly as possible, then learning discernment and relying on our own inner judgment is essential to master.

> Ultimately, you must decide in your own hearts, and these alone. Base your decisions on your perception. To inhabit the new awareness, you are required to be yourself, for when you are, you are a beautiful being, in touch with your eternal dimension, conscious of the generations that will follow you, conscious of the generations that came before, immersed in the love that lights and unites the leaves of all generations upon life's singular tree. (Carey, p. 78)

The second aspect of discernment requires that we learn to get in touch with our intuition and to hear the inner voice that speaks to us. This is perhaps the most difficult step for most of us to learn, because we live in a society that rewards analytical thinking and not intuition. Consequently, most people have shut down their feelings and adopted the attitude that intuition is connected to psychic phenomena and is less than desirable. This attitude has limited our growth. Operating without using all our capabilities is like playing cards with less than a full deck. If we do not honor all aspects of our personalities, we cannot become all that we are meant to be.

Ascended Master Kuthumi says this about intuition and its connection to discernment.

Discernment requires that Initiates learn to go inward and "feel" the vibrational frequency of each thing that confronts them. It makes no difference whether the message received comes through words, actions, or emotions. The skill that separates a Master from a novice is the ability to feel the sound of the message. Once the vibrational level is felt, the Master knows whether or not to accept or reject the message in regard to whether or not the guidance that accompanies the message is helpful or not so helpful for one's path. If the vibrational frequency is high, then following the message will bring greater things to the soul. If the vibrational frequency is low, the Master knows to bless the energy, let it go, and transmute it into a higher tone for the angelic choir to use in singing praises to the Creator.

This was the way of the Atlantean Masters. This will be the way in the Seventh Golden Age.

Decision-making is the third aspect of discernment. This step is perhaps the most critical, for the decisions we make, based on our perceptions and intuitions, determine our actions. Some of our decisions are made instinctively, as we respond to real or perceived threats or dangers. We may make other decisions in a similar way, without considering all choices, by simply "going with the crowd" or taking the easy way. In such cases, we give away our right to make decisions. In all cases, whatever decision we make, we are ultimately responsible for the consequences, for the laws are perfect and will bring to us that which we have owned.

One of the reasons that we do not make decisions that we wish to make is fear—fear of being different, fear of loss of acceptance, fear of being alone. While we need to use caution and judgment, we also must understand that we reduce ourselves when we do not consider our own values and perceptions as we make decisions.

We should never judge ourselves harshly if the decisions we make are not the best—nor should we judge others. Unconditional love and acceptance of our frailties are the goals we are striving to achieve. We need to accept what is and continue to move forward, making new decisions regarding the tests that face us. Adopting this process only enhances the practice of refining our discernment.

One of the lessons we are learning today is that we need to listen to our inner thoughts. We are living in a time of inclusion and collaboration where we understand the importance of listening to, respecting, communicating, and working with others. We must take seriously the importance of trust and responsibility as a motivator of ourselves and others. We must realize that while each human being is unique, we are all children of God and have shared interests, responsibilities, and abilities to teach and learn from each other.

Decisions must be made with the understanding that all decisions create consequences. Every thought and action, even a thought or decision that is not acted upon, creates a reaction. When we make decisions, we need to make them with care and in contact with our Higher Selves.

Decision-making is not simply encountering a thought, situation, or idea and making a decision. Rather, it requires processing the information through our rational, intuitive, and spiritual filters in order to determine the course of action that is best for us.

The final aspect of discernment is to choose and to

take action or actions based on the choice we have made. We may choose a course or direction, but not follow through with the necessary actions, as a result of our lack of skills, discipline, or persistence. This is where our will must come into play. Willing ourselves to learn what is needed, to discipline ourselves, and to persist when achievements do not come quickly is part of the learning process necessary for intellectual, emotional, physical, and spiritual growth.

Our skills of discernment change over time as we develop new values and new abilities. We may hold ideal values but not be able to actualize or live by these values until we learn the skills that are needed to realize them. Brian Hall (1994) identifies four sets of skills that are essential to our personal and spiritual growth. They are:

Instrumental Skills. Instrumental skills include our intelligence and manual dexterity to care for ourselves, to read and write, and to carry out the tasks of daily life.

Interpersonal Skills. Interpersonal skills are the skills we need to express and manage our emotions so that we gain cooperation from those with whom we relate and work.

Imaginal Skills. Imaginal skills include the skills needed to learn from our experiences, to choose and to act creatively on complex alternatives, and to see and act on new ideas not previously considered.

System Skills. System skills are the skills needed to see and manage all parts of a system, and to design and manage change in ourselves, in groups, or in organizations.

In order to become integrated beings we must develop at least minimal skills in all four areas. Skills and values are interrelated. When we change perceptions, this often leads to new values. These values are acted upon as we use existing skills or develop new skills.

The importance of developing these skills is highlighted by the challenges we will experience over the next several decades as Earth moves into the Fifth Dimension. In the past, change was more gradual and we were able to use our abilities of discernment in a more deliberative manner. We will need to recognize the need for rethinking our perceptions and values, for monitoring our decision-making, and for disciplining our actions as we use our discernment skills.

Development of our discernment skills gives us the opportunity to move toward becoming one with the Light and reaching the next level of our spiritual growth. This is the goal for all of us to achieve.

Summary

Discernment is often considered narrowly as the ability to discern or select the "rightness" or higher vibrations inherent in a situation. Discernment is much more than this. Discernment is the ability to make discriminations, make choices, make decisions, and take actions which contribute to our growth and the creation of a better world. It involves four basic processes:

＊ Perception
  While we always have perceptions of situations, they may be limited to those perceptions which fit our self-interests. Quality perceptions require the ability to develop a mind-set based on the intents of ourselves and others. It is a perception of what is needed for the advancement of self and others.

＊ Intuition
  Intuition is our ability to connect with our Higher Selves and hear the inner voice that speaks to us.

＊ Decision-Making
  Decisions must be made with the realization that decisions create consequences and that not deciding also creates consequences. Decisions need to be made with care and with contact with our Higher Self.

＊ Action
  Discernment requires action. Follow-through requires discipline and the will to learn the skills that are needed to be successful in our courses of action.

Learning the skills needed for spiritual and effective lives is a lifetime task. Learning instrumental, interpersonal, imaginal, and systems skills is an integral part of our personal and spiritual development.

Chapter 27

THE POWER OF
FORGIVENESS

*Inner peace can be reached
only when we practice forgiveness.
Forgiveness is the letting go of the past,
and is therefore the means for correcting
our misperceptions.*
Gerald G. Jampolsky
Love Is Letting Go of Fear

orgiveness is THE KEY to transformation. It is the gateway to the Fifth Dimension. "One must master a forgiving state of mind to obtain eternal life in the higher kingdoms," says Sananda, the teacher who chose to come through to deliver the message for this chapter.

Who better to deliver instruction on this topic than Sananda himself, Jesus the Christ, the Master of forgiveness? While his teachings encompassed many subjects, forgiveness was always at the heart of all that he taught. Even as long ago as two thousand years, his essence comprehended the power of forgiveness and the reason why humanity must achieve this state of mind.

Today Sananda, THE Master of metaphysics, reveals the science behind the power of forgiveness.

To My Most Distinguished Colleagues in the Light.

I come forward from my Father's House to deliver guidance on the meaning and intent of "forgiveness." It is with pleasure that I deliver this message, for the information, if understood and followed, will deliver all who have the capacity to understand into the Light of the Fifth Dimension.

I AM Sananda, Jesus the Christ, known to others as the Lion of Judah, come forth to bring freedom to you, my Brothers and Sisters.

Forgiveness emanates from the heart, the area and chakra that connect with my essence. It is the state of mind that pierces a hole in the heart, allowing Light to penetrate consciousness.

Although forgiveness is taught by definition and through example, few on Earth understand how important it is to live the process of forgiveness. That is because the ego's strength is strong, and it is the ego that is the controlling force placed between the Higher Self and the mind. The ego is likened to a film or shield of energy that works constantly to keep the power and Light of the Higher Self from penetrating the lower mind and bodies. It is often connected to forces of darkness that can influence decisions that the individual will make. The ego is closely aligned with the lower three bodies (the physical, mental, and emotional) and enjoys "ruling" this area. It is like a dictator in some respects, as it does not welcome competition. Often it will play games and tricks on the individual just to keep its position of power, even though the individual constantly experiences pain, frustration, and depressing states of mind from following the ego's advice.

The "battle for the soul," currently witnessed on Earth, is one in which the Light of the Higher Self is challenging the will of the ego for control of the individual's soul. The arenas and Tests of Initiation are presently being experienced worldwide by less than ten percent of the world's population. By 1997, an additional fifteen percent of the world's population will be elevated to the arenas. By the year 2000, nearly sixty percent will be awakened and in the process of understanding entry into the Fifth Dimension; and in 2011, the entire population on Earth will have heard the cry. Therefore, the importance of this message will be significant for all in the years to come.

My heart measures much pain and frustration within many individuals in embodiment. The cries for help are delivered daily by the angelic kingdom, and the Ascended Realms work endlessly to plan and assist within the guidelines stating that we cannot interfere unless invited to do so. Since so many have invited our presence and welcome our words and guidance, we assist through the hearts of those who choose freely to work with our essence.

Those who are the messengers of our hopes and wisdom stand before the world ready to accept all Karma for their actions. Their strength and Light hold firm and will continue to be anchored in the years to come through additional souls linked to the Light, creating a strong shield for the Command. For their strength, I am grateful, as is the entire Celestial Command. If it were not for their courage, messages such as this one could not be realized.

As I measure the pain from the souls who cry out, I understand the dilemma that they face. The soul is trapped within the body which is primarily controlled by the ego, and the mind and emotions are then manipulated like puppets.

The dilemma is that the weakest of the nine bodies composing human form are the mental and emotional bodies. These are also the two that the ego rules, because these bodies are closest to the physical. The ego is clever, and it is skilled. It understands every weakness and strength within a person's composition and is out to win the battle of control.

The mental and emotional bodies have literally been in control for many lifetimes because of karmic debts that had to be paid. Enlightenment, and the teachers who come with this process, do not appear to the student until the majority of karmic debts have been forgiven and the candidate begins to rise on the path, thereby acquiring a higher frequency of Light. When this occurs, the mind begins to resonate on a higher frequency, one which matches the Light of the Command. At that moment, the individual calls through his or her consciousness to the teachers, using the Law of Attraction, and the teachers gently come to provide the answers to questions. This state of mind means that the person is ready to undergo the Tests of Initiation.

Enlightenment can be acquired in one lifetime if the candidate is truly motivated and disciplined to acquire the understanding and wisdom. Normally, the process of enlightenment takes thousands of lifetimes. It frequently takes that long for the soul to acquire the volume of lessons needed to purify and merge with the Higher Self. That is the goal *all individuals strive to achieve, and that is the victory all see within the mind's eye—the soul merging with the Higher Self. Not achieving this victory is THE ONLY THING that keeps a person in separation. Not achieving this state causes pain and delays the harmony and peace longed for within.*

So, once again, allow me to repeat: The ego (which is the individual personified) is the shield between the soul and the Higher Self. It works to rule the lower kingdom, of which the individual IS the kingdom. Once this is understood, the questions then become:

Whom do you serve: God or man?
Whom do you trust: God or mammon?

If you wish to free the lower self from pain, suffering, and anguish, then there is only one choice. You must merge with the Higher Self; that is the only way to accomplish this. Each soul must choose freedom for the process to begin. But, as always, the choice is yours.

Because humanity has been primarily preoccupied in completing karmic debts, the teachings that have been sent to begin the enlightenment process have, for the most part, fallen on deaf ears. It is my observation that the words from the teachings are analyzed primarily through the mind. This process assists many to understand the meaning of the teachings. While this is a first step, and we are grateful that many do this, it is not enough to experience fully the freedom that is offered through the teachings. The teachings must also be experienced with the heart. Analyzing and dissecting only with the mind are insufficient.

Forgiveness is the key to purifying the soul. Since this state of mind rests at the heart of transformation, allow me to explain, in energy terms, why this is so.

The universes collide and form one pulsating field of energy that is the God Force. This energy field constitutes the life support system for individuals in embodiment. The connecting point to this power is through the Higher Self. This field of energy is intense and it radiates a pure force comprised of Light particles that make up the variances of all creation, including the eight lower bodies that make up the human form.

Anything that vibrates less than this God Force, while still a part of this force, is considered to be of a lower form and, therefore, can be described as "contaminated" (although this term is used in an exaggerated form to make this point). Important to remember here is that, in order to connect with the power contained within the Higher Self, all lower forms of energy (such as those held within the lower eight bodies) must be cleared and raised into the collective frequency of this God Force.

Emotions like hate, envy, jealousy, anger, remorse, suspicion, and even mild dislike vibrate at lower frequencies. Any one of these feelings serves to contaminate individuals, keeping them from realizing their full potential and power.

The ego, which controls the dark side of humanity, must make choices as to what to do with every experience encountered. Remember that forces of both darkness and Light will try to influence the ego's choices by whispering things into consciousness. The difference will be that the Higher Self will pro-

vide the higher guidance, which will always require more strength and discipline to follow. It is easier to hate, feel righteous, and "win" than to humble thyself before thine enemy and forgive the trespasses that have come upon you. Although I strive not to judge, it is my humble observation that the ego usually chooses the path of least resistance.

The ego will frequently listen to anything that gives justification for why the person should continue to hold on to the lower feelings, for, remember, the ego's only chance for ruling is to keep the individual trapped in the lower kingdoms. Be mindful and know that the dark forces to which the ego can connect are very clever. When the ego listens to and obeys the lower directives, convincing the mind to do the same, the individual's vibrational frequency stays low because vibrations are directed by one's state of mind. Maintaining a lower frequency assures that the person will remain in the kingdom that the ego controls. "Victory" is accompanied by the ups and downs of life, often bringing depression and frustration. Yet all is perfect because it has been chosen.

When the individual chooses not to hold on to lower feelings any longer and begins to rise above them (even though it was easier to behave that way in the past), the vibrational frequency of the soul is raised. This always causes a consciousness shift. CHOOSING TO LET GO of the past habits and patterns begins in the mind.

The path to freedom is a CHOICE. Freedom commences the moment the individual chooses to control the mental and emotional bodies and to follow a higher path, rather than to follow the path that the ego wishes. Once the choice is made to control the mental and emotional bodies (rather than the mental and emotional bodies controlling you), a new world emerges and hope springs forth like the lilies in the spring. This moment of decision begins the process of initiation whereby the person is reunited with an "old" friend, the Higher Self, who quietly instructs on another way to live.

The statement for eternal life and entry into the Fifth Dimension is:

"Ego is dead; ego is dead; ego is dead!"

The ego uses the mind and emotions, coupled with ingrained habits and traditions, to keep people from letting go of lower beliefs, attitudes, and feelings. The ego frequently wins because the control mechanism employed is often fear.

Here is a test to follow in determining which of the two forces directs inner guidance:

When presented with new information or asked to accept information unconditionally, it is advisable to take a moment, breathe deeply, and examine how this new information resonates within. If the vibration of fear is present, then know that the information has been cleverly delivered by the lower forms of ego, and its intent is to control the soul by keeping it trapped in the lower kingdom. All is vibration.

Anything that resonates of fear and directs decisions to be made as a result of that feeling is not of the highest. Instead, it is a clever simulation, usually using the mental body to try and convince one to move in a specified direction. Often, logic is disguised and used as the means by which to cover up the presence of fear.

In God's universe, there is only one law—love. Out of this law come Oneness and unity, not separation and fear. If you do not feel this vibration, then you are being coerced by a strong and clever force that wishes for you to maintain an emotional and mental state of the past that resonates with the vibrational frequency compatible with the specified agenda. (Thus, the Law of Vibration explained again.) Courage is often the trait that is needed for the soul to proceed forward and stand in the truth of what one feels inside.

Now, allow me to return to the topic of forgiveness.

Examine how it feels when the mind is in control and cannot forgive another for what he or she has done. The feeling within is likened to those described above—hate, anger, or frustration. Also, when one is unforgiving, the notion that he or she is "winning" can also be present. Am I not right?

If you agree, then examine this state of mind from a vibrational frequency. When a mind resides in these lower states of consciousness,

* ❋ *Are the mind and heart illumined or are they darkened?*
* ❋ *Are the lower eight bodies empowered or are they weakened?*
* ❋ *Are the mental and emotional bodies controlling the person, or is the person controlling the mental and emotional bodies?*

To answer the last question, record how much mental energy is consumed when an individual is kept in this state and how often the thoughts of the incident are replayed within the mind, causing greater and greater sores to fester. In what vibra-

tional frequency is the individual kept suspended when the heart cannot forgive? The deeper question is what prevents the victim from letting go?

FORGIVENESS IS NOTHING MORE THAN LETTING GO

A FIRST GREAT PARADOX

A first great hidden paradox to this situation is that the person who trespasses against another is considered to be, by the "victim," the lesser quality soul. Often this is not the case, because events present themselves in life for two reasons: karmic debts and dharmic destinies. Dharmic destinies include Tests of Initiation. In addition, situations can occur that are not intended to cause harm, yet are perceived by individuals as being harmful because the mind and ego are in control. Circumstances can then arise that evolve into additional Tests of Initiation for individuals to pass. When these occur, such tests are always orchestrated by the Higher Selves of the individuals involved. Therefore, there are many situations that can occur in any moment to place a person in an arena for advancement and learning. This is truth.

Since all souls must be strengthened on the path to initiation, it is reasonable to conclude that all must be tested. Often the tests will come through individuals whom the person least suspects. This assures that the lessons will be even more difficult to achieve.

The saying that holds for this level of initiation is:

"You can tell the level of spiritual mastery you have attained by the level of the test or opponent who will be brought to you."

The logical conclusion to this is the greater the test, the greater the compliment to the person being tested; for the test is a direct correlation to the level of mastery of the soul. From this perspective, then, is your most hated "enemy" or "opponent" your greatest friend? Is this individual placed in your life to become your greatest teacher and to help you learn lessons that you have not yet learned? Think about it. If you agree that thine "enemy" could be so described, does that then make the soul of the opponent lesser, greater, or equal to thine own?

Each test is never what it appears to be on the surface. Tests are never the paperwork, the mannerisms of the boss, the mate leaving, or the slanderous statements made by another. The tests are of a higher nature and they ALWAYS concern mastery of the Universal Laws. For is that not what each Initiate has come to Earth to master? The activities one is involved with are part of the illusion, or the maya, as it is termed in the Far East.

For example, if a mate chooses to leave, the test might actually be to measure one's ability to BE unconditional love in the midst of all adversity. Or, for another who has already passed that test, the test could be to balance the female and male characteristics within. It all depends upon what the soul needs to grow.

The perceived weaknesses within the soul determine what the lessons will be. The weaker patterns within will determine the arena in which the person will be placed. The arena (situation) will provide the individual with opportunities to practice strengthening that part of the personality that needs strengthening. If the person has a predominant amount of feminine energy within and is not a "fighter," then there is a strong likelihood that the test will require the individual to display assertive behavior, thus assisting the individual to align with the male energies within and bring a more perfect balance to the inner energy fields. If the person does not choose to accept the challenge because the former habits of relying on the feminine energy patterns are too great, then he or she will most assuredly face the test again in the future. This is so because the test relates to a particular vibrational frequency and must be passed before the soul can reach a higher level of vibration. This pattern—and the test—will then repeat itself until the lessons are learned. Each time the test appears, however, it comes with new faces. Each new scenario will also bring lessons ten times more exaggerated than before, allowing the individual many opportunities to practice the lessons until they are learned.

Once the lessons are learned, however, and the individual is actually behaving on a higher level, the soul radiates this higher frequency of Light and, because of the Law of Vibration, will NEVER HAVE TO UNDERGO THOSE TESTS AGAIN. When one's vibrational frequency is increased, the soul is free to take on tests of a higher nature that reside on the new level of frequency it has accomplished.

Knowing this to be true, now observe those who have trespassed against you. Because their deeds have served to raise your soul to a higher level, are they among those who have come to serve you or to harm you? If one forgives another for the illusions that appear to be so intense and goes inward to master the lessons of the tests, then the individual progresses on the path to the Light at a much faster pace. Entry into the Fifth Dimension then is almost assured.

Only you can harm yourself, Dear Children of Light. No deed of another can harm you unless you give your power away. If you surpass all limitations and rise above illusion, you will give no power away and the Light shall protect and serve you. This is my promise to you.

Does this explanation provide you with another viewpoint regarding how important it is to forgive?

A SECOND GREAT PARADOX

The second great paradox is that "victims" who believe they are "winning," because they smugly declare they cannot forgive and choose to hold onto their anger, are actually losing. The individuals who have caused them pain still control their souls' vibrational levels by keeping them at lower vibrational states. When one cannot master forgiveness, the reality is that the other individual holds power over the soul by keeping it vibrating at a lower level. This continues for as long as an individual holds on to that lower state of mind that blocks him or her from seeing through the illusion. Therefore, the one who has trespassed against the other continues to hold the soul in bondage for as long as the "victim" allows this to happen. Of course, this pleases the ego immensely.

How simple is the solution, Dear Children of Thoth. How difficult to master the solution, however, when one is the plaything of the ego.

Let go! Let go! Let go!

By letting go and not allowing another's deed to imprison the soul, the individual experiences a higher state of consciousness and freedom, not yet experienced. In letting go and experiencing forgiveness, a lighter, happier feeling begins to overcome consciousness and the mind begins to open to new ideas. This shift of consciousness fills the heart and soul with new hope. The heart's capacity for charity is then activated. A stronger faith results. All is guaranteed. Forgiveness then is THE KEY to understanding and experiencing the three ancient mysteries of faith, hope, and charity. Therefore, I say unto Ye:

Let go of all hatred and anger, and say thank you for the lessons and the opportunities to raise your soul's vibrational frequency into the Light. Without such an experience you would never be self-realized. Then love your opponent for making you the Master you are today. See your greatest enemy as your greatest friend, and rejoice that you have been sent such powerful teachers for they shall deliver you unto the Lord.

Adonai, My Beloved Sisters and Brothers of the Light. I AM Sananda, sent by my Father to once again deliver you from bondage. Hear my words with your heart and allow my essence to penetrate your minds, and you shall see the Light all around.

Qadoish, Qadoish, Qadoish. Adonai Tsebayoth.

Go in peace.

Summary

Forgiveness, or letting go of past grievances or actions, is the key to spiritual growth. When we cling to old hurts or wounds we imprison ourselves in a life ruled by lower vibrations, and we are destined to repeat the problems of the past. Forgiveness allows us to move to higher levels and to evolve in our spiritual growth.

* Forgiveness is the key to transformation.
* Forgiveness emanates from the heart. It is a state of mind that pierces a hole in the heart, allowing Light to penetrate consciousness.
* Ten percent of the world's population is currently experiencing Tests of Initiation; by 1997 another fifteen percent will begin the process; by 2000 nearly sixty percent will be awakened; and by 2011, the entire population on Earth will be involved in the Tests of Initiation.
* Enlightenment, a state of mind that normally takes thousands of lifetimes to achieve, can be achieved in one lifetime if the person is motivated and disciplined.
* The statement "Ego is dead" is the statement for eternal life and entry into the Fifth Dimension.
* The strength of the opponent or the difficulty of the Tests of Initiation is a measure of the challenges that you are expected to overcome and master. Your enemies can be considered to be your best friends, for without these challenges to overcome, how would you ever earn mastery?
* Forgiveness is nothing more than "letting go."

Chapter 28

JOINING FORCES WITH THE ANGELS

Angels and ministers of grace defend us.
William Shakespeare
Hamlet

Throughout time, history has recorded encounters with beings who reside in other dimensions and magical kingdoms. It is not by chance that every culture on Earth and every geographical area of the world has stories to tell about these enchanting beings. These beings have many names ranging from fairies, elves, and sylphs to cherubim, seraphim, and archangels. They are not of human form; instead they are distinct life forms of their own, residing on other dimensions of time/space. In Sanskrit, one word summarizes the entire range of these kingdoms, and that word is *Deva,* meaning God, good Spirit, or beings of Light.

Although mystics and sensitives always have been able to "see" these beings, the majority of humans cannot. The Third Eye of the average person is not opened, which prevents contact or awareness of their presence. Because most people cannot see these beings of Light, they receive little "press" or recognition by the masses.

So what are the normal responses when questions about these beings are raised? Well, these responses seem to fall within the following three categories:

1. **All stories about these beings are fiction**. The beings have been created by storytellers, including Biblical writers, over thousands of years. For example, the Angel Gabriel really did not appear to Mary, and that story was invented by one of the most creative minds of the day.

2. **All stories about these beings are imagined**. Even though communication networks were not present until this century, a miraculous coincidence has occurred that created nearly identical stories in every major civilization on Earth. (Obviously, regardless of physical boundaries or distances between individuals, the human psyche has the remarkable ability to imagine in identical ways.)

3. **Stories about these beings are real**, even though the majority of individuals cannot see them with their physical sight. They do exist in another dimension of time/space, but science does not yet have the technology to measure their presence.

It is clear that these traditional responses fit the options for a Third Dimension steeped in duality—yes or no, imagined or real.

This chapter approaches the topic with a clear recognition that the Devic kingdoms are real. Because the authors frequently communicate with these beings, no further debate regarding their authenticity will be presented.

The purpose of this chapter, then, is briefly to describe the membership of this kingdom and then to go one step farther and tell the reader how to make contact with these beings of Light. The intent is to foster an awareness of these beautiful beings with the hope that communications can be expanded in the future and more assistance can be obtained from them.

The unfoldment of the Devic Kingdoms is intricately intertwined with our evolution. Devas are a part of the feminine energy rising to meet us on our journey. The Fifth Dimension will bring us more of an awareness of the beautiful creatures residing in God's kingdoms. We must begin now to prepare the way for new realities to enter our lives and open to the joy that awaits us on the path. The house of the Father has many rooms.

Angels have been around since the beginning of time. Their existence is recorded as fact in the Bible. They have been the objects of numerous works of art and are the subjects of classical paintings worldwide. The word angel comes from the Greek *angelos*, meaning messenger. The angelic kingdom was created to serve God and to work in every capacity to fulfill this responsibility. Their job is to assure that God's entire kingdom runs smoothly and in accordance with the Divine Plan.

Angels are called Gods, watchers, servants, the holy ones, Spirits, the heavenly army, and hosts. In the Bible, they are referred to as morning stars in the Book of Job, and as Chariots of God in the Book of Psalms. There are angels of:

The Devic Kingdom. These angels work with the elements of nature. Here, there are Devas of the earth, air, water, animals, fish, and birds, and even sunsets and sunrises, to name but a few.

Thoughts, Prayers, Virtues, and Enlightenment. These angels expand the positive thoughts that we emit and apply the right energy to those thoughts to assure their appropriate usages.

Healing. These angels provide clarity and love and create the conditions necessary for humans to perform healing.

Churches, Organizations, Cities, Territories, Countries, and Races. These angels are responsible for assuring that all evolutionary patterns and responsibilities will be completed for the assigned group. The angel in charge of America, for example, is named Americus.

Protection and Guardianship. These angels protect individuals in large group memberships.

Evolutionary Patterns. These angels oversee each individual's evolutionary plan through all incarnations.

Karma. These angels supervise all karmic patterns and debts that one has to experience in order to evolve and reach a higher consciousness.

The Service to Christ. These angelic beings are preparing the way for the return of the Most Radiant One. They focus their energies on sending the Christ energies to Earth to raise its vibrational frequencies and to assure that the Divine Plan will indeed be fulfilled.

Technology and Equipment. These angels oversee equipment, facilities, and technology. They report to the Hierarchy if technology and its uses are not being used in accordance with the higher plan. For example, Kuthumi stated that when the atom bomb was developed and detonated in World War II, a cry was heard around the universe that Earth needed assistance in its evolutionary cycle. It was these angels who sounded the cry that called the celestial forces to come forth to provide assistance to humanity.

Angels have been heard, spoken to, listened to, and observed by visionaries, prophets, and a few ordinary people. They are the messengers of God. Angels can appear in earthly or etheric form. Our children, the pure of heart, accept them unconditionally.

Some individuals see angels in their dreams, where their guidance is known to have helped many people through difficult situations. Their messages have come in many mysterious forms, including "coincidences" and analogies. Angels often guide souls by sending them messages in their dreams.

Further, angels have been known to facilitate spontaneous healings, especially with terminally ill patients. When these incidents are reported (and often not until years later, for a variety of reasons), people claim that their energy and lives suddenly changed. One common occurrence is a shift in consciousness in which the person loses interest in worldly possessions and acquires a new interest in spirituality and a sense of mission.

Although numerous reportings of contact with angels have been logged, something happened over the centuries to diminish our belief in these beings of Light. In the past, few individuals paid attention to angels or even acknowledged their existence. When movies were made about them, there was an underlying, unspoken assumption that the movies were fiction. People scoffed and called these Spirits fantasies.

Today, however, there seems to be a renewed interest in these beings of Light. Television shows, books, and magazine articles abound with stories and testimonials of angels and their magical presence. At least this is true in America.

In spite of this renewed interest, many scientists and medical personnel believe that people who report sightings of angels are only experiencing hallucinations due to endorphins in the body. In their research, these scientists have found suggestions that the functions of the brain produce chemicals and patterns in the mind. They therefore assume that angelic sightings are merely imaginings—some type of chemical brain activity. Despite the fact that only five percent of individuals are diagnosed as being fantasy-prone, the scientists tend to dismiss all explanations for these reportings other than scientific ones.

How sad this state of mind is for humanity. The mystic and wise Initiates know that some things simply cannot be measured. They understand that measuring experiences is not the only way to prove their validity. Some things can only be experienced, such as love, for example.

What has happened to create this state of mind that closes so many individuals down to their natural awareness? How could humanity, with all its advanced technology and knowledge, actually evolve to shutting out this Light and assistance? What dark force has been at work that has so successfully closed minds, reducing humanity to cynicism? The success of such a force is apparent when one looks at the condition of the world today. The good news is that it is not too late to change.

Since humanity is in charge of creating its destiny, and ultimately that of Earth, and since there is a spiritual awakening occurring on the planet, we can collectively change things. The fact is that angels are real, and they do intervene for us on Earth. They are a part of our force field of power and are here to assist us to become Spiritual Masters. Their Light is a chief Source of our power because their Light is a Source of extraordinary love. Because of free will, however, we must choose to connect with them.

In one message, Master Kuthumi spoke of the employment status of the Celestial Command.

We await to be called into action by the Legion of Light Workers on Earth. The edict decrees we cannot interfere because of the condition of free will. This is a sacred condition, and we honor it.

The angels grow especially restless for they have so many gifts to bring. Their full potential lies as dormant as the trees in winter while they await the calls from Earth's Spiritual Warriors to join forces with their strength.

Call, Dear Ones, and call soon. Reduce the unemployment rate in the Heavens. If you oblige, we shall continue to serve you in acquiring new jobs to fulfill your mission.

According to Kuthumi, the angels are underemployed because humanity is not choosing to connect with their power and use their full potential to combat the negativity of Earth. He goes on to explain further that, when we call them to assist:

1. They are obligated to come.
2. They will come.
3. They command unique job functions and responsibilities.
4. They will assist us with our needs and wants.
5. They are smiling and kind, and Masters at giving love.

When connecting to the angelic kingdom, it is important to make our requests specific. For example, if we need assistance with healing, we should call upon the angels who tend to that specific area or need. Our prayers can send angels to help if their assistance does not interfere with karmic or dharmic law. Sometimes individuals are in situations to learn lessons designed to strengthen their souls. When this is the case, the angelic kingdom seldom will interfere; to do so could actually retard the soul's development and progress to the Light.

Never make a blanket call for all the angels in the universe to assist. Remember that they are obligated to come. Call only upon those whose assistance you require.

Psalm 91, verses 11 and 12, reads:

11 For to his angels He [God] has given command about you, that they guard you in all your ways.

12 Upon their hands they shall bear you up, lest you dash your foot against a stone.

Angels take care of everyone and protect us from

harm. They often take care of the spiritual body more than the physical one. At the time of death, they prepare one for the journey after life and then serve as guides on the way. Every major city also has a chief power (angel) guiding it, just as every major territory or country has an Ascended Master watching over its development.

There are nine orders in the hierarchy of angels and the Celestial Hierarchy. These are, from the lowest to the highest: angels, archangels, principalities, powers, virtues, dominions, thrones, cherubim, and seraphim. Each order has special duties that it performs.

Angels and archangels command a high rank in the hierarchy. They guard people and all physical things and are also sent as messengers. Often they come to a planet or star system just to observe and collect wisdom. Sometimes they remain until the inhabitants reach a certain level of illumination, lending their Light to assist in this transformation.

Principalities protect religion and spirituality and serve as the angelic rulers of the nations of the world.

Powers thwart the efforts of demons to overthrow the world. They have received special authority from the Celestial Command to provide protection.

Virtues bestow excellence and merit in grace and valor. They also work miracles on Earth and are the principal beings who assist in healing.

Dominions are regulators of angelic duties. It is through them that the Majesty of God is manifested.

Thrones bring the justice of God to us.

Cherubim each have innumerable subordinates in the hierarchical order who are charged with fulfilling the law according to the twofold principles of equilibrium and cause and effect. They sometimes are called the Recorders, and also the Rulers of North, South, West, and East. Often they appear in units of four. In Christianity, they are personified as the Recording Angels whose job it is to record each human's deeds in a great book. It is by these deeds that each individual is judged. The Cherubim also protect the throne of God.

Seraphim have six wings and surround the throne of God, where they ceaselessly sing, "Holy, Holy, Holy." They are the angels of love, Light, and fire. The Seraphim are the most ardent in Divine love and strive to inspire that quality in human beings.

We can invoke angels at any time and request their assistance.

Jesus said in Matthew 21:21,22:

Therefore I say unto you, if Ye have faith and doubt not...whatsoever Ye shall ask in prayer, believing, Ye shall receive.

Master Kuthumi was asked to describe the angelic kingdom and its role on Earth today. He sent through the following message.

It is with great pleasure that I, Kuthumi, deliver a message about my distinguished celestial colleagues, the angels. Without fail, they sing the praises of the Most High and, for this reason alone, I am honored to deliver information that shall help even the most casual observer.

The angelic kingdom is considered to be the cosmic glue that assists all dimensional beings to become the Light. These beings have the patience of Job and understand the path to the Light even better than many on the Ascended Realms. Since most of them have never been embodied on Earth, they do not resonate with the remembrance of the five senses and how these tools for learning impact a soul's path to the Light.

Members of the angelic kingdom are the stepping stones to higher worlds. They compose the dimensional frequency that affects the soul and its ability to hear. All that is spoken by the Ascended Masters is heard by humans only because of the angelic assistance which adjusts the vibrational patterns of the causal body.

The term "guardian angel" is a truth, for each soul in the universe is assigned a guardian angel. This higher Light being is actually one with the Higher Self, which is what each soul in embodiment actually is. This concept is understood by few, and acknowledged by fewer, but that is of no consequence for this instruction. The point I make is that each individual, regardless of color, creed, or gender, is assigned the presence of a being from the angelic kingdom.

The angels are dutiful and they are committed to one thing: the Light. For them, there is no other purpose for being. They see all and understand that each experience is designed for the soul's lessons to understand and integrate with the Light. That is all. Their agenda is easy to understand.

The radiance that shines from them emanates from pure God Force energy. It is so strong and intense that it cannot be perceived with the human eye. It can only be seen with the inner eye and the eye of the soul unless an individual has purified himself or herself through many lifetimes and moves to the vibrational frequency closer to theirs.

The angels are likened to work horses. They perform their responsibilities with great dedication and joy, for they understand that to fill the hearts with Light and love is the only purpose for exist-

ence. *They are the guardians of the Light and understand that there is only one law: love.*

Love is an elusive concept, but, for the angelic kingdom, it is the only thing they understand. They are incapable of judgment and can only administer the higher truths that vibrate on the spectrum of power that embraces the Christos energy. They are also the ambassadors of the Creator and perform flawlessly to assure that Divine Will rules.

The angelic kingdom is divided among a hierarchy that comprises precision and order. The layers of the hierarchy understand how to coordinate responsibilities to facilitate the master plan for Earth's transition into the Fifth Dimension. They are skilled in completing the responsibilities in the Light matrix and work to bring maximum benefits to Earth through all Children of Light who are connected to their essences.

It is the responsibility of the membership of the Order of Melchizedek in embodiment to make the connections to the angelic kingdom and begin to coordinate with them to bring God's plan to Earth. That is why both groups have come. They have come to unite to do God's will before the will of the ego. All have come to raise the vibrations of the planet into the stream of consciousness that will eventually catapult the world into the higher dimensions of the new millennium.

The four Archangels blow the trumpets as the games now begin. Michael, Gabriel, Raphael, and Uriel stand positioned in the four directions to usher in the triumphant. They rejoice at the reawakening as the remembrance of victory moves to the forefront of consciousness.

Hear my words with your hearts, Dear Children of Light, and see with your inner eye the angelic kingdom standing ready to do your bidding. Unite with these chariots of fire and begin to do battle with the forces of darkness that try to consume your souls. Know that victory is assured through love and Light, and begin to embrace the darkness with the power that you know to be yours.

Learn of the hierarchy in the angelic kingdom and how to connect to their power. Then carry the sword of Archangel Michael for your protection in the days to come. You are assured victory if you follow this plan.

Good tidings of great joy shall be yours in the days ahead.

Adonai, My Celestial Sisters and Brothers of the Command. I AM Kuthumi, your Messenger for the Divine.

John Randolph Price, in his book *The Angels Within Us*, says he believes there are twenty-two angels charged specifically with guiding us as we travel our spiritual paths. Randolph cautions, however, that before we call these angels to us, we must prepare ourselves to work with them by clarifying our minds and intentions. He says there are four critically important steps we must take:

Step one: Forgive ourselves for our past errors of thought and the negative things we have created in our lives.
Step two: Evaluate ourselves—our personality traits and our attitudes.
Step three: Totally surrender our minds, emotions,

bodies, and personal lives to the Spirit within.

Step four: Meditate, bringing our awareness into the presence of God.

After we have done this, we are ready to call the angels to us and ask for their loving help. This help frequently shows itself in uncomfortable or unexpected ways. Why? Because angels lovingly (and fearlessly) cut us loose from whatever is stopping our spiritual growth and progress toward the Fifth Dimension. You can suspect they are at work when:

* Life suddenly takes a new direction. You might be discovering new adventures and creativity or you may feel like you are losing everything you have accomplished over time.
* You feel an intense pull to move elsewhere, but you don't know why or where you should be going.
* You suddenly change careers in spite of a drastic cut in pay.
* You start taking responsibility for your own actions and feelings. You stop blaming other people, fate, or circumstances for things that go wrong in your life.
* You have a solid sense of knowing and of strength, peace, guidance, and renewed energy. You find life refreshing and exciting instead of stagnant.
* You laugh more and see yourself and everything around you through the delighted eyes of a child.

The time has come for us to reopen our Third Eyes and to see with the same vision as the prophets of old. We must train our inner eyes to see what we cannot see with our physical eyes. When we strengthen our faith, we will "see" angels all around us. We can command angelic intervention and bring back the mysticism of the higher days.

Summary

The point has often been made that we are never alone and that we have a variety of resources to call upon for reassurance, assistance, or learning. Angels constitute one of the groups that are available to us. Each of us has a guardian angel or a higher Light being that is actually one with our Higher Self. They watch over us and provide us guidance on a continuing basis.

There are several other categories of angels who are assigned specific tasks. Angels communicate with the soul and help us to hear the messages of the higher realms. Angels are able to assist in combatting the negativity of Earth. When called upon, they will come and assist us with our needs.

＊ Angels are messengers of God, and they can appear in earthly or etheric form.

＊ Angels intervene for us on Earth. Their Light is a chief Source of our power when we choose to connect with them, because their Light is a Source of extraordinary love.

＊ The angelic kingdom is the cosmic glue that assists all dimensional beings to become the Light.

＊ There are nine orders in the hierarchy of angels known as the Celestial Hierarchy:
  ◆ Angels and Archangels—guard people and things and are sent as messengers;
  ◆ Principalities—protect spirituality and serve as the angelic rulers of the nations of the world;
  ◆ Powers—stop the demons from overthrowing the world;
  ◆ Virtues—work miracles on Earth and assist in healing;
  ◆ Dominions—regulate angelic duties;
  ◆ Thrones—bring the justice of God;

- ◆ Cherubim—fulfill the Law according to equilibrium and cause and effect and protect the Throne of God;
- ◆ Seraphim—angels of love, Light, and fire.

❋ Members of the Order of Melchizedek in embodiment are here to connect with angels and coordinate with them to bring about God's plan on Earth. Ultimately, this membership will teach others how to do the same.

Chapter 29

==⧓==

THE
ELECTROMAGNETIC
GRID

*We are made wise not by the recollections of our
past but by the responsibility for our future.*
George Bernard Shaw

n Atlantis, an etheric energy matrix existed beneath the Earth's surface, providing a lattice network for such activities as telepathic communication and healing. This matrix was known as a
grid, which is defined as a network of uniformly spaced hori-
zontal and vertical bars or lines, especially one for locating
points when placed over a map, chart, building plan, etc.

This grid was a system of electromagnetic frequencies
created through worldwide linkages made by human thought
waves and energy transmitted by the Earth and through crystals. The system followed a carefully designed global plan
that was obviously intelligently thought out and detailed. It
embodied the study and form of *geomancy*, which means the
divination of lines drawn at random.

This electromagnetic grid existed for centuries and

346

supported the higher-dimensional existence of the Atlanteans. It enabled life to exist in a higher form on the planet. It was an empowering system situated several feet beneath the Earth's surface. The electromagnetic grid was built by the Thrice-Greatest Geomancer and Master of Earth known as Hermes Trismegistus and the High Priests and Priestesses of Atlantis who came to Earth to build a great civilization for this part of the galaxy.

The intricate landscaping produced by their efforts to connect the Heavens to Earth was completed in cooperation with the Elohim and the Devic kingdoms. It was based on the Hermetic Principles that form the basis for all manifestation. These principles are included in the Universal Laws, described earlier in this book. The effect of this grid ultimately was to connect humans to the Earth through the power of Spirit.

Today, we see the remnants of this miraculous accomplishment in the form of ley lines. These electromagnetic currents of energy once encased the Earth, connecting land masses and traveling under the seas. Architects, scientists, archaeologists, mystics, and others know these lines to be real, but have little physical evidence to support their existence. Some people believe that they can be located using the spiritual trigonometry techniques of Buckminster Fuller. Even if they can, it is impossible to create an acceptable scientific explanation of how these lines were created. Evidence of their existence and the power of their intersection points, however, can be tracked to such uses as:

* Guiding focal points for positioning cathedrals, pyramids, sacred structures, and other mystical objects, such as Stonehenge
* Organizing Earth energies
* Facilitating UFO activities and sightings
* Guiding the migration patterns for birds
* Dictating volcanic activity
* Directing gravity and antigravity activities

❋ Defining the ridges on mountain tops
❋ Directing the movements of ocean currents

The electromagnetic grid was the greatest spiritual accomplishment ever completed on the planet. It exemplified the highest human thought-forms of love interfacing with Mother Earth.

The primary purposes of the electromagnetic grid were to:

1. connect the spiritual Light Bodies of individuals; and
2. supply a free and unending amount of energy to those who were connected to it.

This was done by synchronizing brain-wave patterns to the currents of energy emitted by thoughts that were linked with the heart centers of individuals. Thus, frequencies were created that were connected directly to the Higher Selves and, consequently, the Divine Plan. As a result, Earth's grid lines and the auric frequencies of individuals were clarified and purified, for all are connected in the macrocosm/microcosm.

Since the energy field created by these steps aligned with a higher frequency or spiritual attunement, this frequency automatically connected to Earth's Light network called "Christ consciousness" (another term for the God Force). This created a web of Light resembling a massive brain and nervous system, signalling and connecting the physical world to the etheric existence of the Higher Self. In this way, a highly evolved spiritual telecommunications system was created that could be used by all who had reached an enlightened state of consciousness.

Since there were so many awakened individuals in Atlantis who were connected to the God Force, it was relatively easy to bridge connections of thought, mind, and heart through the Higher Selves. All individuals who walked the Earth with their Third Eyes open were connected to this energy field because the resonance patterns of the Third Eye equaled that of Christ consciousness.

Hermes and other beings of Light first implanted celestial crystals within the etheric bodies of the High Priests and Priestesses and then within those of the Light Workers of the hierarchy. These crystals contained symbolic and geometric coding from the Universal Language of Light that sent out frequencies to connect signals emanating from points of Light. This effort formed lines of Light radiating from their etheric bodies which connected to the Earth, forming the illumined web of Divine energy.

To determine which crystals would be implanted within the etheric bodies, the High Priests and Priestesses were matched using a selection process that assured compatibility to other souls. Matching was completed based upon membership in the individual's soul group and the ray upon which each entered embodiment. Crystals that matched select criteria were then implanted etherically within the lower eight bodies of these high Initiates.

After all etheric coding was completed, Hermes' team then positioned crystals (primarily clear quartz, although other stones such as rose quartz and amethyst also were used) beneath the Earth's surface. This step connected the High Priests and Priestesses, who carried the etheric implants, to the electromagnetic energies emitted from the crystals buried beneath the Earth. Individuals were then "charged" accordingly with a higher current of energy and eventually sent around the world, connecting designated points to sacred sites. Connections were accomplished by touch, and also by the physical presence of the High Priests and Priestesses, because their auras emitted energy rays that were higher than those of the other citizens of Atlantis.

These select emissaries of the Divine journeyed to various lands and sites. Each time they visited foreign places, the currents of energy were made stronger. Throughout the centuries this process strengthened the ley lines, making them nearly impenetrable. The Light traveling through these lines was so pure and radiant that mystics and high adepts could see them with their Third Eyes. Earth's radiance could be tracked by Celestial Beings in the Heavens, and all who resided on this frequency used this grid for higher purposes. The grid truly connected the Heavens to Earth and formed the perfect Oneness. Consequently, peace, love, and Light abounded everywhere, for all of these attributes were connected to the Divine Plan.

That was the state of affairs when Atlantis was in its glory. But as history often reveals, things began to change. Certain individuals, not of the priesthood, began to rise to power and change the systems, which resulted in disaster. In time, Atlantis fell, and when it did, many of these great accomplishments were buried with the land underneath the ocean floor.

Reports (such as those written by Plato) reveal that Atlantis was magnificent during its height and glory. Some of the survivors, who were the keepers of this sacred knowledge on geomancy, settled in Egypt and the Yucatán, keeping a portion of the mysteries and knowledge alive. That is why these civilizations were able to rise to great heights, also. Other souls drifted off into "the deep sleep," holding the sacred information within their Akashic Records until the time when history would reveal that the souls of the High Priests and Priestesses would reincarnate to rebuild Atlantis in the form of the Seventh Golden Age. That time is now.

The High Priests and Priestesses from Atlantis have risen. The souls of these beings who ruled Atlantis have reincarnated and presently are remembering what this electromagnetic grid was and what it stands for. Even now, they are traveling the world creating a NEW grid matrix for Earth.

Atlantis IS rising, just as the great "sleeping prophet" Edgar Cayce prophesied decades ago. This time, the purpose of the priesthood is to assist Earth to enter the Fifth Dimension.

For the past several years, these souls (representing the Order of Melchizedek) have been actively involved in establishing a new electromagnetic grid, situated this time not under the Earth, but approximately three to four feet above its surface. Much of the old grid has been destroyed or desecrated, making it virtually unusable for the new world that is coming. Therefore, sacred sites are being created all over the world as energy fields to support the new matrix.

Rainbow energy fields are slowly emerging from Earth's crystalline structures deep below its surface. Gaia (Mother Earth) is awakening and moving out of slumber into a heightened state of consciousness. As more and more souls choose to receive the Universal Language of Light programming from etheric crystals implanted within the lower eight bodies, assurances arise that the New Jerusalem is emerging on Earth and humans are the co-creators of this celestial temple.

Soon the new electromagnetic grid will be complete. When this occurs, the etheric, cosmic doors that emerge will create entrance and exit points that facilitate interdimensional travel. Communication with the gods, just as in Atlantis, will become "business as usual," and all who earn the higher vibrational frequency connected with the Higher Self will have access to this communications channel network.

Since Atlantis fell, the Order of Melchizedek periodically has sent to Earth some of its finest members who have incarnated to assist humanity to evolve. This was especially important during the Dark Ages, when consciousness was at its lowest. Usually only one soul embodied at a time, but occasionally they would incarnate in groups, supporting each other when an important mission, such as mass enlightenment or a great invention or literary work, had to be completed. Every time they embodied, these souls were so pure that they could remember how to connect to the Order's membership remaining on the etheric (the Ascended Masters). They would do so for the purpose of channelling great works, writings, and legacies for humanity's benefit and growth.

One need only review history to read the names of these great Masters who came to Earth. Souls like Pythagoras, Socrates, Plato, Hippocrates, Athena, Akhnaton, Isis, Jesus, Mother Mary, Buddha, Krishna, Mohammad,

Shakespeare, Solomon, Moses, Sai Baba, Gandhi, and Quan Yin are only a few who were sent to Earth by the Order. Jesus is called Melchizedek King in the scriptures because of his purity and perfect mastery of the laws.

The Order of Melchizedek has been guiding Earth's development from the beginning of time and will continue to do so in the future. Today, the Order is providing instruction and assistance to all who have the hearts to hear. It teaches individuals how to be free of limitations and pain, thus ending the struggle to evolve. The Age of Aquarius has promised this. It has been written; so shall it be done!

Hermes has returned, too, and once again is directing the establishment of the new electromagnetic grid that is destined to surround the Earth. The new matrix will be likened to a tuning fork as it vibrates and connects the higher consciousness of humans all over the world. It will facilitate the development of the Adam Kadmon, or the emergence of the new human who is destined to walk the face of the Earth in the Seventh Golden Age.

Just as when Atlantis existed, conditions on Earth and in the universe are synchronized once again to support this endeavor. It has taken over 10,000 years for this higher frequency to be reached, because the Heavens have not been able to experience such an alignment until now. This perfect alignment has called forth the Great One himself to direct this miraculous project.

The electromagnetic grid is not intended to be part of a new religion. Instead, it is being created to develop humanity's potential by linking higher consciousness centers to the Christos energy. The grid will create a web of Light and focused human consciousness, vibrating on wave lengths that use the Universal Language of Light to transmit messages. It will be the super highway for evolution in the years to come. Some of the uses for the electromagnetic grid are to:

* Send love
* Heal oneself and others
* Increase telepathic powers

* Open the Third Eyes of Initiates on the path to enlightenment
* Link the world in the concept of Oneness
* Send support to others
* Increase the soul's ability to do soul travel
* Access the Universal Language of Light
* Increase manifestation powers for self and others
* Empower individuals
* Strengthen Earth's magnetic field in the Light
* Support spiritual development
* Link humanity with Mother Earth
* Contact the Celestial Command (including the angels)

The Universal Language of Light contains 144,000 geometric symbols. It is the frequency coding that humans need to transcend third-dimensional thinking. It comes to us through our own Higher Selves and filters down to our lower eight bodies. This language carries the Divine blueprint for our individual missions that replaces the will of the ego with the Will of God.

These geometric symbols presently are being encoded into human consciousness and our etheric bodies. This is being completed by the Celestial Hierarchy with all who have given permission to have it done. Coding resides on various wave lengths, so that individuals receive only the symbolic coding that matches their levels of consciousness. The lower the consciousness, the fewer the codes that can be downloaded. The higher the consciousness, the more the codes that are implanted. The more symbols that one receives, the more responsibility for world service he or she is given in fulfillment of the Divine Plan.

The goal for Earth's ascension into the Fifth Dimension is to connect as many Light Workers to the grid as possible. We are connected to the grid through the solar plexus area. We can focus our energy, meditate on the Light, and send and receive important messages, energies, and manifestations.

THE ELECTROMAGNETIC GRID
CANNOT BE MISUSED

The electromagnetic grid is an instrument of peace, co-operation, and love, and will be used to build this kind of world in the coming millennium. It cannot be misused because one must reside on a higher frequency to use it. No one residing on a lower frequency (for example, people who are greedy or wish to inflict harm on others) will be able to connect to it. When a person evolves to a higher level of consciousness, he or she will be incapable of inflicting harm, for the soul's new vibrational frequency will carry an agenda that no longer supports the lower behaviors.

The importance of the electromagnetic grid is that it provides Light Workers everywhere a tool for sending and receiving information and energies that can result in manifestations to serve the move toward the Fifth Dimension.

Here is an exercise sent through from Kuthumi to assist you in accessing this electromagnetic grid:

1. Sit with your spine straight and breathe deeply.
2. Calm your mind, body, and emotions. Stay perfectly centered at all times when using this force field.
3. Invoke the Light and your Higher Self to protect you.
4. Meditate on the Light.
5. Illumine the Third Eye by visualizing a bright golden Light within your head. Connect this Light with your heart center.
6. Connect to the Great Central Sun and the Earth Star through your twelve chakras and ground this higher radiant energy within your heart.
7. Visualize the electromagnetic grid connecting to

your solar plexus area with a golden Light of energy. See yourself as part of this web and feel grounded in this sea of love and Light.

8. Send out impulses of energy and begin to receive, as well.

9. Expect that it is so! So Be It! So It Is!

Summary

Hermes Trismegistus, with the Elohim and Devic Kingdoms, built an electromagnetic grid system several feet below the Earth's surface that was used for centuries to support a higher-dimensional existence on Atlantis. After the fall of Atlantis the grid was damaged, and the remnants are known to us as ley lines. The grid connected the Light Bodies of individuals to each other and to the Earth, provided a free and unending amount of energy to those connected to the grid, and connected the physical world to the etheric existence of the Higher Self. It also formed a telecommunications system which could be used by all who had reached an enlightened state of consciousness.

For the first time in 10,000 years, Earth has reached a frequency that supports a new electromagnetic grid, to be built in support of the Seventh Golden Age and upon entering the Fifth Dimension. The new grid will be approximately three to four feet above Earth's surface, and sacred sites are being created as energy fields to support the new grid matrix.

The new grid will:

* Create entrance and exit points for interdimensional travel;
* Facilitate communication with etheric beings;
* Facilitate communication with other Initiates and enlighten people worldwide;
* Generate wave lengths that use the Universal Language of Light to transmit messages;
* Transmit our Divine blueprints for our life missions.

Chapter 30

INITIATION

That which we do not confront in ourselves we will meet as fate.

Carl Jung

Newar 12/12/15

N o book on self-empowerment such as this one would be complete without an explanation of the Levels of Initiation. Levels of Initiation are the tests that all spiritual seekers must complete on their journeys. They are tests of the soul.

These tests are completed through a step-by-step process and are designed to strengthen the physical, mental, spiritual, and emotional bodies while facilitating change within each of them. Each individual's tests are unique, depending on the lessons needing to be learned. One of the conditions for passing these tests is, ultimately, self-control.

Initiation means acquiring spiritual consciousness and using this knowledge to guide higher energies and powers into and through one's body. It also implies omniscience and omnipotence. Therefore, command over the mental and

emotional bodies is imperative, and the male and female energies within must be balanced. Initiation is also the merging of the Higher Self with the lower eight bodies to facilitate
the flow of this power.

Remember this quotation:

OF ME I DO NOTHING.
IT IS THE FATHER (MOTHER)
WITHIN ME THAT DOES IT ALL

This statement by Jesus is an excellent example of his
understanding of this merger and the power that comes with
it. In Far Eastern religions, this power is often called Kundalini. It is *buddhi* and considered an active principle. It is
an electromagnetic force that, when aroused, has the power
to kill as easily as it can create.

In the past, few souls passed their Tests of Initiation
because there were not many opportunities to learn them nor
were there Master teachers from whom to receive help. For
centuries, this knowledge was deemed so threatening to those
in power that rulers often attempted to destroy both it and
the teachers who were perpetuating it. In some parts of the
world, individuals were forced to move underground and conduct secret meetings to keep the knowledge alive. In other
areas, mystery schools were formed that allowed only those
who had reached a certain level of spiritual consciousness to
be admitted. These schools often were reserved for the High
Priests and Priestesses who incarnated for the sole purpose
of perpetuating this knowledge for the world.

At present, most individuals are conscious to a degree
that corresponds to the resistance of their nerves and physical bodies. When higher spiritual powers begin to flow
through the physical body, many patterns, beliefs, and emotional blockages will be changed. Since this must be accomplished without injury to the physical body, the person must
be ready to receive this power.

Initiation should never be requested until the person has experienced all of life and is in a position to control this power as it enters the lower nerve centers. If all is not in alignment, the energy can be so powerful that it actually can harm the individual and the lower, subtle bodies. If individuals seek initiation too soon or too quickly and do not pass their Tests of Initiation, the soul may sink to a state even lower than that in which it originally incarnated.

Achieving initiation takes years of dedication, discipline, and concentration. It requires that one learn the lower curricula before the higher are introduced. For most individuals, this process takes thousands of incarnations. The soul needs to experience all aspects of life, while choosing a different role each time. For only a few can initiation be accomplished in much less time.

Many old souls have incarnated on Earth today for one purpose—to pass their Tests of Initiation, which will grant them ascension to higher levels. Deep down, each of these souls knows that this is the last lifetime in which they must come back to Earth. Next time, if they return, it will be by choice. The race is not won yet, however, because each time a soul returns, it must be tested. No one is granted safe passage until the tests are completed successfully.

The Levels of Initiation through which we all must pass to enter the higher realms and dimensions are described in this chapter. Never before has this knowledge been revealed in such a form for all to see. THE TIME IS NOW, says Ascended Master El Morya, for this information to come forth. In this age of transition into the Fifth Dimension, all souls must choose which path they will follow. This information is brought into the Light for all to read, with the intent that this firsthand knowledge will help more souls to choose the path of the Spiritual Warrior.

There are twelve Tests of Initiation. They are:

Level 1   The state of beingness that allows the individual's nine bodies to maintain normal functions. This is the time of birth (and general awareness), where the world is seen as an extension of oneself.

The decision concerns unfoldment.

Level 2   The moment one first senses detachment from the Source of the All. This constitutes the moment when the individual begins the journey in the physical world.

The decision encompasses the development of ego.

Level 3   The cry for assistance from the innermost reaches of the mind, when individuals believe that they are separate from one another and begin to search for ways to belong once again.

The decision constitutes selection of companions.

Level 4   The shift of awareness when one understands that there is a greater power and looks to the Heavens with sincerity and asks to become one with this power once again.

The decision demands integrity of purpose.

Level 5   The state of consciousness when one makes a commitment to serve the Creator of the All, and understands that this commitment will require many things in life to change.

The decision includes walking the path of higher truths, and eliminating past weaknesses and blockages that only nurture the illusions around.

Level 6   The moment of action when one stands by the new truths and values and moves into the physical world with new-found courage.

The decision includes making a statement in the physical world which supports the choice.

Level 7   The period when the Initiate undergoes a test of power which is designed to strengthen the will and which brings about an understanding of Universal Laws.

The decision involves searching the soul for answers and listening to one's inner voice for guidance on the right direction to follow.

Level 8   The time when relationships are challenged and the Initiate learns that the only true relationship of significance is the relationship he or she has with God.

The decision requires that one learns unconditional love.

Level 9   The test that develops manifestation powers from within and includes the period of examination which reveals how one will use these powers in the world.

The decision encompasses the choice to let go of ego completely and to serve humanity in the name of the One.

Level 10   The period of stillness within the heart that allows the universe to work through the Higher Self in the creation process.

The decision involves a state of higher consciousness called euphoria, and the relationship this has to the physical, manifest world around.

Level 11   The state of beingness whereby one journeys

interdimensionally to other places of the Most High and uses these experiences for benefiting humanity.

The decision requires one to separate the nine bodies and to commit to the One.

Level 12 The state of enlightenment whereby the One is within and the Light permeates the essence.

The decision requires one to begin the process of unfoldment once again, only on higher planes of existence. It demands that the Initiate assume responsibility for the commitment made and to journey to other worlds to assure that a higher vibration will encompass the world whence he or she has come.

The first five levels are normally acquired quite naturally in our earlier years. It is at the sixth level that the Initiate is required to make a commitment to the path of spiritual consciousness. The decision made here is critical because it determines the course of the entire journey thereafter. (These Tests of Initiation are detailed in the newsletter *Celestial Voices*. See the back of the book for further information on how to order these.)

Once a person embarks on the spiritual path, many challenges and tests, in addition to those described here, are brought to the individual. These are not to be considered forms of punishment. Instead, they are to be received as opportunities for growth. The saying goes:

> *You can tell the level of spiritual mastery you*
> *have achieved,*
> *by the level of the test that will be brought to*
> *you.*

So, if you are a person who has been greatly challenged lately, and you feel that the whole world is caving in around you, feel honored! The greater the tests, the greater the compliment. In order to pass the tests, the individual must go inward and find out what lesson is to be learned. The lessons never include the obvious. They always concern issues relating to the soul's growth, such as learning patience, forgiveness, or unconditional love, or acquiring sensitivity, strength, or assertiveness to strengthen the will. One must journey inward to find these answers, and will not escape the tests until the appropriate level of behavior is mastered. If you do not learn the lessons the first time around, the test comes again with new faces and situations. The only drawback is that it arrives ten times stronger. Therefore, learn the lessons as quickly as possible. Begin now to control your mental and emotional bodies and stay calm and centered at all times, and you will accelerate your path into the Light and into mastery. It is then that *The Light Shall Set You Free.*

Have a wonderful journey!

Summary

Our spiritual journey, like our life journey, is developmental. We experience various steps or levels as we progress through stages of mastery. The Levels of Initiation are the tests that the souls of the spiritual seekers must complete. The tests are provided to strengthen our physical, mental, emotional, and spiritual bodies while facilitating change in them. Passing the tests requires discipline and command over our mental and emotional bodies and the balancing of female and male energies. Initiation also is the merger of the Higher Self with the lower eight bodies to support the flow of power.

Initiation requires years and lifetimes of effort. One must learn the lower curricula before the higher are introduced. For most individuals, this process requires many incarnations.

Tests of Initiation are tailored to meet the needs of the soul, but there is an overall pattern or sequence of twelve levels of Initiation. The first five levels of initiation are passed by most persons as they are born, develop their sense of self or ego, seek belongingness with a companion, develop a desire to become one with God again, and make changes which are needed for their spiritual development.

Levels six through twelve are more difficult, requiring intentional effort and discipline. Briefly, they move through taking a stand and speaking one's truth; undergoing a test of power that assists understanding of the Universal Laws; learning unconditional love; using one's power to serve humanity; waking through the Higher Self in the creation process; seeing interdimensionally; and achieving enlightenment.

We make our journeys easier when we control our emotional and mental bodies, stay calm and centered at all times, and learn the lessons the first time they appear. Passing the Tests of Initiation and meeting higher levels of mastery prepares us for new and higher levels of service and mastery.

EPILOGUE

If we live the right way
    and let the Light into our hearts and minds,
    the whole world becomes alive.

The world is a lovely garden,
    full of dreams, life, and beauty.
It is a special place shared by many kingdoms,
    and the one place where all can connect
    and grow together.

GLOSSARY

Adam Kadmon
Sons and daughters of Light who are evolved beyond the body form and are manifestations of Light. In this exalted state, they are the extensions of God and exist as energy Beings of Light who have the ability to create with thought and word.

Adonai
Hebrew word for the Lord. A manifestation.

Angels
Supernatural beings who have great intelligence and power. They are guiding influences and spirits, such as the Guardian Angels, who watch over each soul in embodiment. Angels are generally regarded as good, innocent, powerful, and beautiful, and may intervene to protect us from harm. There is a hierarchy within the angelic realms that constitutes many levels of power: Angels, Archangels, Principalities, Powers, Virtues, Dominions, Thrones, Cherubim, and Seraphim.

Negative forces also claim to have angels, such as Lucifer, the fallen angel, who was cast out of heaven at God's command by Archangel Michael.

Akashic Records
Chronicles of all that occurs in one's life. Everything is inscribed in the akasha, which is etheric energy vibrating at a frequency that records all of the impressions of life, whether created in or out of embodiment. Any individual can learn to access these records by developing inner sight.

Arcturians
Fifth-dimensional beings who claim they are from the star Arcturus in the Bootes constellation.

Ascended Masters
Those who have mastered time and space and gained mastery of the self, fulfilled their divine plan, and ascended into the presence of God. There, because of their great love, they receive new directions to teach in many worlds.

Atlantis
A highly evolved ancient civilization which developed and used advanced technologies such as those we are learning about today. The civilization misused some of the technologies by not integrating spiritual practices into their use and was destroyed by earthquakes and other cataclysms. The continent of Atlantis sank into the Atlantic Ocean on three separate occasions. Some Atlanteans escaped and went to such places as Greece, Egypt, and Central America.

Beings
A term used to denote the existence of Light beings, such as the Ascended Masters, Arcturians, or other species from different star systems. A life form, just as humans are one of the life forms ensouled on Earth.

Bodhisattvas
Buddhas-to-be. Those who aspire to become Buddhas have to perfect within themselves the following characteristics during several lifetimes: morality, charity, renunciation, wisdom, patience, truth, effort, determination, universal unconditional love, and composure.

Celestial
The Heavenly realms which are beyond third-dimensional sight. The home of beings not incarnated.

Chakras
The ethereal body's sense organs, as defined by such Far Eastern organizations as the Theosophical Society. Chakras resemble energy vortices. There are several in the body, visible to clairvoyants only. Of these, it is advisable to use only seven when aligning the spiritual body on a daily basis. Each of these seven chakras vibrates at the frequency of one of the seven colors in the rainbow, which combine to create white Light.

Children of Light
Humans progressing on their paths of spirituality who seek the Light and are guided by it.

Christ Consciousness
One of the early stages of spiritual development. The intellectual capacity for knowing Christ and our Creator. It leads to the spiritual urge to find God or Christ (Christ-seeking) and the craving to do Christ's and God's will.

Codes
The symbolism used by the Tribunal Council of the Galactic Command to deliver the keys that contain the secrets to the power held by the Atlantean Masters of over 10,000 years ago.

Commanders
Starseeds working for the Galactic Command to help carry out the plan for assisting planet Earth and her inhabitants in the transition into the Fifth Dimension.

Cosmic Beings
Beings from other universes and galaxies.

Creator of the All
Another name for God.

Dharma
The cosmic law defining the natural and moral principles and order that apply to everything in existence. Dharma defines the destiny of each soul that comes into Earth embodiment.

Dimension
A plane of existence that can be subdivided into seven primary parts, each comprising a specific agenda that makes up the curricula of that plane.

Electromagnetic Gridline
An ancient Atlantean underground grid (developed by Hermes) for mental and spiritual communication, which was energized by crystals, special stones, and objects. It is now being reconstructed around the world as a crystalline web of Light, above the surface of

the Earth, to be used as a source of connection and communication among spiritual Light Workers who believe in its power and worth.

Energy Field
Area charged with electromagnetic energy that surrounds a being or object. It may be positive, negative, or both.

Etheric
The all-pervading essence of creation, filling all space and interpenetrating all matter. The holder of all unseen events. All things exist first as ideas or thought-forms in the etheric before manifesting into the physical. Also referred to as ethers.

Ethers
See etheric.

Galactic Command
A fleet of starships composed of Masters and Celestial Beings from numerous galaxies and ruled by the Ascended Masters of the Great White Brotherhood (White meaning white Light) who are helping Earth enter the Age of Aquarius. These beings travel the universes and have the capability to influence and direct God's plan for continued evolution. They are highly advanced, and do not necessarily appear in a third-dimensional form. They have assisted Earth on her evolutionary path since the beginning.

Golden Age
Any age when Earth moves to a higher consciousness and the people on Earth live in greater peace, harmony, love, and abundance.

Golden Liquid Light
A phrase synonymous with God. It is the pool of electromagnetic energy that is the creator of everything that exists. It is called liquid because it moves continuously like a fluid and cannot be contained. See also Prana.

Great Central Sun
The center or core of white fire from which the spiritual/material universes emanate. In the past, Sirius, the Dog Star, has been the focal point of the Great Central Sun in our section of the universe. Over time, however, this position changes because of the precession of the equinoxes.

Guides
Those who walk beside our souls and assist our spiritual growth.

Higher Self
The Christ Self, the I AM presence, the exalted form of selfhood. The Light body that surrounds our physical bodies and contains the power of the God Force.

I Am Presence
Same as the Higher Self.

Karma
A universal law of cause and effect summarizing the totality of an individual's actions in any single successive state of existence. Karma also is defined as the physical, mental, and spiritual lessons that return in any lifetime to provide opportunities for the soul's growth. Loosely used, it means fate. Karmic paths are the journeys humans take that teach many lessons.

Keys
The clues that unravel the mysteries of the secrets of the power of Atlantis and, ultimately, creation.

Law of Attraction
This Universal Law demonstrates how we create the things, events, and people that come into our lives. Our thoughts, feelings, words, and actions produce energies which, in turn, attract like energies. Negative energies attract negative energies and positive energies attract positive energies.

Law of Cause and Effect
This Universal Law states that nothing happens by chance or outside the Universal Laws. Every action has a reaction or consequence and we "reap what we have sown."

Law of Compensation
This Universal Law is the Law of Cause and Effect applied to blessings and abundance that are provided for us. The visible effects of our deeds are given to us in gifts, money, inheritances, friendships, and blessings.

Law of Correspondence
This Universal Law states that the principles or laws of physics that explain the physical world—energy, Light, vibration, and motion—have their corresponding principles in the etheric or universe. "As above, so below."

Law of Gender
This Universal Law states that everything has its masculine (yang) and feminine (yin) principles, and that these are the basis for all creation. The spiritual Initiate must balance the masculine and feminine energies within himself or herself to become a Master and a true co-creator with God.

Law of Perpetual Transmutation
This Universal Law states that all persons have within them the power to change the conditions in their lives. Higher vibrations consume and transform lower ones; thus, each of us can change the energies in our lives by understanding the Universal Laws and applying the principles in such a way as to effect change.

Law of Polarity
This Universal Law states that everything is on a continuum and has an opposite. We can suppress and transform undesirable thoughts by concentrating on the opposite pole. It is the law of mental vibrations.

Law of Relativity
This Universal Law states that each person will receive a series of problems (Tests of Initiation) for the purpose of strengthening the Light within. We must consider each of these tests to be a challenge and remain connected to our hearts when proceeding to solve the problems.. This law also teaches us to compare our problems to others' problems and put everything into its proper perspective. No matter how bad we perceive our situation to be, there is always someone who is in a worse position. It is all relative.

Law of Rhythm
This Universal Law states that everything vibrates and moves to certain rhythms. These rhythms establish seasons, cycles, stages of development, and patterns. Each cycle reflects the regularity of

God's universe. Masters know how to rise above negative parts of a cycle by never getting too excited or allowing negative things to penetrate their consciousness.

Law of Vibration
This Universal Law states that everything in the universe moves, vibrates, and travels in circular patterns. The same principles of vibration in the physical world apply to our thoughts, feelings, desires, and wills in the etheric world. Each sound, thing, and even thought has its own vibrational frequency, unique unto itself.

Light Body
The individual's electromagnetic body existing in the etheric. It is the real body that provides the blueprint for the physical body and allows interdimensional communication.

Light Workers
Spiritual believers who actively work to bring love and Light to Earth.

Lion of Judah
A name given to Jesus signifying that his teachings were Divine truths emanating from the Tribe of Judah. The Prophet Daniel recorded the vision of a winged lion rising out of the sea. An interpretation of this vision is that, in the coming millennium, Divine wisdom and truth will rule and a new spiritual world will be born

Love
An electromagnetic force which encompasses the totality of the All. Energy emanating from God that creates life.

Mandala
A circular pattern with concentric, geometric symbols and forms that represent the universe. Although traditionally from the Hindu and Buddhist religions, mandalas are used in many traditional practices for meditation purposes.

Masters
Men and women who have evolved spiritually, transcended their fellows, and who assist in ruling the world. Adepts.

Merkabah
Vehicle of Light structure encasing the Earth that is used as the means of communication between the Ascended Masters and the members of the Order of Melchizedek in embodiment. According to some, this structure includes individual units situated over and around individual Light Workers. Each unit is approximately fifty-five feet in diameter. These units are tetrahedrons with the two halves spinning contrary to each other, and must be activated to receive the maximum benefit of their use. In other instances, these units of Light resemble teardrop diamond cuts.

Metaphysics
The philosophy that applies the laws of physics to the spiritual world. The belief that the world above and the world below are in correspondence.

Most Radiant One
The Ascended Master who is said to be Jesus the Christ or Sananda. The Supreme Commander of the Celestials who oversee Earth's transition into the millennium.

New Age
An age of spirituality and Oneness. Some refer to this age as the millennium that is approaching in connection with the Second Coming of Christ.

New Jerusalem
The emerging title of the United States for the future. According to the Ascended Masters, the people in the United States are responsible for processing information and spiritually awakening people worldwide so that collectively we may bring Earth into the Fifth Dimension.

Order of Melchizedek
A bonded group of spiritual and incarnated souls working in the Light to carry out God's plan for the universe.

Prana
The life support energy system of the universe. Also called the Golden Liquid Light.

Precession of the Equinoxes
An astronomical effect of the gradual shift in the Earth's axis of rotation which produces a westward movement and shifting of constellations around the celestial sphere. Approximately 25,800 years are required to complete the cycle. The Earth stays in each "age" (Pisces, Aquarius, etc.) for over 2,000 years. The precession is caused by the sun's and moon's attraction as a result of bulges around the Earth's equator.

Qadoish, Qadoish, Qadoish, Adonai Tsebayoth
Holy, Holy, Holy, Lord God of Hosts. One of the most powerful phrases that can be uttered to glorify God.

Reincarnation
The rebirth of the soul in a new body. This concept also incorporates the belief that the soul reappears in another form after death.

Sai Baba
In the late 1800's a fakir, who could perform miracles, lived in India. His name was Sai Baba, a name given in respect to those who have earned it. He offered spiritual teachings to many of various religious backgrounds. Upon his death, he told one of his followers that he would return in eight years in male embodiment and implied that they should look for him. On November 23, 1926, eight years following Sai Baba's death, a male child was born with great supernatural powers. He has risen once again in India and is presently sharing his wisdom, miracles, and spiritual teachings with millions of devotees from all over the world. An Avatar, presently on Earth, who holds the Christ consciousness for the world.

Seventh Heaven
The Seventh Dimension and home of highly spiritually evolved souls.

Shamballa
The etheric city, said to be over the Gobi Desert, that is the home of the Ascended Masters.

Soul
An entity regarded as being the immortal or spiritual part of a person. The moral or emotional nature of humans. Though it has neither physical nor material reality, the soul is credited with the

functions of thinking and willing, and, hence, of determining all behavior. The vehicle that transports the memories, lessons, and accomplishments of the individual. The soul holds together the Light
of our nine bodies; the physical body, mind, emotions, and actions of
an individual reflect the soul's evolutionary progress.

Spirit
The animating principle carrying with it the idea of power. It is a
living energy and mystic force emanating out of the etheric realms.

Spiritual
Matters having to do with the soul and connection to the spirit of
the Creator.

Starseeds
Souls from other planets, star systems, or universes who answered
a call for assistance and agreed to come to Earth to help with the
healing and transformation of this planet. Individuals in embodiment who presently are working with the Ascended Masters and the
Galactic Command to help fulfill God's Divine Plan of bringing
peace, harmony, and love to Earth.

Terra
Another name for Earth, sometimes used to describe Earth after the
completion of the planet's transformation into a star.

Third Eye
The "psychic" eye located in the middle of the forehead between the
eyebrows. Also, the location of the sixth chakra. A connection to
spiritual energy that can be activated by meditation and awareness
to produce second sight or extrasensory perception. The inner eye
of God.

Vibrational Frequency
The rate at which the atoms and subparticles of a being or object
vibrate. The higher this vibrational frequency is, the closer it is to
the frequency of Light.

Vortex
A magnetic grid system entrance and exit point where magnetic and
spiritual energies flow back and forth at vibrational levels outside
of Earth's normal operations and physical time. Sensitive individu-

als, upon entering these areas, feel the differences in their energy levels. Some experience lightheadedness, loss of concentration, or other such sensations.

Yin and Yang
The broad or universal expression of female (yin) and male (yang) energies. The yin expression is creative thought, and is receptive, nurturing, and intuitive. The yang expression is outer-directed, seeking, and questing, and is the action that carries out creation.

BIBLIOGRAPHY

Brennan, B. *Hands of Light*. New York, NY: Bantam Books, 1987.

Brennan, B. *Light Emerging: The Journey of Personal Healing*. New York, NY: Bantam Books, 1993.

Carey, K. *The Third Millennium*. San Francisco, CA: Harper, 1991.

Haich, E. *Initiation*. Palo Alto, CA: Seed Center, 1974.

Hall, B. *Values Shift*. Rockport, ME: Twin Lights Publishers, Inc., 1994.

Harmon, Willis. *Global Mind Change*. Indianapolis: Knowledge Systems Inc. 1988.

The Holy Bible. Chicago: Good Counsel Publishing Co., Inc., 1965. (Published with the approbation of His Excellency Walter A. Coggin, O.S.B., Ph.D., D.D.)

Hurtak, J. J. *Keys of Enoch*. Los Gatos, CA: The Academy for Future Science, 1977.

Milanovich, N. J., Rice, B., & Ploski, C. *We, the Arcturians*. Albuquerque, NM: Athena Publishing, 1990.

Newton, M. *Journey of Souls: Case Studies of Life between Lives*. St. Paul, MN: Llewellyn Publications, 1994.

Price, J. R. *The Angels Within Us*. New York, NY: Bantam Books, 1993.

Stone, D. J. *The Complete Ascension Manual: How To Achieve Ascension in this Lifetime*. Sedona, AZ: Light Technology Publications, 1992.

Webster's New World Dictionary of the American Language. Second college edition. D. B. Guralnik, Editor in Chief. New York, NY: Simon and Schuster, Inc., 1984.

Webster's New Lexicon Dictionary of the English Language. Encyclopedic Edition. B. S. Cayne, Editorial Director. New York, NY: Lexicon Publications, Inc., 1989.

ABOUT THE AUTHORS

Norma J. Milanovich—Norma lives fulfilled in the best of two worlds—the business and corporate world and the world of metaphysics. After a successful career in academia for nearly twenty years at two major universities, Norma embarked on a spiritual journey that changed her life. Her awakening ultimately connected her to the Ascended Masters and other Celestial Beings who have freely given instruction and knowledge that gave her the understanding for integrating the long-elusive concepts of body, mind, and Spirit. The instruction taught her tools for empowerment that, for the first time in her life, provided her the freedom to be, with no stress or fears.

Today, Norma is president of a training and organizational development corporation. She conducts workshops and training for individuals from major corporations, both nationally and internationally. She specializes in needs analysis, job task analysis, strategic planning, organizational development (conducting effective meetings, team building, etc.), and personal empowerment training. Helping people learn and excel and seeing them become all that they can be is what motivates her to continue her educational pursuits.

In the metaphysical world, she continues her journey by integrating the teachings of the Ascended Masters into her everyday life. She is a popular speaker at conventions and conducts workshops and training on such topics as Universal Laws, empowerment, connecting with the Ascended Masters, connecting to our Light Bodies, developing telepathic abilities, using Earth's electromagnetic grid line, and journeying interdimensionally. Her work brings her to countries worldwide. She also conducts numerous spiritual journeys annually, which bring her to every corner of the world.

Back home, Norma stays busy bringing through messages from the Masters, and publishes two quarterly newsletters, *Celestial Voices* and *Majestic Raise*. The former provides instruction from the Ascended Masters for humanity's empowerment and the latter contains current messages of concern from the Celestial Beings regarding Earth's entrance into the Fifth Dimension. She is presently working on another book, guided by Ascended Master Kuthumi, which will describe the fascinating journeys she and hundreds of others have taken with the Ascended Masters to activate Earth's electromagnetic grid and axis.

Perhaps the most glorious and exciting project of all that consumes her time is The Templar, a structure designed by the Ascended Masters for Earth and her inhabitants. It is a pyramid that is described as the "Twelfth Wonder of the World." To realize this accomplishment, Norma works with a Council of Twelve and meets with architects and Masters Kuthumi and El Morya to receive architectural details and instructions on how to build this incredible edifice. To date, hundreds of messages and numerous drawings have been received, depicting a structure of such perfection and beauty that seeing the drawings brings tears even to the eyes of unbelievers.

Shirley D. McCune—Shirley is an educator who has worked at national, regional, state, and local levels in the improvement of educational systems and opportunities for children and adults. Currently, she is a consultant and provides research, technical assistance, and training to educational and governmental organizations. She is the author of numerous monographs, technical assistance materials, and research reports.

Shirley's spiritual journey began in earnest when she developed a life-threatening illness. Her healing activities moved her into metaphysical philosophy and thinking. Since the healing experience she has continued her efforts to gain knowledge to continue on her spiritual path.

WE, THE ARCTURIAI

WE, THE ARCTURIANS *was written by Dr. Norma Milanovich, Betty Rice and Cynthia Ploski. The book is a selected compilation of messages transmitted through Dr. Milanovich via a microcomputer from beings who identify themselves as Celestials from the star Arcturus and members of the Galactic Command. These transmissions describe, in detail, their home, starship, mode of functioning, way of life, their mission, and Earth's transition into the New Age.*

One of the more unique features of this book is that the Arcturians state they are preparing the way for the return of the Most Radiant One, who they call Sananda, Jesus, the Christ.

To obtain a copy of **WE, THE ARCTURIANS,** fill out and mail the coupon below.

Please send me _____ copies of **We, The Arcturians** at $14.95 each, S&H $5.00. New Mexico residents **only** add $0.83 per copy sales tax. (Outside the US and Canada $17.95 each, S&H Air rates $12.00, Surface rates $7.00. US funds only).

Name _____

Address _____

City _____State _____ Zip _____

☐ MasterCard ☐ VISA (check one)

#_____/_____/_____/_____ Exp. Date: ____/____

Signature _____

Send check, money order, Visa or Mastercard to:
**Athena Leadership Center, Mossman Center, Suite 204,
7410 Montgomery Blvd. NE, Albuquerque, NM 87109-1584
Orders only: 1-800-970-9701   FAX: (505) 880-1623**

SACRED JOURNEY TO ATLANTIS

This is the story of an incredible adventure experienced by 34 men and women who, in February 1991, traveled on a sacred journey to the Bahamas and the storied lost continent of Atlantis to discover the "Wisdom of the Ancients." The adventure was completed in only three days, but profoundly affected individual lives and altered the vibrational patterns of the world.

Read the book and perhaps you will discover that you also are destined to regain the knowledge known only by the ancient of the ancients who ruled the lost continent of Atlantis. Fifteen coded messages from the Ascended Masters are in the book which unlock the secrets of the Atlantean Masters.

Please send me _____ copies of **Sacred Journey To Atlantis** at $12.95 each, S&H $5.00. New Mexico residents **only** add $0.72 per copy sales tax. (Outside the US and Canada $15.95 each, S&H Air rates $12.00, Surface rates $7.00. US funds only).

Name _____

Address _____

City _____State _____ Zip _____

☐ [MasterCard] ☐ [VISA] (check one)

#_____/_____/_____/_____ Exp. Date:____/____

Signature _____

Send check, money order, Visa or Mastercard to:
**Athena Leadership Center, Mossman Center, Suite 204,
7410 Montgomery Blvd. NE, Albuquerque, NM 87109-1584
Orders only: 1-800-970-9701   FAX: (505) 880-1623**

Celestial Voices is a quarterly newsletter containing messages sent from the Ascended Masters. The instruction details such things as the six-steps to enter the Fifth Dimension (six issues), how to manifest abundance (three issues), the twelve Levels of Initiation (eight issues), and the seven Tests of Empowerment (seven issues). The Ascended Masters continually transmit profound information in these newsletters that contain practical ideas for changing our lives.

To order your subscription of *Celestial Voices,* fill out and mail the coupon below. Subscription rates (check your choice):

☐ 1 yr. $12.00 ☐ 2 yrs. $22.00

Price outside the US and Canada: 1 yr. $18.00 2 yrs. $33.00

Back issues: *Celestial Voices* started quarterly in January of 1991 and back issues can be obtained for $3.00 an issue. Outside the US and Canada $4.50 an issue. (US funds only).

Name _____

Address _____

City _____State _____ Zip _____

☐ MasterCard ☐ VISA (check one)

#_____/_____/_____/_____ Exp. Date: ___/___

Signature _____

Send check, money order, Visa or Mastercard to:
Athena Leadership Center, Mossman Center, Suite 204,
7410 Montgomery Blvd. NE, Albuquerque, NM 87109-1584
Orders only: 1-800-970-9701 FAX: (505) 880-1623

Majestic Raise Newsletter

*Share The Vision Of Tomorrow Through the Eyes Of The
Ascended Masters*

Dr. Milanovich's **NEW** quarterly newsletter *Majestic Raise*, contains
transmissions from the Ascended Masters including:

* ❋ *Current messages from the Hierarchy*
* ❋ *Information on the magnificent and life-changing
  journeys, designed by the Ascended Masters*
* ❋ *Visions of tomorrow*
* ❋ *Updates and schedules of key events*
* ❋ *Practical guidance for self-empowerment*

Majestic Raise is produced to assist Light Workers to
clarify missions and leadership roles and to keep the
network informed of the Celestial changes.

☐ 1 yr. $19.00   ☐ 2 yrs. $35.00

Price outside the US & Canada: 1 yr. $25.00   2 yrs. $43.00

Name _____

Address _____

City _____State _____ Zip _____

☐ [MasterCard] ☐ [VISA]   (check one)

#_____/_____/_____/_____ Exp. Date: ____/____

Signature _____

Send check, money order, Visa or Mastercard to:
**Athena Leadership Center, Mossman Center, Suite 204,
7410 Montgomery Blvd. NE, Albuquerque, NM 87109-1584
Orders only: 1-800-970-9701 FAX: (505) 880-1623**

AWAKENING THE SPIRITUAL MASTER WITHIN
Level II Workshop on Audio Cassettes

This powerful two-day workshop (on audio cassettes) provides further knowledge and skills on how to accelerate your electron spin and how to obtain a higher consciousness working with the Ascended Masters. Instruction focuses on detailed information that provides the listener with practical skills on living in the third-dimensional world as a fifth-dimensional being. Gateways to higher portals of wisdom are opened when one participates in this instruction.

Included:

❖ *Acquire empowerment techniques that accelerate the connection to your Light Body*
❖ *Acquire an understanding of the Sub-laws of the Universe*
❖ *Discover ways to connect to the Higher Self*
❖ *Discover ways to increase your telepathic abilities*
❖ *Gain knowledge about your mission on Earth*
❖ *Learn about the electromagnetic grid - Your lifeline to the future*

Please send me _____ copies at $129.00 each, S&H $5.00. New Mexico residents **only** add $7.18 per copy sales tax. (Outside the US and Canada, S&H Air rates $12.00, Surface rates $7.00. US funds only).

Name _____

Address _____

City _____State _____ Zip _____

☐ MasterCard ☐ VISA (check one)

#_____/_____/_____/_____ Exp. Date: ____/____

Signature _____

Send check, money order, Visa or Mastercard to:
**Athena Leadership Center, Mossman Center, Suite 204,
7410 Montgomery Blvd. NE, Albuquerque, NM 87109-1584
Orders only: 1-800-970-9701   FAX: (505) 880-1623**

Sacred Journey To Atlantis Poster
Art Work by David Gittens

Sacred Journey to Atlantis
By David Gittens

A striking full-color poster based on the original art work that illustrates the cover of **Sacred Journey to Atlantis.**

This beautiful reproduction measures 12 by 16 inches and depicts the magic and mystery of the Atlantean spirit.

To order your copy or copies, fill out and mail in the coupon below.

Please send me _____ copies of the **Sacred Journey To Atlantis poster** at $7.95 each, S&H $3.00. New Mexico residents **only** add $0.44 per copy sales tax. (Outside the US and Canada, S&H $5.00. US funds only.)

Name _____

Address _____

City _____ State _____ Zip _____

☐ [MasterCard] ☐ [VISA] (check one)

#_____/_____/_____/_____ Exp. Date: ___/___

Signature _____

Send check, money order, Visa or Mastercard to:
**Athena Leadership Center, Mossman Center, Suite 204,
7410 Montgomery Blvd. NE, Albuquerque, NM 87109-1584
Orders only: 1-800-970-9701 FAX: (505) 880-1623**

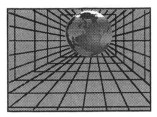

THE FIFTH DIMENSION
EARTH'S CHANGING REALITY

Video Tape

On this video tape, Dr. Norma Milanovich gives a presentation dealing with metaphysical / spiritual knowledge and phenomena, expanded interpretations of ancient knowledge, the crop circle enigma, the transition of humans and Earth into the Fifth Dimension, and explanations of the unified field of intelligence, energy, vibrations, and frequencies. These concepts are presented in relation to human spiritual evolution, along with an introduction to the Ascended Masters and guidance from the Arcturians.

Please send me _____ copies of the video tape *The Fifth Dimension—Earth's Changing Reality* at $29.95 cach, S&H $5.00. New Mexico residents **only** add $1.67 per tape sales tax. (Outside the US and Canada $34.95 each [PAL format], S&H Air rates $12.00, Surface rates $7.00. US funds only.)

Name _____

Address _____

City _____State _____ Zip _____

☐ MasterCard ☐ VISA (check one)

#_____/_____/_____/_____ Exp. Date: ____/____

Signature _____

Send check, money order, Visa or Mastercard to:
Athena Leadership Center, Mossman Center, Suite 204,
7410 Montgomery Blvd. NE, Albuquerque, NM 87109-1584
Orders only: 1-800-970-9701 FAX: (505) 880-1623

THE TEMPLAR

IN THE SEVENTH GOLDEN AGE

Video Tape

The Trinity Foundation, organized in 1991 to implement the Templar project, presents a video tape entitled **The Templar in the Seventh Golden Age**. *This tape documents the speech given about the Templar project by Dr. Norma Milanovich to the United Nations Parapsychology Society on October 3, 1991.*

Please send me _____ copies of the video tape *The Templar in the Seventh Golden Age* at $29.95 each, S&H $5.00. New Mexico residents **only** add $1.67 per tape sales tax. (Outside the US and Canada $34.95 each [PAL format], S&H Air rates $12.00, Surface rates $7.00. US funds only.)

☐   I wish to be placed on a mailing list to receive further information about the Templar Project.

Name _____

Address _____

City _____State _____ Zip _____

☐ MasterCard ☐ VISA (check one)

#_____/_____/_____/_____ Exp. Date: ____/____

Signature _____

Send check, money order, Visa or Mastercard to:
Athena Leadership Center, Mossman Center, Suite 204, 7410 Montgomery Blvd. NE, Albuquerque, NM 87109-1584 Orders only: 1-800-970-9701 FAX: (505) 880-1623

SIRIUS ART

This print and other artwork done by Richard Pulito may be obtained from

Sirius Art
545 Benton Rd.
East Meadow, NY 11554-5465

(516) 783-8589